Linguistic Studies
of Text and Discourse

Collected Works of M. A. K. Halliday

Volume 2 in the Collected Works of M. A. K. Halliday

Linguistic Studies of Text and Discourse

M. A. K. Halliday

Edited by Jonathan Webster

continuum
LONDON • NEW YORK

Continuum

The Tower Building, 11 York Road, London, SE1 7NX

370 Lexington Avenue, New York, NY 10017-6503

First published 2002

British Library Cataloguing-in-Publication Data
A catalogue record for this book is available from
the British Library.

ISBN 0-8264-5868-8 (hardback)

Typeset by SetSystems Ltd, Saffron Walden, Essex
Printed and bound in Great Britain by
MPG Books Ltd, Bodmin, Cornwall

CONTENTS

PREFACE

This volume, *Linguistic Studies of Text and Discourse*, focuses on the application of Systemic Functional Grammar to the analysis of texts, both highly valued and everyday, both written and spoken. The works in this volume present a framework for pursuing the practice of linguistic description and analysis of language in use in context of situation. Understanding better the grammar at work creating meaning, we appreciate more the work of the grammarian, whose task it is to explore for evidence as the basis of a linguistically sophisticated interpretation of the text under investigation.

The first part of this volume provides the foundation for subsequent chapters dealing with detailed analysis of specific texts, ranging from the highly valued by such authors as William Golding, J. B. Priestley, Alfred Lord Tennyson, and Charles Darwin, to the more everyday variety, such as a fund-raising letter and part of a doctoral defence. All are meaningful; each an instance formed from the total network of meaning potential; each accessible through the categories of the description of the language as a whole. A text achieves reality against an infinity of shadow texts that might have been; a literary work only has meaning against the background of the language as a whole.

The last sentence of this volume reads, 'There can be no semiotic act that leaves the world exactly as it was before.' Such is the power of grammar at work. With it we are enabled to create meaning, to change our lives for better or for worse. The grammarian explores the features whereby this potential for meaning and impact on our world are realized and experienced.

ACKNOWLEDGEMENTS

'Descriptive linguistics in literary studies', from *English Studies Today: Third Series*, edited by Alan Duthie, Edinburgh University Press, 1964, pages 23–39. Reprinted by permission of Edinburgh University Press.

'The linguistic study of literary texts', from *Proceedings of the Ninth International Congress of Linguists*, edited by Horace Lunt, Mouton, 1964, pages 302–7. Reprinted by permission of Mouton de Gruyter.

'Linguistic function and literary style: an inquiry into the language of William Golding's *The Inheritors*', from *Literary Style: A Symposium*, edited by Seymour Chatman, Oxford University Press, 1971. © 1971 Oxford University Press. Reprinted by permission of Oxford University Press.

'Text as semantic choice in social contexts', from *Grammars and Descriptions*, edited by Teun A. van Dijk and János S. Petöfi, Walter de Gruyter, 1977, pages 176–225. Reprinted by permission of Mouton de Gruyter.

'The de-automatization of grammar: from Priestley's *An Inspector Calls*', from *Language Form and Linguistic Variation: Papers Dedicated to Angus McIntosh (Current Issues in Linguistic Theory 15)*, edited by John M. Anderson, John Benjamins, 1982, pages 129–59. Reprinted by permission of John Benjamins.

'Foreword' and 'The nuclear sections of Tennyson's "In Memoriam"', from *Functions of Style*, edited by David Birch and Michael O'Toole, Pinter, 1988, pages vii–ix, 31–44.

'The construction of knowledge and value in the grammar of scientific discourse: with reference to Charles Darwin's *The Origin of Species*', from *La rappresentazione verbale e iconica: valori estetici e funzionali*. Atti del XI Congresso Nazionale dell'A.I.A., Bergamo, 24–25 October 1988, edited by Clotilde de Stasio, Maurizio Gotti and Rossana Bonadei, Guerini Studio, 1990, pages 57–80. Reprinted by permission of Guerini Studio.

'Some lexicogrammatical features of the "Zero Population Growth Text"', from *Discourse Description: Diverse Linguistic Analyses of a Fundraising Text* (*Pragmatics and Beyond, New Series 16*), edited by William C. Mann and Sandra A. Thompson, John Benjamins, 1992, pages 327–58. Reprinted by permission of John Benjamins.

'So you say "pass" . . . thank you three muchly', from *What's Going on Here? Complementary Studies of Professional Talk*, edited by Allen D. Grimshaw, Ablex, 1994, pages 175–229. Reprinted by permission of Greenwood Publishing Group.

Extracts from *The Inheritors* by William Golding (pages 121–4) are reprinted by permission of Faber and Faber Ltd.

PART ONE

LINGUISTIC ANALYSIS AND TEXTUAL MEANING

EDITOR'S INTRODUCTION

'It is part of the task of linguistics to describe texts,' states Halliday in 'The linguistic study of literary texts'. What is a text? For sure, size does not matter when defining what counts as a text. Rather, in 'Text as semantic choice in social contexts', a text is described as 'a semantic concept', 'a sociological event, a semiotic encounter'; it is 'the means of exchange', 'the primary channel of the transmission of culture', 'the semantic process of social dynamics'. Halliday stresses 'the essential indeterminacy of the concept of "a text"'; nevertheless, be it long or short, prose or verse, spoken or written, literary or non-literary, any text is accessible to linguistic analysis. Particularly if that linguistic analysis is grounded in a theory which recognizes the 'textual' systems of the language.

The first chapter, 'The linguistic study of literary texts', combines two of Halliday's earlier works, both originally published in 1964: *Descriptive Linguistics in Literary Studies*, and *The Linguistic Study of Literary Texts*. Halliday emphasizes the point that the linguistic study of literature, or "linguistic stylistics", 'is no different from any other textual description; it is not a new branch or a new level or a new kind of linguistics but the application of existing theories and methods.' As he explains, 'A literary text has meaning against the background of the language as a whole, in all its uses; how can its language be understood except as the selection by the individual writer from the total resources at his disposal? Yet all too often the observations about the language of a work of literature bear no relation to any descriptive account of those resources.' Only objective linguistic scholarship using the categories of the description of the language as a whole, not '*ad hoc*, personal and arbitrarily selective statements', can contribute to the analysis of literature and allow for 'the comparison of each text with others, by the same and by different authors, in the same and in different genres.'

Halliday analyses W. B. Yeats' poem *Leda and the Swan* in terms of 'the "cline of verbality", and the structure of the nominal groups', and compares the findings with those from another Yeats poem *His Phoenix*, Tennyson's *Morte d'Arthur*, and a passage of prose from the *New Scientist*. Halliday also examines three short passages of modern English prose, by John Braine, Dylan Thomas, and Angus Wilson, in terms of nominal groups, lexical sets and cohesion. The concept of cohesion, described as an alignment or grouping of various descriptive categories, was developed particularly for literary textual analysis.

On the role of linguistics in literary analysis, Halliday concludes, 'Linguistics is not and never will be the whole of literary analysis, and only the literary analyst – not the linguist – can determine the place of linguistics in literary studies. But if a text is to be described at all, then it should be described properly; and this means by the theories and methods developed in linguistics, the subject whose task is precisely to show how language works. The literary analyst is not content with amateur psychology, armchair philosophy, or fictitious social history; yet the linguistics that is applied in some accounts of literature, and the statements about language that are used as evidence, are no less amateur, armchair and fictitious.'

First published in 1977, the second chapter in this part, 'Text as semantic choice in social contexts', begins by describing in detail the semantic system, with particular attention to the textual (or text-forming) component, and its corresponding structure-generating systems and cohesive relations. Halliday defines a text as 'an instance of social meaning in a particular context of situation.' Text is the means of exchange of meanings among societal members in the context of situation. Halliday's notion of text encompasses the traditional and the spontaneous, both literary and conversational. By way of illustration, Halliday focuses on a narrative entitled *Fables for Our Time*, presenting a situational interpretation of the text, and concluding with a systemic description of a single sentence from the same text. A sentence, after all, is the product of 'numerous micro-acts of semantic choice'. It is a lexicogrammatical structure, which has 'its origin in the functional organization of the semantic system.' In so doing, Halliday illustrates the semiotic cycle: 'the network that extends from the social system, as its upper bound, through the linguistic system on the one hand and the social context on the other, down to the "wording", which is the text in its lexicogrammatical realization.'

4

Chapter One

THE LINGUISTIC STUDY OF LITERARY TEXTS
(1964)

The starting point could be Jakobson's observation: "Insistence on keeping poetics apart from linguistics is warranted only when the field of linguistics appears to be illicitly restricted."[1] It is part of the task of linguistics to describe texts; and all texts, including those, prose and verse, which fall within any definition of "literature", are accessible to analysis by the existing methods of linguistics. In talking of "the linguistic study" of literary texts we mean, of course, not "the study of the language" but "the study (of the language) by the theories and methods of linguistics". There is a crucial difference between the *ad hoc*, personal and arbitrarily selective statements offered, frequently in support of a preformulated literary thesis, as "textual" or "linguistic" statements about literature, and an analysis founded on general linguistic theory and descriptive linguistics. It is the latter that may reasonably be called "linguistic stylistics".

It is a prerequisite of such a study that both the theory and the description should be those used in the analysis of the language as a whole. Linguistic stylistics must be an application, not an extension, of linguistics; this is the only way to ensure the theoretical validity of the statements made. The justification for using linguistic methods in literary analysis is that existing grammatical, lexical, phonological and

---

Two works are combined in this chapter:

'Descriptive linguistics in literary studies', first published in *English Studies Today: Third Series*, edited by Alan Duthie. Edinburgh: Edinburgh University Press, 1964, pp. 23–39.

'The linguistic study of literary texts', first published in *Proceedings of the Ninth International Congress of Linguists*, Cambridge, MA, 1962, edited by Horace Lunt. The Hague: Mouton, 1964, pp. 302–7.

phonetic theory is already valid and relevant for the purpose. At the same time the descriptive statements made about a literary text are meaningful only in relation to the total "pure" description of the language concerned: if the linguist hopes to contribute to the analysis of English literature he must first have made a comprehensive description of the English of the period at all levels. (It can presumably be taken for granted that the categories of such a description will be formally defined, and that the description will not be restricted to below the rank of the sentence.) If for example all clauses of a particular poem are shown to have the same structure, it is essential to know whether or not this is the only permitted clause structure in the language; and if not, what its relative frequency is in a large sample representative of "the language in general".

Moreover, a text is meaningful not only in virtue of what it is but also in virtue of what it might have been. The most relevant exponent of the "might have been" of a work of literature is another work of literature. Linguistic stylistics is thus essentially a comparative study. To pursue the example above, we also need to know the relative frequency of this clause structure in other works of the same period and the same genre. The more texts are studied, the more anything said about any one text becomes interesting and relevant.

We can therefore define linguistic stylistics as the description of literary texts, by methods derived from general linguistic theory, using the categories of the description of the language as a whole; and the comparison of each text with others, by the same and by different authors, in the same and in different genres.

While insisting that stylistic studies use the same methods and categories as nonliterary descriptions, we must make the proviso that such studies may require new alignments or groupings of descriptive categories, through which the special properties of a text may be recognized. This may include the bringing together of categories and items described at different levels as well as those scattered throughout the description of any one level. An example of such a grouping, in which various grammatical and lexical features are brought together, is *cohesion*.

The principal categories subsumed under cohesion are:

    A. Grammatical
        1. Structural (clauses in sentence structure)
           (a) Dependence
           (b) Linking

2. Non-structural
   (a) Anaphora
      (i) deictics and submodifiers
      (ii) pronouns
   (b) Substitution
      (i) verbal
      (ii) nominal
B. Lexical
   1. Repetition of item
   2. Occurrence of item from same lexical set

The grammatical categories are drawn from a comprehensive description of the grammar of Modern English. A brief account of the underlying theory is given in my paper 'Categories of the theory of grammar'.[2] Some commentary on these categories is given here.

Cohesion is of course a syntagmatic relation and, insofar as it is grammatical, it is partly accounted for by structure. Structure is the ordered arrangement of one or more items of the same rank to form an item of the rank above: in English, the ways in which a sentence can be made up of clauses, a clause of groups, a group of words and a word of morphemes. All structure is thus in the broadest sense cohesive. But with the smaller units there is little consistent variation between texts. A more delicate treatment of cohesion would certainly include at least some relations in clause or group structure, for example apposition and *rankshift*; but in the first instance structural cohesion can be limited to the relations between clauses in sentence structure. These take various forms, of which the most significant for literary texts are *dependence* and *linking*. Very roughly, these can be glossed in traditional terms as "subordination" and "co-ordination", the former including non-defining but not defining relative clauses.[3]

Structure, however, is not the only cohesive factor operating at the level of grammar. There are certain grammatical categories whose exponents cohere with other items in the text, items to which they do not stand in a fixed structural relation or indeed necessarily in any structural relation at all. Principal among these are the anaphoric items in the nominal and adverbial group: deictics, submodifiers and adverbs, of which the most frequent are *the*, *this*, *that*, the personal possessives, *such*, *so*, *there* and *then*; and the (personal) pronouns. These items are regarded as cohesive only in their anaphoric use; this accounts for the majority of occurrences of all except *the*, which is most frequently

7

cataphoric. Deictics and pronouns used cataphorically, pointing forward to a modifier or qualifier as in *the tall man, the man who came to dinner, he who hesitates, it is useful to ask,* are not cohesive; nor is the homophoric *the* in *the moon.* Secondary in importance to anaphora, because much less frequent in written English, is substitution: the use of *do* as lexical item in the verbal group and *one* as head of the nominal group, as in *he might have done* and *a long one.*

Lexical cohesion in its clearest form is carried by two or more occurrences, in close proximity, of the same lexical item, or of items paradigmatically related in the sense that they may belong to the same lexical set. For example, in a passage by Leslie Stephen one paragraph ends *I took leave, and turned to the ascent of the peak*; the next paragraph begins *The climb is perfectly easy.* Thus in the new paragraph the first lexical item, *climb,* coheres with *ascent*; later occur *mountain* and *summit* cohering with *peak.* The lexical set is identified by privilege of occurrence in collocation, just as the grammatical system is identified by privilege of occurrence in structure; the set is a grouping of items with similar tendencies of collocation. The occurrence of a high frequency collocation, like *ascent . . . peak,* is not here regarded as being itself a cohesive feature, since there seems no reason for assuming that such a collocation is any more cohesive than one of low frequency: too many variables are involved, such as the lexical power of the items and their grammatical relations. But in any case a valid assessment of lexical cohesion depends on the study of collocations in very large samples of text, this being necessary to the recognition of lexical sets; work of this kind on English texts is only just beginning.

The features outlined in the last three paragraphs may be regarded as the main types of cohesion in modern written English.[4] Frequently, of course, cohesion is lexicogrammatical, as in *the climb,* quoted above, with anaphoric deictic. It includes also other features, not listed here but required by a more delicate analysis: for example, lexical variation within a constant grammatical frame, and vice versa.

But it must not be thought that all statements in linguistic stylistics require special alignments of categories. On the contrary, a straightforward linguistic description of a literary text, in which the text is treated in exactly the same way as any other text that is being subjected to linguistic analysis, reveals a great deal both about that text in particular and about literary language in general. To quote Jakobson again:[5] "The set (*Einstellung*) toward the MESSAGE as such, focus on the message for its own sake, is the POETIC function of language." It is this "set toward the message" that determines the particular type of linguistic patterning that is characteristic of literature.

If we keep the word "pattern" as a general, non-technical name for all the organization, at all levels, that is a crucial property of language as such, then the special property of literary language is the patterning of the variability of these patterns. In other words, the creative writer finds and exploits the **irregularity** that the patterns allow, and in doing so superimposes a further **regularity**. It is this "regularity", as we may reasonably call it provided we avoid giving the term an arithmetical interpretation, that marks the "focus on the message". This is clearly displayed by any good linguistic description of a text – provided there exists already a good description, textual or otherwise, of that language.

All illustrations in linguistics are misleading. Language does not operate except in the context of other events; even where these are, as with written texts, other language events, any one point made about a piece of text which is under focus raises many further points extending way beyond it into the context. This does not mean that no linguistic statements can be self-sufficient, but that the only ultimately valid unit for textual analysis is the whole text. It takes many hours of talking to describe exhaustively even the language of one sonnet.

However, if students can be asked to comment on the language of literary texts within the time limits of an examination, it should be possible to give selective illustrations of what would be regarded as a good answer to a question on the language of particular short texts. I propose here to refer to W. B. Yeats' poem *Leda and the Swan*, and to three short passages of modern English prose by John Braine, Dylan Thomas, and Angus Wilson.

Leda and the Swan

A sudden blow: the great wings beating still
Above the staggering girl, the thighs caressed
By the dark webs, her nape caught in his bill,
He holds her helpless breast upon his breast.

How can those terrified vague fingers push
The feathered glory from her loosening thighs?
And how can body, laid in that white rush,
But feel the strange heart beating where it lies?

A shudder in the loins engenders there
The broken wall, the burning roof and tower
And Agamemnon dead.

> Being so caught up,
> So mastered by the brute blood of the air,
> Did she put on his knowledge with his power
> Before the indifferent beak could let her drop?

W. B. Yeats

The first example will be the use of *the* in *Leda and the Swan*. The relevant grammatical background can be summarized as follows. The primary (least delicate) structure of the English nominal group is (M)H(Q): a head, which may or may not be preceded by a modifier and followed by a qualifier. Nearly everything occurring in the qualifier is rankshifted: that is, is of a rank (in fact always clause or group) above or equal to the unit in whose structure it is operating (here the group). In the modifier, on the other hand, only compound "Saxon genitives" and some modifiers of measurement are rankshifted; in general the modifier is an ordered sequence of words (the word being the unit immediately below the group in rank), proceeding from the most grammatical to the most lexical. The first place in the structure of the modifier is occupied by the word class known as "deictics", consisting more delicately of three subclasses of which one contains the items *the*, *a*, *this*, *that*, the personal deictics *his*, *her*, etc., and certain other words. The contextual function of the deictics is to identify, and among them *the* is unmarked and specific: that is, its function is to identify a **specific** subset but to do so by reference to something other than itself; unlike *his* or *that*, *the* carries no power of identification but indicates that something else present does. This "something else" may be either (1) in the M/Q elements of the nominal group, (2) in the context, linguistic or situational, or (3) in the head of the nominal group itself. There are thus three distinct relations into which *the* as deictic enters, respectively **cataphoric**, **anaphoric**, and **homophoric**. These can be illustrated from the following passage:

> Accordingly, after a peace-offering of tobacco, in return for a draught of foaming milk, I took leave, and turned to the ascent of the peak.
> The climb is perfectly easy, though I contrived to complicate matters by going the wrong way. The absence of guides generally enables one to enjoy a little excitement, the more agreeable because not contemplated beforehand. Indeed, to confess the truth, a former attempt upon the mountain had failed altogether by reason of my ingeniously attacking it by the only impracticable route. It was with all the more satisfaction that I found myself on the present occasion rapidly approaching the summit, and circumventing the petty obstacles which tried to oppose my progress.

Leslie Stephen

10

For example:

Cataphoric:
The absence *of guides*
the only impracticable route
Anaphoric:
turned to the *ascent* of the peak. *The* climb
Homophoric:
the truth

In two instances, *the more agreeable* and *all the more satisfaction, the* is not a deictic at all but a distinct formal item which operates as submodifier in the nominal group.

The complete statement of the formal properties of these relations, such that they can be recognized as distinct structures, is complex and involves lexis as well as grammar – though in spoken English, since tonicity (the placing of the tonic in the tone group) can be observed, it is possible to make a purely grammatical statement that accounts for most occurrences. In written English the general picture is as follows: there is a high probability that

(*a*) if there is a modifier (other than *the*) or qualifier in the nominal group, *the* is cataphoric,

(*b*) if there is no modifier or qualifier, then

(i) if in the preceding context there has occurred a lexical item which is either the same item as, or from the same lexical set as, the head of the nominal group, *the* is anaphoric,

(ii) if not, *the* is homophoric.

Table 1 (p. 20) shows all the nominal groups, other than those consisting only of pronoun or personal name, in *Leda and the Swan*. Out of a total of 25, no less than 15 have **both** a specific deictic (10 *the*, 5 others) **and** a modifier (other than the deictic) or qualifier or both. This contrasts, for example, with Yeats' poem *His Phoenix*, which contains 81 nominal groups of which only 17 are of this type. In nominal groups with modifier or qualifier, if *the*, or other specific deictic, is present it is usually cataphoric; moreover, samples of modern English prose writing show that the most frequent use of *the* is in fact cataphoric reference to modifier or qualifier, not anaphoric reference ("second mention") as often supposed. In *Leda*, however, out of ten nominal groups having *the* and a modifier or qualifier, only one, *the brute blood of the air*, had *the* in cataphoric use. The remainder, although they have both (*a*) items whose place in structure

11

(at M or Q) makes them potentially defining, and (*b*) the item *the* whose function is usually to show that such potentially defining items are in fact defining, yet have non-cataphoric *the*. That is to say, in spite of the *the*, *the dark webs* are not identified by their being dark – like *the loins*, they are to be identified anaphorically, in fact by anaphoric reference to the title of the poem. The only other type of writing I can call to mind in which this feature is found at such a high density is in tourist guides and, sometimes, exhibition catalogues. (I hope I need not add that this is in no sense intended as an adverse criticism of the poem.)

The second example is the distribution of verbal items in *Leda and the Swan*. Most of this poem, especially the first ten and a half lines, is organized in nominal groups; they account for 69 of the 83 words in this first part. There are 14 verbal groups in the poem, and in addition four words of the class "verb" operating directly in the structure of (as opposed to being rankshifted into) nominal groups (*staggering, loosening, broken, burning*).

The table below represents a sort of scale of "verbness" in the use of verbal items – the "cline of verbality", to give it a jargonistic label. On the extreme left, most "verbish" of all, is the finite verbal group in free clause; the further over to the right, the more the status of verb is attenuated, until finally it is subordinated altogether to the nominal element without even the formality of a rankshift. In *Leda*, with its preponderance of nominal groups, the verbal items are considerably deverbalized: contrast again *His Phoenix*, and also the 16 lines from Tennyson's *Morte d'Arthur* beginning *Then quickly rose Sir Bedivere, and ran* (columns as in Table 2 on p. 21):

	1	2	3	4	5	6
Leda	5	2	3		4	4
His Phoenix	30	12	2	6	2	2
Morte d'Arthur (extract)	17		3		2	

Of various short passages examined for comparative purposes, the only one showing a distribution at all comparable to that of *Leda* was a passage of prose from the *New Scientist* concerning the peaceful uses of plutonium.

I am not of course saying that the language of *Leda* is like that of the *New Scientist*. The two passages are alike **in this respect**: that is all. Again, no evaluation is implied: even if one criticized the highly nominal style of much scientific writing this is quite irrelevant to *Leda*, since (i) the two are quite different registers, and what is effective in one register may not be effective in another, and (ii) this feature cannot be isolated from other features in which the two are quite different – for example the lexical items concerned.

It is worth examining the lexical items in more detail. In the *New Scientist* passage, and also in *His Phoenix* (where, however, the **grammatical** use of verbs is, as we have seen, highly "verbal"), the **lexical items** operating as verbs are in general weak: that is, they are items like *be* and *have* which are collocationally neutral. In *His Phoenix*, for example, out of 48 finite verbal groups, 40 are accounted for by the following items: *be* (13), *have* (12), *know* (4), *do, go, say, find, hear, live, walk and talk, pick and choose,* and *please.* By contrast many of those in the Tennyson passage are powerful items: that is, items with restricted ranges of collocation, like *plunge, brandish, wheel,* and *flash.* In *Leda*, the few verbal items are varied in power, though medium rather than extreme. But they get lexically more powerful as they get grammatically less "verbal": in finite verbal group in free clause we have *hold, push, put on, feel;* while at the other end of the scale, not operating in verbal group at all, are *stagger, loosen,* and *caress.*

Lexical power is the measure of the restriction on high probability collocations: the fewer the items with which a given item is likely to collocate (put another way, the more strongly the given item tends to be associated with certain other items), the more "powerful" it is said to be. This, of course, has no evaluative connotations, nor has it anything to do with a denotation of violence or movement. But in fact in *Leda* the more powerful of the verbal lexical items are items of violence; and it is precisely these that perform nominal rather than verbal roles. Thus while the Tennyson passage, a straightforward narrative, is characterized by a succession of fairly powerful lexical items denoting movement, each constituting by itself a (generally monosyllabic) finite verbal group in free clause, in *Leda*, where there are lexical items of movement which are likewise fairly powerful, these either are not verbs at all or are themselves verbs but subordinated to the nominal elements in clause structure.

The third example is a comparison of one or two features in three short passages of prose, which have in common the fact that each is the description of a room. The passages, which are reproduced below, are taken from *Room at the Top* by John Braine, *Adventures in the Skin Trade* by Dylan Thomas, and *The Middle Age of Mrs Eliot* by Angus Wilson; they are referred to by the abbreviations JB, DT, and AW.

I looked at it with incredulous delight: wallpaper vertically striped in beige and silver, a bay window extending for almost the whole length of the room with fitted cushions along it, a divan bed that looked like a divan and not like a bed with its depressing daylight intimations of sleep and sickness, two armchairs, and a dressing-table, wardrobe and writing-table all in the same pale satiny wood. On the cream-painted bookcase was a bowl of anemones and there was a fire burning in the grate, leaving an aromatic smell, faintly acid and faintly flower-like, which I knew but couldn't quite place ... There were three small pictures hanging on the far wall: *The Harbour at Arles*, a Breughel skating scene, and Manet's *Olympe*.

John Braine

Every inch of the room was covered with furniture. Chairs stood on couches that lay on tables; mirrors nearly the height of the door were propped, back to back, against the walls, reflecting and making endless the hills of desks and chairs with their legs in the air, sideboards, dressing-tables, chests-of-drawers, more mirrors, empty bookcases, wash-basins, clothes cupboards. There was a double bed, carefully made with the ends of the sheets turned back; lying on top of a dining table on top of another table there were electric lamps and lampshades, trays and vases, lavatory bowls and basins, heaped in the armchairs that stood on cupboards and tables and beds, touching the ceiling. The one window, looking out on the road, could just be seen through the curved legs of sideboards on their backs. The walls behind the standing mirrors were thick with pictures and picture frames.

Dylan Thomas

Her little bedroom at the hotel was ugly – the more hideous for having been recently redecorated with a standard 'contemporary' wallpaper. All over the walls floated gay little blue and pink café tables, around them a few Vermouth and Pernod bottles and the word 'Montmartre' in pretty childish script. The design was no doubt carefully chosen to enchant cross-Channel travellers; it had no message for Meg. In the first weeks she had sought every excuse to be away from the room; but now suddenly the wallpaper, the pink, bevel-edged, modern-istic mirror, and the furniture of shaded pink and silver began to give her a sense of anonymity. They were so remote from anything she knew or cared for that she felt free, safe, and hidden.

Angus Wilson

(*a*) Nominal groups. In DT, all 49 nominal groups have lexical item as head: there are no pronouns or other grammatical heads. Of these only 11 have any lexical modification or qualification, and of a total of 5 lexical modifiers only *empty* has the value "epithet" in the group structure. By contrast in JB, which has 36 nominal groups of which 4 have grammatical heads, of the remaining 32 with lexical heads 16 have modifier or qualifier (or both) and 22 have deictics. Likewise in AW, with 37 nominal groups of which 9 have grammatical heads, 12 of the 28 with lexical heads are lexically modified or qualified and 15 have deictics. The DT passage is a heap of mainly simple nominal groups (that is, ones consisting of a noun only), with also some heaping of clauses; in AW and JB we have the compound nominal group as the centre of attention. All this is obvious; but the fact that it is obvious does not excuse us from stating it accurately. Nor is it useful to count items or patterns without a linguistic analysis to identify what is to be counted.

The following table shows the number of nominal groups with lexical heads, and with lexical and grammatical modifiers and qualifiers, in the three prose passages. The last part of the table shows the distribution of "head" items in the principal lexical sets (see next paragraph).

	JB	DT	AW
Nominal groups	36	49	37
Nominal groups with lexical head	32	49	28
with M/Q (lexical)	16	11	12
with D	22	19	15
Head from 'room' set	19	40	9
from 'furniture and décor'	14	34	5
from 'constructional'	5	6	4

(b) Lexical sets. Of the 49 lexical items as head of the nominal groups in DT, 40 are assignable to a lexical set under the heading *room*: 34 of these to a set (subset of *room*) *furniture and décor*. Of the 32 lexical heads in JB, only 14 are furniture; and of AW's 28, only 5. Constructional items, however, such as *wall*, are distributed fairly evenly among the three passages. In AW especially the furniture is of little interest: even of the 5 non-constructional items, two are occurrences of *wallpaper* and one, *tables*, refers to the design of the wallpaper – the tables *float*; the other two items are *furniture* and *mirror*. It is interesting to note the different parts played by lexical items from the sets associated with the *room* theme in the three passages.

(c) Cohesion. The principal types of cohesion are shown in Table 3 (p. 21). The passages are too short to allow much to be said about their relative degrees, and use of different types, of cohesion; but some differences do emerge. In DT there is no grammatical cohesion at all across sentences or across orthographic sub-sentences (and only one instance even within a sentence: presupposition of "bondage" beginning at *reflecting*). Cohesion is entirely lexical, by constant repetition of items or occurrence of items from within one set. JB is likewise not cohesive grammatically, except for some "linkage" between clauses and the anaphoric *it* in the first sentence (and cohesion by structural parallelism, an important type of grammatical cohesion about which too little is yet known to permit accurate assessment); nor, however, is there much lexical cohesion in the passage. AW on the other hand is more grammatically cohesive; apart from clause linkage, there are the anaphoric pronouns *it, she, they*, and the anaphoric *the* in *the walls* and *the design*; at the same time there is, as often in Angus Wilson, lexical cohesion by occurrence of items within a set, for example *ugly . . . hideous*.

Other points of interest include: the distribution of lexical items in nominal groups as subject in clause structure; the use of original and of familiar collocations – compare JB: *picture/hang* with DT *picture/thick*; the use of items from the lexical sets of colour and smell; the distribution of verbal groups and words in the "cline of verbality" and the choice of lexical items, weak and powerful, operating in the verbal groups. But enough has been said to illustrate textual analysis, and by now perhaps the pass mark has been awarded. That the linguist can suggest how to describe a text is perhaps, from the point of view of the literary analyst, the main justification for his existence.

At the very beginning of this paper I used the term "application" to refer to the study of literary texts by the theories and methods of linguistics, and I would stress that it is in fact an application of linguistics that is under discussion. We can be more specific than this. One branch of linguistics is descriptive linguistics, the study of how language works; this contrasts both with historical linguistics, the study of how language persists in time, and with institutional linguistics, the study of the varieties and uses of, and the attitudes to, language. Within descriptive linguistics, one kind of description is textual: the linguist describes a text, written or spoken; this contrasts with exemplificatory description, which presents the categories of the language and illustrates them, or if formalized, generates a set of described sentences and derives others from them. The linguistic study of literature is textual description, and it is no different from any other textual description; it is not a new branch or a new level or a new kind of linguistics but the application of existing theories and methods. What the linguist does when faced with a literary text is the same as what he does when faced with any text that he is going to describe.

But all description involves institutional considerations, and literary description is no exception. When we describe language we have to find out and specify the range of validity of the description; this means taking into account the variety represented, both dialect (variety according to user) and register (variety according to use). Register and dialect differences are of course variable in delicacy: we may talk of the register of literature, subdivided into the registers of prose and verse, each subdivided further into the various genres. At any particular point on the scale of delicacy the total set of registers may form a continuum, and there will certainly be a great deal that is common, linguistically, to all; but there are also linguistic differences between them – otherwise they would not be recognized as different registers. And just as in dialect we eventually, when we get delicate enough, reach the individual: every speaker his own idiolect, or bundle of available individual dialects: so also in register we come finally to the individual – every speaker, and writer, his own bundle of individual registers. Again, it does not need a new branch of linguistics to recognize and account for individual styles: all language is individual activity in a given variety, and thus there is an institutional basis, in the technical sense of institutional linguistics, in all description, literary or otherwise.

This does not mean, however, that for each text or individual writer we start again with a totally new description, with a new set of categories unrelated to what has gone before. Indeed, if many of the things written about the language of particular works of literature are much less useful than they might have been, this is more often than not because the writer, having neither made a description of the language himself nor used one made by someone else (other than the misty image of English that is still so often given in our schools), has invented a set of *ad hoc* categories for each text he has examined. What is said has therefore no relation to what was said about any other text, still less to any description of the language as a whole. If the linguistic analysis of literature is to be of any value or significance at all it must be done against the background of a general description of the language, using the same theories, methods and categories. A literary text has meaning against the background of the language as a whole, in all its uses; how can its language be understood except as the selection by the individual writer from the total resources at his disposal? Yet all too often the observations about the language of a work of literature bear no relation to any descriptive account of those resources.

The same point applies to the comparison of texts: it is impossible to compare one text with another unless both have been described in the

17

same way. All literary analysis, if one is at all interested in the special properties of the language of literary texts or of a particular genre, is essentially comparative. This makes it all the more essential to be consistent, accurate and explicit: to base the analysis firmly on a sound, existing description of the language. While this means restraining oneself from inventing new categories, a temptation to which the literary analyst must be especially exposed, it does not of course preclude new alignments of established categories, such as Professor McIntosh's use of "involvement" in studying Shakespearean dialogue.[6] These may be required in any linguistic study, but they are perhaps especially fruitful in comparative literary studies. Another example is the relation of cohesion referred to above, which is very valuable in comparing long texts. The concept of cohesion has been developed especially for literary textual analysis; but every category brought together under this heading is drawn from the total description of English and has exactly the same range of application whatever the text to which it is applied.

Of course no amount of faithful adherence to the same description will be of any use if the description is not a good one in the first place. We are still plagued with steam grammars, with their ragged categories, their jumbled criteria and their fictions; descriptions of English which give little insight into the way the language works or indeed the way any language works, except perhaps the Latin they were originally modelled on. This kind of pre-linguistic linguistics is no use for literary studies. It is no paradox that it is modern scientific, including statistical, linguistics that proves really illuminating when applied to the study of literature – no paradox at least to anyone who studies language seriously, since the study of language perhaps more than anything else shows up the artificial nature of the dichotomy between arts and sciences. Not only do we need to be able to state accurately the role of a particular pattern or item in the language, what it contrasts with, what it may and may not combine with and so on; we may want to know its probability of occurrence under various definable conditions. It is of no interest to show that nine-tenths of all clauses in a certain poem are, say, of the class "interrogative" unless we know how this relates to the probabilities of occurrence of this and the other terms in the mood system. The originality of a person's use of his language consists in his selecting a feature not where it is impossible (has not been previously selected) but where another would be more probable – and even more in his balanced combination of the improbable with the probable, as in the lexis of *Leda and the Swan*, which is an interesting blend of old and new collocations.

18

I have stressed grammar, but this is of course only one of the levels involved, and the usefulness of linguistic theory in application to literary studies depends on its ability both to comprehend and to integrate all the levels of language. That is another reason for insisting on the need for up-to-date linguistics: not only must the literary analyst have access to theories for the description of all levels of linguistic patterning – grammar, lexis, phonology and phonetics, and their graphic parallels – but he must be able to see them in interaction as they must always interact in any language event. He may want to analyse, for example, *her loosening thighs* as a grammatical item, with a certain structure – is it the same as *the staggering girl*, or not?; as a collocation in lexis – is *loosen* the same lexical item as *loose*?; as a piece of English phonology – how does it exploit the patterns of English rhythm and intonation?; and in terms of its phonetic properties. He may feel he needs to do all this so that he can see what it is doing in the poem. I have not, for lack of time, given illustrations of phonological and phonetic analysis; but this is a good place to point out that when we speak of "linguistics" in literary studies, this is really a shorthand for "the linguistic sciences", and is to be taken to include them both – linguistics and phonetics.

If it is considered that the meaning of a piece of literature lies between rather than within the lines, it seems likely that linguistics has no message. This is not to say that the literary allusion is outside the scope of linguistic analysis; on the contrary, all use of language is allusion, and textual allusion is only one endpoint on a scale the other end of which is the context of our whole previous experience of the use of an item or pattern: hence the insistence that a work of literature, like any other piece of language activity, is meaningful only in the perspective of the whole range of uses of the language. Similarly it is not to say that literary "figures of speech" cannot be analysed; it is true, however, that they do need rigorous linguistic definition. Again there is no sharp line to be drawn between metaphor and non-metaphor; but if linguistics cannot describe certain parts of language it is likely to be of little use for any application. Linguistics is not and will never be the whole of literary analysis, and only the literary analyst – not the linguist – can determine the place of linguistics in literary studies. But if a text is to be described at all, then it should be described properly; and this means by the theories and methods developed in linguistics, the subject whose task is precisely to show how language works. The literary analyst is not content with amateur psychology, armchair philosophy, or fictitious social history; yet the linguistics that is applied in some accounts of literature, and the statements about language that are used as evidence, are no less amateur, armchair and fictitious. It is encouraging that literary scholars are coming more and more to reject such statements, and to demand a standard of objective linguistic scholarship that is no less rigorous than the standard of literary scholarship which they expect, and exact, from themselves.

Table 1 Deixis in nominal groups in *Leda and the Swan*

+/- M/Q	+ M/Q			− M/Q
+/- D	M	Q	MQ	
+D specific	the staggering girl the dark webs the feathered glory the broken wall the burning roof and tower the indifferent beak those terrified vague fingers that white rush her helpless breast her loosening thighs	the thighs caressed by the dark webs her nape caught in his bill	the great wings beating above the staggering girl the strange heart beating the brute blood of the air	the loins the air his bill his breast her nape his knowledge his power
+D non-specific	a sudden blow	a shudder in the loins		
- D				body

Table 2 Verbal items in *Leda and the Swan* and the fifteen lines from Tennyson's *Morte d'Arthur*

	Items in verbal group (i.e. operating at 'predicator' in clause structure)					Items in nominal group (i.e. not operating at P.)
	1	2	3	4	5	6
Clause class (system: status)	Independent	Dependent		Rankshifted		(irrelevant)
Group class (system: finiteness)	Finite	Finite	Non-finite	Finite	Non-finite	
Leda and the Swan	hold push feel engender put on	lie let	drop catch up master		beat caress catch lay	stagger loosen burn break
	5	2	3	–	5	4
Morte d'Arthur	rose (2) ran plung'd clutch'd wheel'd threw made shot flash'd fell caught brandish'd drew went	shock dipt	leaping flashing whirl'd		seen cloth'd	
	15	2	3	–	2	–

Note: Compare the narrative style in Tennyson (the most 'active' verbs in the most 'verbal' setting) with the tension set up in *Leda* (the most 'active' verbs in the least 'verbal' setting, as if describing a picture rather than recounting an event).

Notes

1. See Thomas A. Sebeok (ed.): *Style in Language* (Cambridge, MA: MIT Press, 1960), p. 352.
2. *Word*, 17 December 1961 (see Volume 1, Chapter 2).
3. A more correct theoretical statement of structural cohesion is that it is presupposition at the rank of the sentence. Presupposition is the special relation between elements of a non–chain-exhausting structure that have as their exponents terms in a non–choice-exhausting system. Thus in *I'll come if you want me* the structural relation of "conditioning" clause and "conditioned" clause, which is a type of dependence, is one of presupposition.
4. I omit here phonological cohesion: that with grammatical categories expounded directly by phonology, for example (British English) tone 4 in anaphoric use.
5. *Op. cit.*, p. 356.
6. See Angus McIntosh, '"As You Like It": a grammatical clue to character', *Review of English Literature*, 4.2, April 1963.

Chapter Two

TEXT AS SEMANTIC CHOICE
IN SOCIAL CONTEXTS
(1977)

1 The semantic system

1.1 Initial assumptions

First, and least controversially, let us assume that the semantic system is one of three levels, or strata, that constitute the linguistic system:
  Semantic (semology)
  Lexicogrammatical (lexology: syntax, morphology and lexis)
  Phonological (phonology and phonetics).
These are strata in Lamb's "stratificational" sense.

Second, let us assume that the semantic system has the four components experiential, logical, interpersonal and textual. The first two of these are closely related, more so than other pairs, and can be combined under the heading of "ideational" (but see 1.3 below):

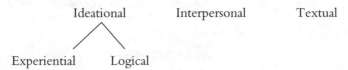

Third, let us assume that each stratum, and each component, is described as a network of options, sets of interrelated choices having the form "if a, then either b or c". Variants of this general form include: "if a, then either x or y or z and either m or n; if x, or if m, then either p or q; if both y and n, then either r or s or t" and so on. The description

First published in *Grammars and Descriptions*, edited by Teun A. van Dijk and János S. Petöfi. Berlin: Walter de Gruyter, 1977, pp. 176–226.

is, therefore, a paradigmatic one, in which environments are also defined paradigmatically: the environment of any option is the set of options that are related to it, including those that define its condition of entry. The description is also open-ended: there is no point at which no further sub-categorization of the options is possible.

Fourth, let us assume that each component of the semantic system specifies its own structures, as the "output" of the options in the network (each act of choice contributes to the formation of the structure). It is the function of the lexicogrammatical stratum to map the structures one on to another so as to form a single integrated structure that represents all components simultaneously. With negligible exceptions, every operational instance of a lexicogrammatical construct in the adult language – anything that realizes text – is structured as the expression of all four components. In other words, any instance of language in use "means" in these various ways, and shows that it does so in its grammar.

Fifth, let us assume that the lexicogrammatical system is organized by rank (as opposed to by immediate constituent structure); each rank is the locus of structural configurations, the place where structures from the different components are mapped on to each other. The "rank scale" for the lexicogrammar of English is:

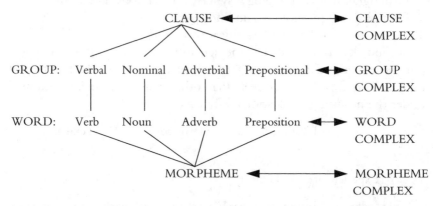

Complexes are univariate (recursive) structures formed by paratactic or hypotactic combinations – co-ordination, apposition, modification and the like – at the rank in question; a clause complex may be formed for example by two clauses in co-ordination. All other structures are multivariate (non-recursive). A "sentence" is defined as a clause complex. See Huddleston (1965), Hudson (1967 and 1971), and Sinclair (1972).

1.2 Structural configurations

It follows from the above that each type of unit − clause, verbal group, nominal group, etc. − is in itself a structural composite, a combination of structures each of which derives from one or other component of the semantics.

A clause, for example, has a structure formed out of elements such as Agent, Process, Extent; this structure derives from the system of transitivity, which is part of the experiential component. Simultaneously it has a structure formed out of the elements Modal and Propositional: this derives from the system of mood, which is part of the interpersonal component. It also has a third structure composed of the elements Theme and Rheme, deriving from the theme system, which is part of the textual component.

For example:

		|the Grays|retired	|to their beds|
Experiential	TRANSITIVITY	Medium	Process	Location: locative
Interpersonal	MOOD	Modal	Propositional
Textual	THEME	Theme	Rheme

It is not the case that the same constituent structure (same bracketing) holds throughout, with only the labels differing. This is already clear from this example: the thematic and modal structures are simple binary ones, whereas the transitivity structure is not. In any case, the representation just given is oversimplified; the Modal constituent includes the finite element in the verb, and consists of Subject plus Finiteness, yielding an analysis as follows:

Clause: \| the Grays \| 'did \| retire' \| to their beds \|

	the Grays	'did	retire'	to their beds
(1)	Medium	Process		Location: locative
(2)	Modal		Propositional	
	Subject	Finite		
(3)	Theme	Rheme		

There may be differences at other points too; in general it is characteristic of lexicogrammatical structures that the configurations deriving

25

from the various functional components of the semantic system will differ not only in their labelling but in their bracketing also.

The logical component is distinct from the other three in that all logical meanings, and only logical meanings, are expressed through the structure of "unit complexes": clause complex, group complex and so on. For example:

Clause complex:	the Grays stopped maligning the hippopotamuses	and retired to their beds
Logical: (co-ordination)	(Clause) A ⟶	(Clause) B

1.3 Functional components of the system

The grouping of semantic components differs according to the perspective from which we look at them.

From the standpoint of their realization in the lexicogrammatical system (i.e. "from below"), the logical component, since it alone is, and it always is, realized through recursive structures, is the one that stands out as distinct from all the others.

From the standpoint of the functions of the linguistic system in relation to some higher-level semiotic that is realized through the **linguistic** semiotic (i.e. "from above"), it is the textual component that appears as distinct, since the textual component has an enabling function in respect of the other components: language can effectively express ideational and interpersonal meanings only because it can create text. Text is language in operation; and the textual component embodies the semantic systems by means of which text is created.

From the point of view of the organization within the semantic system itself (i.e. "from the same level"), the experiential and the logical go together because there is greater systemic interdependence between these two than between other pairings. This shows up in various places throughout the English semantic system (the general pattern may well be the same in all languages, though the specifics are different): for example, the semantics of time reference, of speaking ("X said −"), and of identifying ("A = B") all involve some interplay of experiential and logical systems. To illustrate this from the semantics of speaking, the **process** 'say' is an option in the transitivity system, which is experiential; whereas the **relation** between the process of saying and what is said − the "reporting" relation − is an option in the logical system of interclause relations. The picture is something like the following:

Functional components of semantic systems,
seen from different vantage points:

Semiotic – functional ("from above"):

```
                ┌─────────────────────────────────┐
            (extrinsic)                        (enabling)
        ┌───────────────┐
    Ideational      Interpersonal              Textual
```

Semantic ("from their own level"):

```
                ┌───────────────────┬───────────────┐
            Ideational          Interpersonal     Textual
        ┌───────────────┐
    Logical        Experiential
```

Lexicogrammatical ("from below"):

```
        ┌──────────────────────────────┐
    (univariate)                    (multivariate)
                              ┌──────────────┬──────────────┐
    Logical               Experiential  Interpersonal  Textual
```

Table 1 sets out the principal semantic systems arranged by function and rank, showing their functional location in the semantic system and their point of origin in the lexicogrammar.

1.4 Systems of the spoken language

In considering the nature of text, we have to take note of the fact that certain semantic systems are realized through the medium of phonological systems which have no counterpart in the written language.

In English there are two important systems of this kind: the INFORMATION system, and the system of KEY.

The information system, which derives from the textual component, determines how the text is organized as a flow of messages. It does not operate through a unit on the lexicogrammatical rank scale but specifies a distinct constituent structure of its own, which we refer to as "information structure". The information structure is realized through the intonation system of the phonology; and the structural unit, the **information unit**, is realized as a phonological constituent (i.e. a unit on the phonological rank scale), the one which is generally known as the tone group, or tone unit. This is the carrier

Table 1   Functional components of the semantic system

	IDEATIONAL		INTERPERSONAL		TEXTUAL	
	LOGICAL	EXPERIENTIAL				(COHESION)
		STRUCTURAL				NON-STRUCTURAL
		1. CLAUSE STRUCTURE				
Complexes at all ranks (clause complex, etc.)	expansion	clause: transitivity, modulation; polarity	clause: mood, modality		clause: theme	reference
	identity					
	projection	verbal group: types of process; tense	verbal group: person, polarity	*connotations of attitude etc.*	verbal group: voice; contrast	substitution/ ellipsis
	(paratactic and hypotactic)	nominal group: types of participant; class, quality, quantity, etc.	nominal group: person ('role')		nominal group: deixis	conjunction
		adverbial group: prepositional group: types of circumstance	adverbial group: prepositional group comment		adverbial group: prepositional group: conjunction	lexical cohesion: reiteration, collocation
		2. INFORMATION STRUCTURE				
			information unit: key		information unit: information distribution and focus	

of one complete tone contour. See Halliday (1967b), Elmenoufy (1969), Halliday (1970).

Since it is realized through intonation, which is not shown in the writing system, the information structure is a feature of the spoken language only; and any interpretation of the information structure of a written text depends on the "implication of utterance" which is a feature of written language. There are two aspects to this: (1) the interpretation of the paragraphological signals that the written language employs, such as punctuation, underlining and other forms of emphasis; (2) the assumption of the "good reason" principle, namely that the mapping of the information structure on to other structures will take the unmarked form except where there is good reason for it to do otherwise (or, to put the same thing in another way, that it will take the form that is **locally** unmarked).

This does not mean that we are left with only one possible reading of a text, because in any real text there will be both ambiguities and conflicts in the "co-text", the relevant textual environment at any point. Different features may be counted as relevant; some features will allow more than one interpretation; and some features will run counter to others in the pressures they exert. But there will always be a vast number of theoretically possible readings that are ruled out by the co-text, so that the number of sensible interpretations is reasonably small.

To illustrate this point adequately would take a lengthy article in itself. But a brief illustration of it is given after the discussion of the information system and the systems of "key", at the end of 2.4. Since the information system is part of the textual component it is treated in the context of the discussion of that component, in the next main section (2.3, below).

The system that we are referring to as "key" is not part of the textual component, but of the interpersonal component. It determines the role of each message unit in the interaction of speaker and hearer. In fact there is no single system of key; the term is a covering label for a whole number of specific sub-systems related to the interpersonal system of mood. These systems operate with the information unit as their locus of origin, and are realized through variations in "tone": that is, in the intonation contour that is associated with each tone group. The systems of "key" are referred to briefly in Section 2.4 for the purposes of the illustration.

2   The textual (text-forming) component

2.1   Text-forming resources of the system

The entire semantic system is "text-forming", in the sense that a text is the product of meanings of all four kinds – experiential, logical and interpersonal, as well as textual.

The textual component, however, is the component whose function is specifically that of creating text, of making the difference between language in the abstract and language in use. In other words it is through the semantic options of the textual component that language comes to be relevant to its environment, as distinct from decontextualized language like words listed in a dictionary or sentences in a grammar book.

The Prague school were the first to identify this component, and it came to be known in their work as "functional sentence perspective"; see Daneš (1974). There it has been defined lexicogrammatically, as a component of sentence structure; and in consequence the concept of "FSP" is not taken to include those features which are not aspects of sentence structure – the set of features that has been grouped together under the heading of "cohesion" (see below).

The text-forming resources of language are partly structural (in the sense that they are organized as structure-generating networks of options) and partly not. An example of one that is not structural is anaphoric reference by a third person pronoun such as *he*. The person system itself, in whatever form it appears in the language in question (it will generally be relatable to some idealized norm such as first/ second/third, singular/plural), is a structure-generating system; but it is not the person system as such that is text-forming. The text-forming agency is the relation between *he* and its antecedent; and this is not a structural relation in the defined sense.

The textual component of English is made up of the following: (I) The structure-generating systems (those of functional sentence perspective), which are of two kinds, (i) thematic systems and (ii) information systems; see Halliday (1968). (II) The cohesive relations, which are of four kinds, (i) referential, (ii) substitutive-elliptical, (iii) conjunctive and (iv) lexical; see Gutwinski (1974), Halliday and Hasan (1976). These are what provide texture in the language. There is no implication here that these are universal features; they may be, or they may not. But the systems in each network, and the way the systems are realized, are specific to the language in question.

These systems are outlined in subsections 2.2–2.7.

2.2   THEMATIC *systems*

The thematic systems are systems of the clause, and represent the speaker's organization of the clause as a message. The basic structure through which this organization is realized is that of Theme and Rheme, which in turn is expressed through the order of the elements: the Theme comes first.

The Theme is typically a single element in the clause structure, like *they* in *they called up their friends and neighbors* (s. 16), *late that evening* (s. 12), *to the Grays* (s. 10); including complex elements (group complexes) like *an arrogant gray parrot and his arrogant mate* (s. 1). Often it is foregrounded by being enclosed in a predication, for example *it was long after midnight before* (s. 17).

Very frequently, however, the Theme has the form of a nominalization, a device which allows two or more elements to be taken together as the Theme. There are no examples of this in the text. If, instead of *he calls her snooky-ookums* (s. 2), in which the Theme is *he*, the author had written *what he calls her is snooky-ookums*, the Theme would have been *(what) he calls her*. This is the function of nominalization in the clause: it permits the expression of all possible options in the thematic organization. (Note that *the tender things they said to each other during the monolithic give-and-take of their courtship* is not an example of a multiple Theme; it is a simple Theme consisting of one nominal group only — which happens to have a clause embedded in it as Qualifier).

The thematic system is speaker-oriented, in the sense that the Theme is the speaker's chosen point of departure, and the choice of Theme is independent of what has gone before. In the typical, or unmarked, instance, the Theme is selected from among the elements that are also Given (see 2.3 below): it is something that the speaker is also presenting as environmentally recoverable to the hearer. Hence the most usual type of Theme is a personal pronoun; about half of those in the text are of this kind. But the theme system is not determined by external factors, and with only minor restrictions any alignment of clause elements as Theme and Rheme will be possible.

For each of the principal options in the MOOD system, there is an unmarked choice of Theme. In the declarative and imperative moods, the unmarked Theme is the Subject; and it is important to stress in this connection that the function of Subject in the clause is no less a semantic function than other clause functions such as Agent or Theme. It is a function deriving from the interpersonal component, via the system of mood: the Subject is the "mood-carrying" (modal) nominal, meaning "I state that X . . ." in the declarative and "I want that X . . ." in the imperative.

In the interrogative mood, the unmarked Theme depends on the type of interrogative: it is the WH-element in a WH-type interrogative, and the finite element of the verb in a yes/no interrogative. In either case the meaning is "I want to know X", where X is either the interpretation of the WH-element, or the polarity ("yes or no?", expressed in the finite verb).

Theme	Rheme	
he	calls her snooky-ookums	declarative (s. 2)
("you")	listen to those squawks	imperative (s. 13)
what in the world	can they see in each other?	WH-interrogative (s. 14)
can	you believe that?	yes/no interrogative (s. 3)

The principle that initial position is thematic in function explains a great many features of sequence ("word-order") in the grammar of English, both in the clause and in other units. The unmarked theme of a question is what the questioner wants to know; hence in a WH-interrogative the

31

WH-element comes first, and in a yes/no interrogative the finite element, which is the one that carries the polarity, comes first. The unmarked theme of a command is 'I want (me/you/us) to . . .'; hence the modal Subject comes first – optionally omitted in the unmarked "you" option. The same principle lies behind the tendency for the Subject to come first in a declarative; only here it is much weaker, and more readily overridden by marked themes of various kinds. It also extends to other units than the clause: it is essentially the same thematic principle which determines the assignment of initial position in the group, where it is not subject to choice: the deictic element in the nominal group, the element expressing primary tense or modality in the verbal group, and the preposition in the prepositional group. In each case these are the elements which relate the group to its environment, and so determine its relevance in the message; hence in a language in which initial position is strongly thematic, such as English, they will tend to float to the front and stay there.

2.3   INFORMATION systems

The information systems organize the discourse into quanta of information, or message blocks, called "information units", and determine the internal structure of each information unit.

The structure of the information unit is made up of the elements Given and New. These are realized through the phonological systems of intonation. Each information unit is encoded as one unit of intonation, or "tone group"; and the New element is marked out by the use of tonic prominence as a culminative feature – the syllable on which the tonic prominence falls is the last accented syllable of the New. The element bearing the culminative tonic accent is said to bear the "information focus".

The unmarked place for the New element is at the end of the information unit. In such instances, i.e. when the final element is New, what precedes may be either Given or New. In all other instances, i.e. when some non-final element is presented as New, then every other element in the information unit is thereby signalled as Given.

The meaning of Given is 'treated by the speaker as recoverable to the hearer from the environment'. Conversely, New means 'treated as non-recoverable'. Non-recoverable does not imply that the **item** in question cannot have occurred before, but that if it has, the meaning that is associated with it is non-recoverable in the context. For example,

D' you want to speak to John, or to Mary? – I want to speak to **John**.
Have you met John and Mary Smith? – I know **John**.

In both instances, *John* is shown as New in the response; not because it has not occurred before, but because it is carrying other information ('John is the one I want to speak to', 'John but not Mary') that the speaker assumes to be non-recoverable to the hearer – since otherwise, presumably, he would have asked the question in the first place. It is important not to confuse the concept of New with that of 'no previous mention'.

The intonational prominence – the tonic accent – marks the culmination of the New, so that anything **following** is automatically Given; this includes all inherently Given elements – anaphoric and deictic items – that happen to occur finally in the information unit. The status of what **precedes** is governed by two principles: (1) the system of marking, and (2) the structural hierarchy of the grammar (the "rank scale");

(1) (a) If the information focus falls on an element that is other than the last accented element in the information unit (an "accented" element being any element that is not "inherently Given"), the focus is *marked*.

Semantically this means that the information structure is environmentally specific; there is no indeterminacy, and all else in the information unit is Given. Example (s. 11):

(But they decided instead to . . .) // 1 **gossip** a/bout the / shameless / pair //

Here the focus is on *gossip*, which is non-final; it is therefore marked, and signals *the shameless pair* as explicitly Given. (This happens also to provide an excellent illustration of another cohesive principle, a form of lexical cohesion, whereby a "general word" is introduced as a Given element (here the word *pair*) to serve as the carrier of an attitudinal Epithet (here *shameless*).)

(1) (b) If the focus falls on the last accented element (last element other than any that are "inherently Given"), it is unmarked. Semantically this means that the information structure is not environmentally specific; and indeterminacy results. In this case, the whole information unit may be New; or the New may begin at any structural boundary. The only restriction is that the New cannot be discontinuous: G+N, N+G, G+N+G are all possible structures, but N+G+N is not – the

last can be achieved only by encoding as a sequence of two information units. For an example see below under (2).

(2) The focal element, the element that is defined by the tonic prominence, is the highest-ranking sub-constituent for which the prominence is culminative. That is to say, if the information unit is one clause (this being, as a matter of fact, the unmarked form of the mapping), the focal constituent will be a group – the group being the next-ranking unit below the clause – **provided the tonic prominence falls on the last accented syllable in the entire group**. Example (s. 15):

// I would as / soon / live with a / pair of / unoiled / garden / **shears** //

where the tonic prominence on *shears* marks the entire group a *pair of unoiled garden shears* as being the focal constituent (since the information unit is a clause). If the tonic prominence had been assigned to *unoiled*, the focal constituent would be only the **word** *unoiled* itself, since the prominence would not be culminative for the whole nominal group, but only for the word. In the former instance, with the reading we have assumed, the information structure is unmarked. In the latter, the information structure would be marked, and would therefore presuppose a specific semantic environment, in which the point at issue was 'what kind of garden shears would you as soon live with?'

The information system, in contrast to the thematic system, is hearer-oriented. That is to say, the meaning that is encoded in the Given-New structure is that of 'recoverable, or not recoverable, to the hearer'. This in turn depends on the environment, both verbal and non-verbal; if a meaning is recoverable, it is in some way or other (but there are many possible ways) present in the environment. Since the environment includes the preceding text, the information structure often serves to relate a piece to what has gone before it. But recoverability is not a simple matter of previous mention; and in any case it is the speaker's decision what he is going to **treat as** recoverable. He is free to use the system as he pleases, and frequently uses it to great effect as a means of **constructing** the environment it is designed to reflect.

The speaker has total discretion; he is constructing all the meanings at once. The reader of a written text is in the peculiar position of having discretion at just those points where the written medium happens to be most ambiguous; of which the information system is one. He can, if he chooses, read sentences 2 and 3 as

34

// 4 **he** calls her // 1 snooky / **ookums** said / Mrs. /Gray // 2 can /
you believe / that //

which imposes the interpretation 'Do **you** believe that's her name? –
that's what **he** calls her'. The only grounds for rejecting this are that it
doesn't make sense (of the text; it makes perfectly good sense of the
sentence). There could, of course, be no better grounds than that. But
it illustrates the kind of decision that a reader is making all the time,
whereas a hearer has the solution presented to him readymade.

We tend to think of the information unit as being unlike the
lexicogrammatical units of clause, group and so on, in that while
the latter are specified simultaneously by all semantic components,
the former is defined solely by the textual component. A clause is the
domain of systems of all kinds, experiential (e.g. transitivity), interpersonal (e.g. mood), and textual (e.g. theme); whereas the information
unit is the domain only of the information systems. But this is not
wholly true. The information unit is also exploited by the interpersonal component as the carrier of the systems of KEY: those, related to
mood, whereby the speaker selects the key signature that attaches to
the particular role assignment he is making for himself and for the
hearer. The choice of key is expressed by the tone contour; and the
point of origin for this choice is the information unit – since the
information unit is encoded as a tone group, and one tone group is
one complete tone contour, the two naturally coincide. So the
information structure operates as a kind of distinct but simultaneous
constituent hierarchy, or "rank scale"; one that is mapped on to the
conventional grammatical hierarchy of clause, group, word and morpheme, but realizes a different set of semantic systems. The rationale
for this is very simple: the information structure is simply the phonological system doing extra work. It is the phonological hierarchy that
is being "borrowed" for the occasion.

The various types of phonological contrast, those of intonation, of
rhythm or "pulse", and of articulation, are organized as a distinct
constituent hierarchy, or "phonological rank scale"; in English, tone
group, foot (or stress group), syllable, phoneme. This hierarchy, and the
"phonotactics" that is based on it, functions **as a whole** in the realization
of the lexicogrammatical system. But once it has come into being, so
to speak, particular parts of it function on their own in the representation
of particular semantic systems, which can thus be regarded as "bypassing"
the grammar – as "meanings encoded directly in sounds" – although
for theoretical reasons it is useful to include them in the systematic

representation at the lexicogrammatical level. Prominent among these are the ones that we are referring to as systems of key.

The "key" systems are not part of the textual component. But there is some overlap between them and the information systems, which is of significance for text description. The next subsection explains this point.

2.4   Digression: the systems of "key"

The KEY is expressed by the choice of TONE, the system of pitch contours that is carried by the tone group. In its bare essentials, this is a system of five tones: fall (tone 1), rise (tone 2), low rise (tone 3), fall-rise (tone 4), rise-fall (tone 5).

These tones have different meanings – that is, they realize different semantic systems – according to their modal environment: according to whether they occur in the environment of a declarative, an interrogative, or an imperative, and what kind of declarative, interrogative or imperative it is. For example, a rising tone (tone 2) on a yes/no interrogative means a "straight" question; the same tone on a WH-interrogative means (according to where the prominence is located) either an "echo" question or a question embedded in a request for permission to ask it; and on a declarative it means a contradiction.

The pitch contour as specified in this way begins on the point of tonic prominence (as defined in 2.3 above). This prominence, although often interpreted in terms of stress ("primary stress" in the theory of supra-segmentals), is in fact melodic prominence: the point of concentration of the melodic contour (the main fall, the fall-and-turn, etc.). If there is any part of the tone group before the tonic accent, this is the locus of a sub-melody or "pretone" which adds further specification to the meaning. Since, as already noted, everything that comes **after** the tonic prominence is "Given", there are no "post-tones", but only predictable prolongations of the contour, known as "tails".

For a narrative text with dialogue it is relevant to note that all quoting clauses function as tails to preceding quoted (direct speech) passages:

> // 1 ͺ I would as / soon / live with a / pair of / unoiled / garden / **shears** / said her in/amo/ratus //

There is an optional silent beat at the end of the quoted clause:

> / **shears** ͺ said her in/amo/ratus //.

Once again, in reading a written text we assume unmarked choices: we assume the unmarked key unless there is good reason in the environment for the choice of another one – which then becomes the **locally** unmarked choice, since the environment sets up a local norm. So, for example, on a yes/no interrogative such as *Can you believe that?* (s. 3), taken in isolation, we would assign a tone 2 (rising). However, the text environment shows that here it is to be interpreted not as a straight question but as an exclamation; so it will be assigned a tone that is unmarked for exclamations (tone 5, or a certain variety of tone 1). It could be argued that the specific meanings that are present in the question itself, expressed by the lexical verb *believe* in second person with "potential" modulation, are sufficient to convey the sense of exclamation; but this does not affect the point – rather it illustrates a more general point, that of the flexibility and relative indeterminacy of what it is that constitutes the environment.

It would be out of place here to describe the systems of key in detail; for a fuller account, see Halliday (1967b), and also Halliday (1970). In any case many of them are relevant only to spoken texts in spontaneous verbal interaction, and are not activated in the reading of a written text aloud. But there is one system which lies on the borderline of key and information structure (and hence on the border-line of the interpersonal and textual components) which is, on the contrary, **more** activated in loud reading than in any other variety of English; so we will refer to this in a final illustration from the text.

Given a pair of successive information units, one an unmarked (tone 1) declarative and the other semantically related to it, there is a system of options for the latter, which is realized as a choice among tone 1, tone 3 and tone 4. There is, further, an unmarked association between this and the three syntactic forms which this relation may take: (1) independent (unrelated) clause with parallel structure, (2) paratactically related clause, and (3) hypotactically related clause. These unmarked patterns can be illustrated as follows:

(1) // 1 the hippopotamuses stopped criticizing the Grays;
          // 1 the Grays stopped maligning the hippopotamuses //
(2) // 3 the hippopotamuses stopped criticizing the Grays,
          // 1 and the Grays stopped maligning the hippopotamuses //
(3) // 4 when the hippopotamuses stopped criticizing the Grays,
          // 1 the Grays stopped maligning the hippopotamuses //

Variation in meaning is achieved by means of marked combinations: tone 4 with an independent clause, tone 3 with a hypotactic clause, and so on. And the contrast between tone 3 and tone 4, indicating different degrees of dependence, is available to almost any information unit that is contingent on another one having tone 1.

If now we consider a sentence such as the last one of the main paragraph (s. 11), we find a large number of possible interpretations, including but by no means limited to the following:

But they decided instead	to phone their friends and neighbors	and gossip about the shameless pair
// 3 . . . instead	// 3 . . . neighbors	// 1 . gossip . . . //
// 3 . . . instead	// 1 . . . neighbors	// 1 . gossip . . . //
// 4 . . . instead	// 3 . . . neighbors	// 1 . gossip . . . //
// 4 . . . instead	// 1 . . . neighbors	// 1 . gossip . . . //
// 1	. . . neighbors	// 1 . gossip . . . //
// 4 . . . instead	// 1	. . . . gossip . . . //

each of which includes a number of sub-varieties. All these are different "readings" of the text, and all have different meanings, slight and subtle though these may be. This illustrates the way in which the information structure, and associated systems of key, are supplied by the reader in the loud-reading (and at least in a certain type of silent reading) of a written text. Reading a text is not a purely receptive activity; the reader is also a speaker, even if he is only talking to himself.

2.5 Referential cohesion

Certain elements in the linguistic system have the property that they are interpretable only by reference to something other than themselves. These are the personals, demonstratives (including *the*) and comparatives; for example *she, this, earlier* as in *She's shy. This is what I meant. You should have come earlier.* These are perfectly **intelligible** on their own; but they are **interpretable** only when we know who "she" is, what "this" is, and "earlier" than what.

The reference may be *exophoric*, to some phenomenon located outside the text and in the context of situation; or *endophoric*, to an element within the text, typically something that has preceded (*anaphoric*) but sometimes to something that follows (*cataphoric*). So *she* may refer to someone present and identifiable, or to someone previously mentioned; *this* likewise to some object present and identifiable, or to something – an object or other phenomenon, or a fact – just mentioned or about to be mentioned; *earlier* may involve comparison with the present moment ("than now") or with some time previously mentioned. In a written narrative, all reference can be assumed to be endophoric; but the possibility of exophoric reference appears at one remove in the dialogue that is embedded in the narrative. For example in *He calls her snooky-ookums . . . Can you believe that?* (s. 2/3), *he* and *her* are exophoric to the narrative, whereas *that* is endophoric to the dialogue and refers to "(the fact that) he calls her snooky-ookums".

Reference is a semantic relation and is usually assumed, no doubt justifiably, to be in origin exophoric; and this explains why it takes the forms it does. Personal reference depends on the concept of personal roles in the speech situation ("some person or object other than speaker and addressee"); demonstrative reference is based on proximity ("near" or "not near"; in some languages it is specifically tied to the concept of person, the meanings being "near me", "near you", "not near either of us"); comparative reference involves a conception of likeness and unlikeness between phenomena. The word *the* functions as the unmarked demonstrative; it signals that the referent can be identified, but without locating it on any semantic scale.

Whatever its origin in the linguistic system, reference is a primary text-forming agency, since all endophoric reference contributes to the making of a text. It is a signal that the interpretation is to be sought elsewhere; and if the source lies in some other word or words in the text, cohesion is set up between the two passages in question. This cohesion is independent of the linguistic structure, and so may extend beyond any structural unit; it provides an alternative to structure as a means of cohering one part of the meaning with another.

There are numerous instances in the text of reference as a cohesive relation, across sentence boundaries, both endophoric within the narrative and exophoric from the dialogue to the narrative. Examples from sentences 13–15: (dialogue to narrative) demonstrative *those* [*squawks*], personal *they*, comparative *as soon*; (narrative to narrative) *the* [*male hippopotamus*], *the* [*female hippopotamus*], *her* [*inamoratus*].

2.6   Substitutive and elliptical cohesion

Certain elements which are not referential in the above sense create texture by substitution: they function as alternatives to the repetition of a particular item, and hence cohere with the passage in which that item occurs. For example if the question *Why aren't you listening to the music?* is answered by *I am doing*, the word *doing* is a substitute for *listening to the music*, and hence it signals that the response is in fact an answer to the question. This relation is also independent of structure; there may or may not be a sentence boundary in between.

Substitution, in turn, is a particular form of ellipsis, in which the ellipsis is filled by an explicit counter, or placeholder. Another possible form of response above would be simply *I am*, with *listening to the music* presupposed by ellipsis. Similarly in *What are you doing? – Listening to the music*, the response is an elliptical version of *I'm listening to the music*, this time with the modal element *I am* omitted; and again the ellipsis provides cohesion between the answer and the question that preceded it.

Reference, it was pointed out, is a semantic relation, in which the source of interpretation of some element is to be sought elsewhere; with "elsewhere in the text" as a special case. Ellipsis, by contrast, is a purely formal relation, in which some item is to be transported from elsewhere to fill a designated slot. Ellipsis is essentially a relation within the text, and not, like reference, a relation of text to environment in which the relevant environmental feature may happen incidentally to be located in the text. For this reason substitutive and elliptical relations are not found in semiotic systems other than language, whereas referential relations often are.

Substitution and ellipsis are primarily associated with spoken language, especially spontaneous conversation. The only examples in the text are "*No*", and "*Capsized bathtub, indeed!*" in sentences 4 and 6.

2.7 Conjunctive cohesion

Any pair of adjacent sentences may be related by one of a small set of semantic relations, which may be described in most general terms under the four headings of 'and', 'yet', 'so', and 'then' (additive, adversative, causal, temporal). Each of these covers a wide range of more specific meanings.

Like other cohesive relations, these have their structural counterparts in the form of relations within the sentence, for example in the hypotactic structures with *besides, although, because, after*. But the systems of options are different under these two conditions, the cohesive and the structural.

Each one of the types of conjunctive relation has in principle two interpretations, according to the functional-semantic component from which it is derived. Either the conjunctive meaning resides in the ideational component, as a relation within the thesis; or it resides in the interpersonal component, as a relation within the speech process. These have been referred to respectively as "external" and "internal", taking the communication process as the point of departure: a relation between things – between phenomena that constitute the ideational content of the discourse – is one that is external to the communication process.

The distinction is not totally clear cut, and many instances are indeterminate. It appears clearly in a pair of examples such as the following, where the relation is a temporal one:

(external) First of all the machine broke down. Next it started to make alarming noises inside.

(internal) First of all the machine has broken down. Next it doesn't belong to me anyway.

In the first, the temporal successivity is between the two phenomena which constitute the thesis; in the second, it is between the two steps in the argument, in the speaker's unfolding of his role in the speech situation.

In a narrative text the conjunctive relations are likely to be mainly of the external kind; an example is the adversative in sentences 10 and 11: . . . *they thought of calling the A.B.I.* . . . *But they decided instead to phone their friends and neighbors.* The basic meaning of the adversative relation is unexpectedness: "contrary to the expectation set up by the environment". An example of this relation in its internal sense is possibly to be found in sentences 9 and 10:

The tender things they said to each other . . . sounded as lyric to them as flowers in bud . . . To the Grays, however, the bumbling romp of the lover and his lass was hard to comprehend and even harder to tolerate . . .

where the meaning is 'by contrast', 'on the other hand', and the adversative relation resides not so much in the phenomenon of there being the two attitudes ('seemed good to the hippos but bad to the parrots') as in the narrator's juxtaposing of them as a step in the narrative, brought out by the foregrounded status of *the Grays* as a marked Theme in the second sentence.

2.8   Lexical cohesion

This is the special kind of texture that is achieved by the use of vocabulary, (a) by reiteration and (b) by collocation. Both of these can be exemplified from the text (numerals refer to sentences):

(a)   Reiteration (semantic). Keyword: *lover* (in title)

In system: \ In text:	same referent	including same referent	excluding same referent	unrelated referent
same word	*lover* 1, 8	*lovemaking* 10		*love* 18
synonym	*inamoratus* 15	*courtship* 9	*mate* 1 *endearment* 12	
super-ordinate	*male* 5	*affection* 5	*female* 5, 16 *male* 16	
general word		*creatures* 10 *pair* 11		

The display reflects the fact that the word *lover* is semantically complex; it contains the two components of affection and mating, and both of these elements are reiterated throughout the text. There is a certain arbitrariness in both dimensions of the table, but each is motivated by general considerations, the vertical dimension representing the organization of the system and the horizontal the patterning of the text. The vertical dimension is really a continuity, ranging from (1) repetitions (of the same lexical item – which is itself by no means a determinate concept; here we take the morpheme *love* as criterial), through (2) synonyms at more or less the same level of generality, to (3) related items of greater generality, those which are higher in the lexical taxonomy, up to (4) the class of "general words" that figure at the top, which have very little specific content and occur mainly as cohesive agents. The horizontal dimension shows the referential relationship between the reiterated item and the base word: co-referential, inclusive, exclusive or unrelated.

(b)   Collocation (lexical). Keyword: *lover* (in title). Cohesive chain formed of items related by collocation:

> *lass* (title) – *lover* (1) – *lass* (1) –
> *affection* (4) – *spring* (8) – *lover* (8) –
> *lass* (8) – *young* (8) – *oblivious* (8) –
> *happily* (8) – *tender* (9) – *lyric* (9) –
> *flowers* (9) – *bud* (9)

These are pairs or sets of items that have a strong tendency **in the system** to co-occurrence; hence when they do co-occur in a text, the effect is cohesive. The two concepts of reiteration and collocation are overlapping: lexical items that typically collocate with one another (i.e. are related in the lexical system) are often those which are partially synonymous (i.e. are related in the semantic system). But they are not identical concepts; the relationships are on two different levels. There is no, or only a tenuous, semantic link between *lover* and *spring*: but these are regularly collocated in English writing from Shakespeare to the present day. Conversely, there is no strong collocational bond between *courtship* and *endearment*, or between *lover* and *inamoratus* – it must be rare to find the latter pair in the same text under any circumstances! The lexical structure of a text depends on both types of relationship, and on the interplay that occurs between the two.

The sequences illustrated are probably the most pervasive in the present text, but there are other important strands of lexical cohesion, for example the motifs of derision (*arrogant – scornful – sharp-tongued – mocking – derision*) and of monstrosity. For a detailed study and interpretation of collocational patterning in English, see Sinclair et al. (1970).

Cohesion can be thought of as a **process** in the text, the linking of some element – often but not always an element that is inherently presupposing – to something that has gone before, or in certain instances to something that is to follow. It would be wrong, however, to conceive of it as having no place in the semantic system, as what some linguists call a "surface" phenomenon. Cohesion is also a **relation** in the system. As such it is not directional, though it is ordered in the case of inherently presupposing elements (reference items and substitutes). The meaning of this relation in its most general terms is that of "co-interpretation". This in turn takes on a number of more specific meanings according to the type of cohesion: co-referentiality (identity of reference) is one of these more specific meanings. Co-interpretation refers to the fact that the elements that are "tied" by the cohesive relation are interpreted (not identically but) as a whole, with mutual dependence or "solidarity" between them.

A general treatment of cohesion, covering reference, substitution, ellipsis, conjunction and lexical cohesion, will be found in Halliday and Hasan (1976). This book also contains a scheme of analysis and notation for describing the cohesive properties of a text. For a treatment of cohesion in English literary texts see Gutwinski (1974).

3   The nature of text

3.1   Text and "non-text"

The features discussed in the last section – thematic systems, information systems, and the various types of cohesion – represent the
specifically text-forming resources of the linguistic system. The first
two are structural, in the sense that options in these systems contribute
to the derivation of structure: thematic options to the lexicogrammatical structure, being realized through the clause, and informational ones
to what we have called the information structure, a distinct though
related hierarchy that is realized directly in the phonological system,
through the tone group. The cohesive relations are non-structural, not
being realized through any form of structural configuration.

It should be stressed that all these are aspects of the semantic system.
They are options in meaning, which like other options in meaning are
realized through the organization at other strata.

In order to give a complete characterization of texture we should
have to make reference also to "generic" structure, the form that a text
has as a property of its genre. The fact that the present text is a
narrative, and of a particular kind, as specified in the general title *Fables
for Our Time* – that is, it is a complex of a traditional narrative form,
the fable, and a later form, the humorous essay, to which this has been
adapted – defines for it a certain generic structure, which determines
such things as its length, the types of participant (typically animals given
human attributes, or at least human roles, and engaging in dialogue),
and the culmination in a moral.

The generic structure is outside the linguistic system; it is language
as the projection of a higher-level semiotic structure. It is not simply a
feature of literary genres; there is a generic structure in all discourse,
including the most informal spontaneous conversation; see Sacks et al.
(1974). The concept of generic structure can be brought within the
general framework of the concept of register, the semantic patterning
that is characteristically associated with the "context of situation" of a
text; see Section 4 below, and also Gregory (1967), Halliday (1974),
Hasan (1973). The structure of the narrative genre, especially traditional
forms of narrative, has been extensively studied across a wide range of
different languages, and we shall not attempt to discuss it here; see for
example Taber (1966), Chabrol and Marin (1971).

These three factors – generic structure, textual structure (thematic
and informational), and cohesion – are what distinguish text from

44

"non-text". One does not normally meet "non-text" in real life, though one can construct it for illustrative purposes. Here is a passage in which only the thematic structure has been scrambled; everything else, including all other aspects of the texture, is well-formed:

> Now comes the President here. It's the window he's stepping through to wave to the crowd. On his victory his opponent congratulates him. What they are shaking now is hands. A speech is going to be made by him. "Gentlemen and ladies. That you are confident in me honours me. I shall, hereby pledge I, turn this country into a place, in which what people do safely will be live, and the ones who grow up happily will be able to be their children."

These patterns are not optional stylistic variants; they are an integral part of the meaning of language. Texture is not something that is achieved by superimposing an appropriate text form on a pre-existing ideational content. The textual component is a component of meaning along with the ideational and interpersonal components. Hence a linguistic description is not a progressive specification of a set of structures one after the other, ideational, then interpersonal, then textual. The system does not first generate a representation of reality, then encode it as a speech act, and finally recode it as a text, as the metaphors of philosophical linguistics seem to imply. It embodies all these types of meaning in simultaneous networks of options, from each of which derive structures that are mapped on to one another in the course of their lexicogrammatical realization. The lexicogrammar acts as the integrative system, taking configurations from all the components of the semantics and combining them to form multilayered, "polyphonic" structural compositions.

3.2   The text as a semantic unit

The quality of texture is not defined by size. There is a concept of a text as a kind of super-sentence, something that is larger than a sentence but of the same nature. But this is to misrepresent the essential quality of a text. Obviously one cannot quarrel with the use of the term "text" to refer to a string of sentences that realize a text; but it is important to stress that the sentences are, in fact, the realization of text rather than constituting the text itself. Text is a semantic concept.

The same problem has arisen in linguistics with the conception of the sentence as a super-phoneme. A sentence is not an outsize phonological unit; it is a lexicogrammatical unit that is realized in the phonological system, which has its own hierarchy of units. It may be that the sentence in some language or other is marked off by the phonological system, so that it can be identified at the phonological level; but that does not make the sentence a phonological concept. There is developmental evidence that a child builds up his phonology from both ends, as it were, constructing a phonological system on the one hand and individual phonological representations of lexicogrammatical elements on the other – both particular word phonologies and generalized syllable phonologies at the same time; see Ferguson and Farwell (1973). In other words a system is built up both as a tactic system, in its own right, and as the piecemeal realization of elements of a higher-level system. We find an analogous process taking place at the next level up. The child both constructs a lexicogrammatical system and, simultaneously, lexicogrammatical representations of semantic elements. Just as he develops a word phonology side by side with a syllable phonology, he also develops a text grammar side by side with a clause grammar. The "text grammar" in this sense is the realization, in the lexicogrammar, of particular elements on the semantic stratum; and it explains the important part played in language development by the learning of large stretches of "wording" as uninterrupted wholes.

A text, as we are interpreting it, is a semantic unit, which is not composed of sentences but is realized in sentences. A text is to the semantic system what a clause is to the lexicogrammatical system and a syllable to the phonological system. It may be characterized by certain lexicogrammatical features, just as a clause may be characterized by certain phonological features; but this does not make it a lexicogrammatical unit (given that such a unit is to be defined, as we have defined it, by its being the locus of lexicogrammatical structures).

Whether or not, and in what sense, there is a rank scale, or hierarchy, of semantic units, as some linguists have suggested, must be left undecided. A clause is only one of a number of structure-carrying units in the grammar, and it is not entirely clear why it should be singled out as **the** primary grammatical constituent; the same applies to the syllable, or any unit that is selected as **the** basic unit for phonology. The concept of semantic units is much less clearcut, since the concept of semantic structures is less clearcut. In any case the linguistic system as a whole is not symmetrical, as Lamb pointed out in his review of Hjelmslev; see Lamb (1966). Moreover the distinguishing feature of the semantic system is its organization into functional components. These determine, not units of different sizes, but simultaneous configurations of meanings of different kinds. The semantic analogue of the rank scale would appear to be not some kind of a hierarchy of structural units but the multiple determination of the text as a unit in respect of more than one property, or "dimension" of meaning.

Let us express this more concretely in relation to the text that is under consideration. It constitutes "a text" as defined by the textual component: not only has it a generic structure, but it is also internally cohesive, and it functions as a whole as the relevant environment for the operation of the theme and information systems. In other words it has a unity of what we have called "texture", deriving from the specifically text-forming component within the semantic system, and this is sufficient to define it as a text. But we are likely to find this unity reflected also in its ideational and interpersonal meanings, so that its quality as a text is reinforced by a continuity of context and of speaker-audience relationship. In fact this "artistic unity" is already contained in the concept of generic structure, and reflected in the specific forms taken by the cohesive relations. So there is a continuity in the time reference (every finite verb in the narrative is in simple past tense, every one in the dialogue is in simple present); in the transitivity patterns (the process types are those of perception, cognition, verbalization, and attribution, except for the very last sentence; and there is a rather even distribution among them); in the attitudinal modes, the form of the dialogue, and so on.

In other words, a text is a semantic unit defined by the textual component. This is not a tautology; rather it is the reason for calling the textual component by that name. A text has a generic structure, is internally cohesive, and constitutes the relevant environment for selection in the "textual" systems of the grammar. But its unity as a text is likely to be displayed in patterns of ideational and interpersonal meaning as well. A text is the product of its environment, and it functions in that environment. In Section 4 we shall explore briefly the way in which we can conceptualize the relation of text to its environment, and the processes whereby specific aspects of a speaker's or writer's semantic system tend to be activated by – and hence, in turn, to shape and modify – specific aspects of the environment in which meanings are exchanged.

Meanwhile we should stress the essential indeterminacy of the concept of "a text". Clauses, or syllables, are relatively well-defined entities: we usually know how many of them there are, in any instance, and we can even specify, in terms of some theory, where they begin and end. A text, in the normal course of events, is not something that has a beginning and an ending. The exchange of meanings is a continuous process that is involved in all human interaction; it is not unstructured, but it is seamless, and all that one can observe is a kind of periodicity in which peaks of texture alternate with troughs – highly cohesive moments with moments of relatively little continuity. The discreteness of a literary text is untypical of texts as a whole.

By "text", then, we understand a continuous process of semantic choice. Text is meaning and meaning is choice, an ongoing current of selections each in its paradigmatic environment of what **might have been** meant (but was not). It is the paradigmatic environment – the innumerable sub-systems that make up the semantic system – that must provide the basis of the description, if the text is to be related to higher orders of meaning, whether social, literary or of some other semiotic universe. The reason why descriptions based on structure are of limited value in text studies is that in such theories the paradigmatic environment is subordinated to a syntagmatic frame of reference; when paradigmatic concepts are introduced, such as transformation, they are embedded in what remains essentially a syntagmatic theory. By what at first sight appears as a paradox, since text is a syntagmatic process (but see Hjelmslev (1961), Section 11), it is the paradigmatic basis of a description that makes it significant for text studies. Hence in glossematics, and similarly in the "systemic" version of system–structure theory, the syntagmatic concept of structure is embedded in a theory that is essentially paradigmatic. Here the description is based on system; and text is interpreted as the process of continuous movement through the system, a process which both expresses the higher orders of meaning that constitute the "social semiotic", the meaning systems of the culture, and at the same time changes and modifies the system itself.

3.3 The text as projection of meanings at a higher level

What is "above" the text? If text is semantic process, encoded in the lexicogrammatical system, what is it the encoding of in its turn?

What is "above" depends on one's perspective, on the nature of the enquiry and the ideology of the enquirer. There are different higher-level semiotics, and often different levels of meaning within each.

This point emerges very clearly if one considers literary texts. To say that a text has meaning as literature is to relate it specifically to a literary universe of discourse as distinct from others, and thus to interpret it in terms of literary norms and assumptions about the nature of meaning. The linguistic description of a text which is contextualized in this way attempts to explain its meaning as literature – why the reader interprets it as he does, and why he evaluates it as he does. This involves relating the text to a higher-level semiotic system which is faceted and layered in much the same way as the linguistic system itself. An example of this "layering" from the present text is the use of the generic form of the fable as the vehicle of a humorous essay, already referred to above. The "level of literary execution" is part of the total realizational chain; see Hasan (1971).

When there is foregrounding of lexicogrammatical or phonological features in a literary text, particular forms of linguistic prominence that relate directly to some facet of its literary interpretation, this is closely analogous to the "bypassing" phenomenon that is found within the linguistic system when some element in the semantics is realized directly in phonological terms (cf. 2.3 above). At this point there is isomorphism between two adjacent strata, and the phenomenon can be represented as a straight pass through one of the stratal systems. We have referred to this already in relation to the information and "key" systems in the semantics of English: an example is the bandwidth of a falling tone expressing the degree of "newness" or semantic contrast involved in a statement. It is possible in such a case to set up a grammatical system as an interface between the semantics and the phonology; and there are strong reasons for doing so, since there is a systematic interrelationship between this and other grammatical systems, although strictly in its own terms the grammatical representation is redundant because there is neither neutralization nor diversification at this point.

The point is a significant one because a great deal of stylistic foregrounding depends on an analogous process, by which some aspect of the underlying meaning is represented linguistically at more than one level: not only through the semantics of the text – the ideational and interpersonal meanings, as embodied in the content and in the writer's choice of his role – but also by direct reflection in the lexicogrammar or the phonology. For an example of this from a study of William Golding's novel *The Inheritors* see Chapter 3 of this volume, where it is suggested that the particular impact of this novel on reader and critic may be explained by the fact that the underlying semiotic is projected simultaneously on to the semantics, in the content of narrative and dialogue, and on to the grammar in the highly untypical transitivity patterns that characterize, not so much individual clauses (none of which is in itself deviant), but the distribution of clause types in the writing as a whole.

The present text does not display this feature of multi-level foregrounding to any great extent because it is both short and prose. A verse text, however short, provides scope by virtue of its generic form for the sort of patterned variability of patterns which is involved in this kind of multiple projection; whereas in a prose text it is likely to appear only in rather long-range effects, as deflections in the typical patterns of co–occurrence and relative frequency. But there are minor instances: for example the phonaesthetic motif of the final syllable in *snaffle, bumble, wuffle* and *gurble,* and incongruity involved in the use of synonyms of different "tenor" (see Section 4 below) such as *mate, lover, inamoratus.*

To summarize this point: a text, as well as being realized in the lower levels of the linguistic system, lexicogrammatical and phonological, is also itself the realization of higher-level semiotic structures with their own modes of interpretation, literary, sociological, psychoanalytic and so on. These higher-level structures may be expressed not only by the semantics of the text but also by patterning at those lower levels; when such lower-level patterning is significant at some higher level it becomes what is known as "foregrounded". Such foregrounded patterns in lexicogrammar or phonology may be characteristic of a part or the whole of a text, or even of a whole class or genre of texts, a classic example being the rhyme schemes of the Petrarchan and Shakespearean sonnets as expression of two very different modes of artistic semiotic (patterns of meaning used as art forms).

3.4 The text as a sociosemiotic process

In its most general significance a text is a sociological event, a semiotic encounter through which the meanings that constitute the social system are **exchanged.** The individual member is, by virtue of his membership, a "meaner", one who means. By his acts of meaning, and those of other individual meaners, the social reality is created, maintained in good order, and continuously shaped and modified.

It is perhaps not too far-fetched to put it in these terms: reality consists of meanings, and the fact that meanings are essentially indeterminate and unbounded is what gives rise to that strand in human thought – philosophical, religious, scientific – in which the emphasis is on the dynamic, wave–like aspect of reality, its constant restructuring, its periodicity without recurrence, its continuity in time and space. Here there is no distinction between relations among symbols and relations among the "things" that they symbolize – because both are of the same order; both the things and the symbols are meanings. The fact that aspects of reality can be digitalized and reduced to ordered operations on symbols is still consistent with the view of reality as meaning: certain aspects of meaning are also captured in this way. Pike expressed this property of the linguistic system by viewing language as particle, wave and field; each of these perspectives reveals a different kind of truth about it: see Pike (1959). Linguistic theory has remained at a stage at which particulateness is treated as the norm, and a number of different and not very clearly related concepts are invoked to handle the non-particulate aspects of language. As far as text studies, and text meaning, is concerned, however, we cannot relegate the indeterminacy to an appendix. The text is a continuous process. There is a constantly shifting relation between a text and its environment, both paradigmatic and syntagmatic: the syntagmatic environment, the "context of situation" (which includes the semantic context – and which for this reason we interpret as a semiotic construct), can be treated as a constant for the text as a whole, but is in fact constantly changing, each part serving in turn as environment for the next. And the ongoing text-creating process continually modifies the system that engenders it, which is the paradigmatic environment of the text. Hence the dynamic, indeterminate nature of meaning, which can be idealized out to the margins if one is considering only the system, or only the text, emerges as the dominant mode of thought as soon as one comes to consider the two together, and to focus on text as actualized meaning potential.

The essential feature of text, therefore, is that it is interaction. The exchange of meanings is an interactive process, and text is the means of exchange: in order for the meanings which constitute the social system to be exchanged between members they must first be represented in some exchangeable symbolic form, and the most accessible of the available forms is language. So the meanings are encoded in (and through) the semantic system, and given the form of text. And so text functions as it were as potlatch: it is perhaps the most highly coded form of the gift. The contests in meaning that are a feature of so many human groups – cultures and sub-cultures – are from this point of view contests in giving, in a re-encoded form in which the gift, itself an element in the social semiotic (a "meaning") but one that in the typical or at least the classic instance is realized as a thing, is realized instead as a special kind of abstract symbol, as meanings in the specifically linguistic sense. Such a gift has the property that, however great its symbolic value (and however much it may enrich the recipient), it does not in the slightest degree impoverish the giver.

We can see this aspect of text, its function as exchange, most clearly in the phenomenon of semantic contest: in competitive story-telling, exchange of insults, "capping" another's jokes and other forms of verbal exploit. Oral verse forms such as ballads, lyrics, and epigrammatic and allusive couplets figure in many cultures as modes of competing, and even written composition may be predominantly a competitive act: late Elizabethan sonnets provide an outstanding example. In all such instances the aim is to excel in meaning, in the act of giving and the value of the gift. But it is not too fanciful to see the element of the gift as one component in all literature, and in this way to show how the act of meaning, and the product of this act, namely text, comes to have value in the culture.

The reason for making this point here needs to be clarified. It is natural to conceive of text first and foremost as conversation: as the spontaneous interchange of meanings in ordinary, everyday interaction. It is in such contexts that reality is constructed, in the microsemiotic encounters of daily life. The reason why this is so, why the culture is transmitted to, or recreated by, the individual in the first instance through conversation rather than through other acts of meaning, is that conversation typically relates to the environment in a way that is perceptible and concrete, whereas other genres tend to depend on intermediate levels of symbolic interpretation. A literary text such as the present one creates its own immediate context of situation, and the relating of it to its environment in the social system is a complex and technical operation. Conversation, while it is no less highly structured, is structured in such a way as to make explicit its relationship to its setting; though it is no less complex in its layers of meaning, the various semiotic strategies and motifs that make it up are – by no means always, but in significantly many instances, and typically in the case of contexts that are critical in the socialization of a child: see Bernstein (1971) – derivable from features of the social environment. Hence to understand the nature of text as social action we are led naturally to consider spontaneous conversation, as being the most accessible to interpretation; and to draw a rather clear line between this and other, less immediately contextualizable acts of meaning such as a poem or prose narrative. It is perhaps useful in text studies, therefore, to bring out those aspects of the semiotic act that are common to all, and that encompass what is traditional as well as what is spontaneous, and relate to literary as well as to conversational texts. The very general concept of a text as an exchange of meanings covers both its status as gift and its role in the realization and construction of the social semiotic.

4 Text and situation

4.1 The situation as a determining environment

We have taken as our starting point the observation that meanings are created by the social system and are exchanged by the members in the form of text. The meanings so created are not, of course, isolates; they are integrated systems of meaning potential. It is in this sense that we can say that the meanings **are** the social system: the social system is itself interpretable as a semiotic system.

Persistence and change in the social system are both reflected in text and brought about by means of text. Text is the primary channel of the transmission of culture; and it is this aspect – text as the semantic process of social dynamics – that more than anything else has shaped the semantic system. Language has evolved as the primary mode of meaning in a social environment. It provides the means of acting on and reflecting on the environment, to be sure – but in a broader context, in which acting and reflecting on the environment are in turn the means of **creating** the environment and transmitting it from one generation to the next. That this is so is because the environment is a social construct. If things enter into it, they do so as bearers of social values.

Let us follow this line of reasoning through. The linguistic system has evolved in social contexts, as (one form of) the expression of the social semiotic. We see this clearly in the organization of the semantic system, where the ideational component has evolved as the mode of reflection on the environment and the interpersonal component as the mode of action on the environment. The system is a meaning potential, which is actualized in the form of text; a text is an instance of social meaning in a particular context of situation. We shall therefore expect to find the situation embodied or enshrined in the text not piecemeal, but in a way which reflects the systematic relation between the semantic structure and the social environment. In other words, the "situation" will appear, as envisaged by Hymes (1971), as constitutive of the text; provided, that is, we can characterize it so as to take cognizance of the ecological properties of language, the features which relate it to its environment in the social system.

A text is, as we have stressed, an indeterminate concept. It may be very long, or very short; and it may have no very clear boundaries. Many things about language can be learnt only from the study of very long texts. But there is much to be found out also from little texts; not only texts in the conventional forms of lyric poetry, proverbs and the like, but also brief transactions, casual encounters, and all kinds of verbal micro-operations. And among these there is a special value to the linguist in children's texts, since these tend to display their environmental links more directly and with less metaphorical mediation. (For a description of a short piece of child language, showing its relationship to the context of situation which engendered it, see Halliday (1975)). We find all the time in the speech of young children examples of the way in which they themselves expect text to be related to its environment: their own step-by-step building up of layers of metaphorical meaning affords a clear and impressive illustration of this point.

The question to be resolved is, how do we get from the situation to the text? What features of the environment, in any specific instance, called for these particular options in the linguistic system? It may be objected that this is asking the old question, why did he say (or write) what he did; and that is something we can never know. Let us make it clear, therefore, that we are not asking any questions that require to be answered in terms of individual psychology. We are asking: what is the potential of the system that is likely to be at risk, the semantic configurations that are typically associated with a specific situation type? This can always be expressed in personal terms, if it seems preferable to do so; but in that case the question will be: what meanings will the hearer, or reader, expect to be offered in this particular class of social contexts? The meanings that constitute any given text do not present themselves to the hearer out of the blue; he has a very good idea of what is coming. The final topic that will be discussed here is that of text and situation. In what sense can the concept of "situation" be interpreted in a significant way as the environment of the text?

4.2   Semiotic structure of the situation: field, tenor and mode

It was suggested in the first section that the options that make up the semantic system are essentially of three or four kinds – four if we separate the experiential from the logical, as the grammar very clearly does.

We shall be able to show something of how the text is related to the situation if we can specify what aspects of the context of situation "rule" each of these kinds of semantic option. In other words, for each component of meaning, what are the situational factors by which it is activated?

The question then becomes one of characterizing the context of situation in appropriate terms, in terms which will reveal the systematic relationship between language and the environment. This involves some form of theoretical construction that relates the situation simultaneously to the text, to the linguistic system, and to the social system. For this purpose we interpret the situation as a semiotic structure; it is an instance, or instantiation, of the meanings that make up the social system.

Actually it is a class of instances, since what we characterize will be a situation **type** rather than a particular situation considered as unique. The situation consists of:

(1) the social action: that which is "going on", and has recognizable meaning in the social system; typically a complex of acts in some ordered configuration, and in which the text is playing some part; and including "subject-matter" as one special aspect,

(2) the role structure: the cluster of socially meaningful participant relationships; both permanent attributes of the participants and role relationships that are specific to the situation; including the speech roles, those that come into being through the exchange of verbal meanings,

(3) the symbolic organization: the particular status that is assigned to the text within the situation; its function in relation to the social action and the role structure; including the channel or medium, and the rhetorical mode.

We shall refer to these by the terms "field", "tenor" and "mode". The environment, or social context, of language is structured as a *field* of significant social action, a *tenor* of role relationships, and a *mode* of symbolic organization. Taken together these constitute the situation, or "context of situation", of a text.

We can then go on to establish a general principle governing the way in which these environmental features are projected on to the text.

Each of the components of the situation tends to determine the selection of options in a corresponding component of the semantics. In the typical instance, the field determines the selection of experiential meanings, the tenor determines the selection of interpersonal meanings, and the mode determines the selection of textual meanings.

Semiotic structure of situation	associated with		Functional component of semantics
field (type of social action)	"	"	experiential
tenor (role relationships)	"	"	interpersonal
mode (symbolic organization)	"	"	textual

The selection of options in *experiential* systems – that is, in transitivity, in the classes of things (objects, persons, events, etc.), in quality, quantity, time, place and so on – tends to be determined by the nature of the activity: what socially recognized action the participants are engaged in, in which the exchange of verbal meanings has a part. This includes everything from, at one end, types of action defined without reference to language, in which language has an entirely subordinate role, various forms of collaborative work and play such as unskilled manipulation of objects or simple physical games; through intermediate types in which language has some necessary but still ancillary function, operations requiring some verbal instruction and report, games with components of scoring, bidding, planning, and the like; to types of interaction defined solely in linguistic terms, like gossip, seminars, religious discourse and most of what is recognized under the heading of literature. At the latter end of the continuum the concept of "subject-matter" intervenes; what we understand as subject-matter can be interpreted as one element in the structure of the "field" in those contexts where the social action is inherently of a symbolic, verbal nature. In a game of football, the social action is the game itself, and any instructions or other verbal interaction among the players are **part of** this social action. In a discussion about a game of football, the social action is the discussion, and the verbal interaction among the participants is **the whole of** this social action. Here the game constitutes a second order of "field", one that is brought into being by that of the first-order, the discussion, owing to its special nature as a type of social action that is itself defined by language. It is to this second-order field of discourse that we give the name of "subject-matter".

The selection of *interpersonal* options, those in the systems of mood, modality, person, key, intensity, evaluation and comment and the like, tends to be determined by the role relationships in the situation. Again there is a distinction to be drawn between a first and a second order of such role relationships. Social roles of the first order are defined without reference to language, though they may be (and typically are) realized through language as one form of role-projecting behaviour; all social roles in the usual sense of the term are of this order. Second-order social roles are those which are defined by the linguistic system: these are the roles that come into being only in and through language, the discourse roles of questioner, informer, responder, doubter, contradicter and the like. (Other types of symbolic action, warning, threatening, greeting and so on, which may be realized either verbally or non-verbally, or both, define roles which are some way intermediate between the two.) These discourse roles determine the selection of options in the mood system. There are systematic patterns of relationship between the first-order and the second-order roles. An interesting example of this emerged from recent studies of classroom discourse, which showed that in the teacher-pupil relationship the role of teacher is typically combined with that of questioner and the role of pupil with that of respondent, and not the other way round (cf. *Five to Nine* (1972), Sinclair et al. (1972)) – despite our concept of education, it is not the learner who asks the questions.

The selection of options in the **textual** systems, such as those of theme, information and voice, and also the selection of cohesive patterns, those of reference, substitution and ellipsis, and conjunction, tend to be determined by the symbolic forms taken by the interaction, in particular the place that is assigned to the text in the total situation. This includes the distinction of medium, written or spoken, and the complex sub-varieties derived from these (written to be read aloud, and so on); we have already noted ways in which the organization of text-forming resources is dependent on the medium of the text. But it extends to much more than this, to the particular semiotic function or range of functions that the text is serving in the environment in question. The rhetorical concepts of expository, didactic, persuasive, descriptive and the like are examples of such semiotic functions. All the categories under this third heading are second-order categories, in that they are defined by reference to language and depend for their existence on the prior phenomenon of text. It is in this sense that the textual component in the semantic system was said to have an "enabling" function *vis-à-vis* the other two: it is only through the encoding of semiotic interaction **as text** that the ideational and interpersonal components of meaning can become operational in an environment.

The concept of genre discussed in Section 3 (p. 44) is an aspect of what we are calling the "mode". The various genres of discourse, including literary genres, are the specific semiotic functions of text that have social value in the culture. A genre may have implications for other components of meaning: there are often associations between a particular genre and particular semantic features of an ideational or interpersonal kind, for example between the genre of prayer and certain selections in the mood system. Hence labels for generic categories are often function-ally complex: a concept such as "ballad" implies not only a certain text structure with typical patterns of cohesion but also a certain range of content expressed through highly favoured options in transitivity and other experiential systems – the types of process and classes of person and object that are expected to figure in association with the situational role of a ballad text. The "fable" is a category of a similar kind.

The patterns of determination that we find between the context of situation and the text are a general characteristic of the whole complex that is formed by a text and its environment. We shall not expect to be able to show that the options embodied in one or another particular sentence are determined by the field, tenor and mode of the situation. The principle is that each of these elements in the semiotic structure of the situation activates the corresponding component in the semantic system, creating in the process a semantic configuration, a grouping of favoured and foregrounded options from the total meaning potential, that is typically associated with the situation type in question. This semantic configuration is what we understand by the **register**: it defines the variety ("diatypic variety" in the sense of Gregory (1967)) that the particular text is an instance of. The concept of "register" is the necessary mediating concept that enables us to establish the continuity between a text and its sociosemiotic environment.

4.3   The situation of the present text

The "situation" of a written text tends to be complex; and that of a fictional narrative is about as complex as it is possible for it to be. The complexity is not an automatic feature of language in the written medium: some written texts have relatively simple environments, which do not involve layers of interpretation. An example is a warning notice such as *Beware of the dog.*

The complexity of the environment of a written text arises rather from the semiotic functions with which writing is typically associated. In the case of fictional narrative, this is not even necessarily associated with writing: it is a feature just as much of oral narrative, traditional or spontaneous (in their different ways).

In a fictional text, the field of discourse is on two levels: the social act of narration, and the social acts that form the content of the narration. For our present text the description of the field would be in something like these terms:

1 (a)   Verbal art: entertainment through story-telling
  (b) (i) Theme: human prejudice ("they're different, so hate them!"). Projected through:
    (ii) Thesis ("plot"): fictitious interaction of animals: male/female pairs of hippopotamuses, parrots.

The tenor is also on two levels, since two distinct sets of role relationships are embodied in the text: one between the narrator and his readership, which is embodied in the narrative, and one among the participants in the narrative, which is embodied in the dialogue:

2 (a) Writer and readers; writer adopting role as recounter: specifically as humorist (partly projected through subsidiary role as
moralist), and assigning complementary role to audience.

(b) Mate and mate: animal pair as projection of husband and wife;
each adopting own (complementary) role as reinforcer of
shared attitudes.

Since under each of the headings of "field" and "tenor" the text has
appeared as a complex of two distinct levels, we might be tempted to
conclude that a fictional narrative of this kind was really two separate
"texts" woven together. As a purely abstract model this could be made
to stand; but it is really misleading, not only because it fails to account
for the integration of the text – and in any sensible interpretation this
is one text and not two – but also because the relation between the
two levels is quite different in respect of the tenor from what it is in
respect of the field. As regards the tenor, the text does fall into two
distinct segments, the narrative, and the dialogue; each is characterized
by its own set of role relationships, and the two combine to form a
whole. As regards the field, however, there is no division in the text
corresponding to the two levels of social action: the whole text is at
one and the same time an act of malicious gossip **and** an act of verbal
art, the one being the realization of the other. We could not, in other
words, begin by separating out the two levels and then go on to
describe the field and the tenor of each; we have to describe the field
of the text, and then the tenor of the text, and both in different ways
then reveal its two-level semiotic organization.

The oneness of the text also appears in the characterization of the
mode, the symbolic structure of the situation and the specific role
assigned to the text within it:

3 Text as "self-sufficient", as **only** form of social action by which
"situation" is defined.
Written medium: to be read silently as private act.
Light essay; original (newly-created) text projected on to traditional fable genre, structured as narrative-with-dialogue, with
"moral" as culminative element.

Even a general sketch such as this suggests something of the complexity
of the concept of "situation" applied to a written narrative. The
complexity increases if we seek to make explicit the semiotic overtones
that are typically associated with the interpretation of a literary text; in
particular, as in this instance, the manysided relationship between the

plot and the theme or themes underlying it. If the "context of situation" is seen as the essential link between the social system (the "context of culture", to use another of Malinowski's terms) and the text, then it is more than an abstract representation of the relevant material environment; it is a constellation of social meanings, and in the case of a literary text these are likely to involve many orders of cultural values, both the value systems themselves and the many specific sub-systems that exist as metaphors for them. At the same time, one of the effects of a sociosemiotic approach is to suggest that **all** language is literature, in this sense; it is only when we realize that the same things are true of the spontaneous verbal interaction of ordinary everyday life (and nothing demonstrates this more clearly than Harvey Sacks' brilliant exegesis of conversational texts, which is in the best traditions of literary interpretation) that we begin to understand how language functions in society – and how this, in turn, has moulded and determined the linguistic system.

If therefore there are limits on the extent to which we can demonstrate, in the present instance, that the text has its effective origin in the context of situation, this is only partly because of its peculiarly difficult standing as a complex genre of literary fiction; many other types of linguistic interaction are not essentially different in this respect. There **are** more favourable instances; we have already referred in this connection to children's language, where there is not so much shifting of focus between different orders of meaning. Not that the speech of children is free of semiotic strategies – far from it; but the resources through which their strategies are effected tend to be less complex, less varied and less ambiguous – children cannot yet mean so many things at once. The present text, which is a good example of adult multivalence, is for that very reason less easy to derive from the context of situation, without a much more detailed interpretative apparatus. But certain features do emerge which illustrate the link between the semantic configurations of the text and the situational description that we have given of the field, tenor and mode. These are set out in the subsection which follows.

4.4 Situational interpretation of the text

1 Story-telling – tense: every finite verb in narrative portions is in
   simple past tense
   Theme/thesis – transitivity: predominantly
   (a) mental process: perception, e.g. *listen*; cognition, e.g. *believe*;

reaction, e.g. *surprise, shock*; (b) verbal process, introducing quoted speech. Animal participant as Medium of process (Cognizant, Speaker); note that there is a grammatical rule in English that the Cognizant in a mental process clause is always "human", i.e. a thing endowed with the attribute of humanity,

– vocabulary as content (denotative meanings), e.g. *inamoratus* as expression of "mate".

2 Writer as recounter – mood: every clause in narrative portions is declarative (narrative statement).

Writer as humorist – vocabulary as attitude (connotative meanings), e.g. *inamoratus* as expression of mock stylishness.

Writer as moralist – mood: special mood structure for proverbial wisdom, *laugh and the world laughs . . .*

"Husband and wife" as players in game of prejudice-reinforcement – mood and modulation: clauses in dialogue portions switch rapidly among different moods and modulations, e.g. the sequence declarative, modulated interrogative, negative declarative, moodless, declarative (statement, exclamatory question, negative response, exclamation, statement).

3 Self-sufficiency of text – cohesion: reference entirely endophoric (within text itself). Note reference of *her* to *Lass* in title, suggesting highly organized text.

Written medium – information: no information structure, except as implied by punctuation, but "alternative" devices characteristic of written language, viz (i) higher lexical density per unit grammar, (ii) less complexity, and more parallelism, of grammatical structure, (iii) thematic variation (marked and nominalized themes), which suggests particular information structure because of association between the two systems, typically of the form ([Theme] Given) [Rheme (New)], i.e. Theme within Given, New within Rheme.

Genre: narrative with dialogue – quoting structures: thematic form of quoted followed by quoting, with the latter (*said* + Subject) comprising informational "tail", e.g. *"He calls her snooky-ookums"*, *said Mrs. Gray* expresses "dialogue in context of original fictional narrative".

When the text is located in its environment, in such a way as to show what aspects of the environment are projected on to what features of the text, a pattern emerges of systematic relationship between the two. The linguistic features that were derived from the "field" were all features assigned to the ideational component in the semantic system. Those deriving from the "tenor" are all assigned to the interpersonal component; and those deriving from the "mode", to the textual component.

The logical component enters in to the picture in a dual perspective which we shall not attempt to discuss in detail here. The meanings that make up this component are generalized ideational relations such as co-ordination, apposition, reported speech, modification and sub-modification; as such they form a part of the ideational component. But once in being, as it were, they may also serve to relate elements of the other components, interpersonal and textual. To take a simplest example, the meaning 'and' is itself an ideational one, but the 'and' relation can as well serve to link interpersonal as ideational meanings: *hell and damnation!* as well as *snakes and ladders*. Compare, in the present text, the "and-ing" of alliterative (textual) features in *disdain and derision, mocking and monstrous*.

It should perhaps be stressed in this connection that the interpretation of the semantic system in terms of these components of ideational (experiential, logical), interpersonal and textual is prior to and independent of any consideration of field, tenor and mode. Such an interpretation is imposed by the form of internal organization of the linguistic system. Hence we can reasonably speak of the determination of the text by the situation, in the sense that the various semantic systems are seen to be activated by particular environmental factors that stand in a generalized functional relationship to them.

This picture emerges from a description of the properties of the text, especially one in terms of the relative frequency of options in the different systems. Much of the meaning of a text resides in the sort of foregrounding that is achieved by this kind of environmentally motivated prominence, in which certain sets of options are favoured (selected with greater frequency than expected on the assumption of unconditioned probability), as a realization of particular elements in the social context. The inspection of these sets of options one by one, each in its situational environment, is of course an analytical procedure; their selection by the speaker, and apprehension by the hearer, is a process of dynamic simultaneity, in which at any moment that we stop the tape, as it were, a whole lot of meaning selections are going on at once, all of which then become part of the environment in which further choices are made. If we lift out any one piece of the text, such as a single sentence, we will find the environment reflected not in the individual options (since these become significant only through their relative frequency of occurrence in the text), but in the particular combination of options that characterizes this sentence taken as a whole. As an example, consider the sentence:

"I would as soon live with a pair of unoiled garden shears", said her inamoratus.

This sentence combines the relational process of accompaniment, in *live with*; the class of object, *unoiled garden shears*, as circumstantial element; and the comparative modulation *would as soon* (all of which are ideational meanings) as realization of the motif of human prejudice (field, as in 1 (b) above). It combines declarative mood, first person (speaker) as Subject, and the attitudinal element in *would as soon*, expressing personal preference (these being interpersonal meanings), as realization of the married couple's sharing of attitudes (tenor). Not very much can be said, naturally, about the specific text-forming elements within a single sentence; but it happens that in its thematic structure, which is the clause-internal aspect of texture, this sentence does combine a number of features that relate it to the "mode": it has the particular quoting pattern referred to above as characteristic of dialogue in narrative, together with, in the quoted clause, the first person Theme in active voice that is one of the marks of informal conversation. In fact it displays in a paradigm form the crescendo of "communicative dynamism" described by Firbas (1964, 1968) as typical of spoken English.

We shall not find the entire context of situation of a text neatly laid out before us by a single sentence. It is only by considering the text as a whole that we can see how it springs from its environment and is determined by the specific features of that environment. And until we have some theoretical model of this relationship we shall not really understand the processes by which meanings are exchanged. This is the significance of attempts towards a "situational" interpretation of text. Verbal interaction is a highly coded form of social act, in which the interactants are continuously supplying the information that is "missing" from the text; see on this point Cicourel (1969). They are all the time unravelling the code – and it is the situation that serves them as a key. The predictions that the hearer or reader makes from his knowledge of the environment allow him to retrieve information that would otherwise be inaccessible to him. To explain these predictions requires some general account of the systematic relations among the situation, the linguistic system, and the text.

The text is the unit of the semantic process. It is the text, and not the sentence, which displays patterns of relationship with the situation. These patterns, the characteristic semantic trends and configurations that place the text in its environment, constitute the "register"; each text can thus be treated as an instance of a class of text that is defined by the register in question. The field, tenor and mode of the situation collectively determine the register and in this way function as constitutive of the text.

What is revealed in a single sentence, or other unit of lexicogrammatical structure, is its origin in the functional organization of the semantic system. Each of the semantic components, ideational (experiential and logical), interpersonal and textual, has contributed to its makeup. The final section offers a detailed interpretation of one sentence of the present text, in terms of systems and structures; taking the same sentence as before, and presenting it as the product of numerous micro-acts of semantic choice. This will complete the semiotic cycle, the network that extends from the social system, as its upper bound, through the linguistic system on the one hand and the social context on the other, down to the "wording", which is the text in its lexicogrammatical realization.

5 Analysis of a sentence

"I would as soon live with a pair of unoiled garden shears", said her inamoratus.

5.1 Systemic descriptions

(All system networks are simplified so as to show only those portions that are relevant to the sentence under description. Systems in which only unmarked selections are made in this sentence, such as polarity and voice, are omitted entirely.)

A. Logical
a) Clause complex (= sentence)
  (This sentence is a clause complex consisting of two clauses in "quoting" relation. For the notion of the "complex" (clause complex, group complex, etc.) see 1.1 above. All complexes, and only complexes, display a recursive option of the form

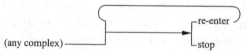

  In other words, they embody recursive options, as distinct from embeddings.)

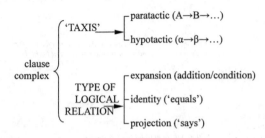

SYSTEMIC   clause complex: (paratactic/projection)
DESCRIPTION

STRUCTURAL   B: Quoted ←A: Quoting
DESCRIPTION

Note: The intersection of these two systems yields the following paradigm of clause complex types:

	paratactic	hypotactic
expansion	co-ordinate	conditional, causal, concessive
identity	appositive	non-defining relative
projection	quoting (direct speech)	reporting (indirect speech)

Examples from the text:

Coordinate (s. 17)

(AA	→ AB)	→ (BA	→ BB)
the hippopotamuses stopped criticizing the Grays	*and fell asleep,*	*and the Grays stopped maligning the hippopotamuses*	*and retired to their beds.*

Appositive (s. 11)

A → B

gossip about the shameless pair, → *and describe them in mocking and monstrous metaphors involving skidding buses on icy streets and overturned moving vans.*

Quoting (s. 15)

B ← A

"I would as soon live with a pair of unoiled garden shears", ← *said her inamoratus.*

Conditional, etc. (s. 10)

α → β

for a time they thought of calling the A.B.I., or African Bureau of Investigation, → *on the ground that monolithic lovemaking by enormous creatures who should have become decent fossils long ago was probably a threat to the security of the jungle.*

Non-defining relative (s. 1)

α → β

An arrogant gray parrot and his arrogant mate listened, one African afternoon, in disdain and derision, to the lovemaking of a lover and his lass, → *who happened to be hippopotamuses.*

65

Reporting (s. 5)

α	→	β
I don't see		*how any male in his right mind could entertain affection for* *a female that has no more charm than a capsized bathtub.*

b) Group complexes: NONE

nominal group	*I*
verbal group	*would live*
adverbial group	*as soon*
prepositional group	*with a pair of unoiled garden shears*
nominal group	*a pair of unoiled garden shears*
verbal group	*said*
nominal group	*her inamoratus*

These groups are all "simplexes"; they contain no logical (paratactic or hypotactic) structures. Examples of group complexes would be:

as soon, or sooner

her inamoratus, the male hippopotamus

one African afternoon at half past four.

c) Word complexes

Note: Verbal, nominal and adverbial groups consisting of more than one element are simultaneously structured both as word constructions (multivariate) and as word complexes (univariate). For example,

	unoiled	garden	shears	
Logical:	γ	β	α	word complex:
	←	Modifier	Head	univariate structure
Experiential:	Epithet +	Classifier +	Thing	multivariate structure

System network

$$
\text{word complex}
\begin{cases}
\text{'TAXIS'} \rightarrow \begin{bmatrix} \text{paratactic} \\ \text{hypotactic} \end{bmatrix} \\[2em]
\begin{matrix}\text{TYPE OF} \\ \text{LOGICAL} \rightarrow \\ \text{RELATION}\end{matrix} \begin{bmatrix} \text{expansion} \\ \text{identity} \end{bmatrix}
\end{cases}
$$

66

Note: The intersection of these two systems yields the following paradigm of word complex types:

	paratactic	hypotactic
expansion	co-ordinate	modifying
identity	appositive	defining appositive

Verbal group *would live*

SYSTEMIC DESCRIPTION	verbal group: (hypotactic/expansion)

STRUCTURAL DESCRIPTION	β:Modifier ←α: Head

Adverbial group *as soon*

SYSTEMIC DESCRIPTION	adverbial group: (hypotactic/expansion)

STRUCTURAL DESCRIPTION	β:Modifier ←α: Head

Nominal group *a (pair of (unoiled garden shears))*

SYSTEMIC DESCRIPTION	nominal group: (hypotactic/expansion)

STRUCTURAL DESCRIPTION	β:Modifier ←α: Head
	(α: Head →β:Modifier)
	(γ←β:Modifier ←α: Head)

Verbal group *said* ('did say')

SYSTEMIC DESCRIPTION	verbal group: (hypotactic/expansion)

STRUCTURAL DESCRIPTION	β:Modifier ←α: Head

Nominal group *her inamoratus*

SYSTEMIC DESCRIPTION	nominal group: (hypotactic/expansion)

STRUCTURAL DESCRIPTION	β:Modifier ←α: Head

Note: The nominal group *I* can be regarded as having a logical structure consisting of α: Head only. A prepositional group resembles a clause in having no logical structure; see C. Interpersonal, below.

B. Experiential

a) Clauses

System network

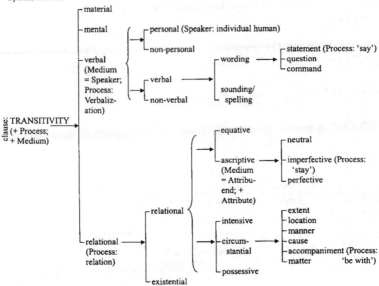

In addition, the Process may be accompanied by a Modulation, realized through (by pre-selection in) verbal group, adverbial group, or both:

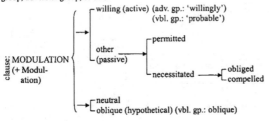

Clause *I would as soon live with a pair of unoiled garden shears*

SYSTEMIC DESCRIPTION	clause: (relational: relational: ((ascriptive: imperfective) / (circumstantial: accompaniment))) / (modulated: (willing/oblique))

STRUCTURAL DESCRIPTION	Process: relation + Modulation + Medium = Attribuend + Attribute

Clause *said her inamoratus*

SYSTEMIC DESCRIPTION	clause: verbal: (personal/(verbal: wording: statement))

STRUCTURAL DESCRIPTION	Process: verbalization + Medium = Speaker: individual

b) Verbal groups

System network

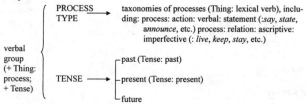

verbal group (+ Thing: process; + Tense)

PROCESS TYPE → taxonomies of processes (Thing: lexical verb), including: process: action: verbal: statement (:*say, state, announce,* etc.) process: relation: ascriptive: imperfective (: *live, keep, stay,* etc.)

TENSE →
past (Tense: past)
present (Tense: present)
future

Verbal group *would live*

SYSTEMIC DESCRIPTION	verbal group: (present / (relation: ascriptive: imperfective))

STRUCTURAL DESCRIPTION	Tense: present + Thing: process

c) Nominal groups

System network

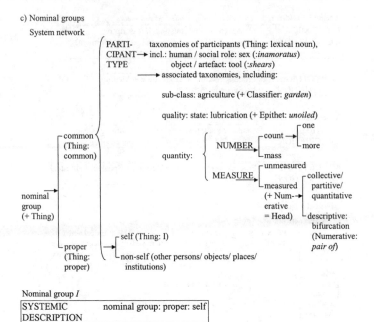

Nominal group *I*

SYSTEMIC DESCRIPTION	nominal group: proper: self

STRUCTURAL DESCRIPTION	Thing: self

Nominal group *a pair of unoiled garden shears*

SYSTEMIC DESCRIPTION	nominal group: common: object: artefact: (tool/ agriculture/ lubrication/ bifurcation)

STRUCTURAL DESCRIPTION	Numerative: measure + Epithet + Classifier + Thing: common: object

Nominal group *her inamoratus*

SYSTEMIC DESCRIPTION	nominal group: common: human: social role: sex

STRUCTURAL DESCRIPTION	Thing: common: human

d) Adverbial group

System network

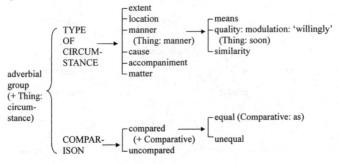

Adverbial group *as soon*

SYSTEMIC DESCRIPTION	adverbial group: (manner: quality: modulation) / (compared / equal)

STRUCTURAL DESCRIPTION	Comparative + Thing: circumstance

e) Prepositional group

System network

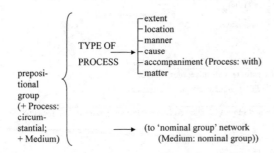

Prepositional group *with a pair of unoiled garden shears*

SYSTEMIC DESCRIPTION	prepositional group: accompaniment

STRUCTURAL DESCRIPTION	Process: circumstantial + Medium

C. Interpersonal

a) Information unit

System network

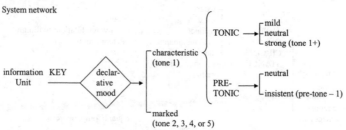

information KEY
Unit

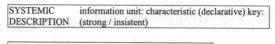

Information unit *I would as soon live with a pair of unoiled garden shears said her inamoratus*

SYSTEMIC DESCRIPTION	information unit: characteristic (declarative) key: (strong / insistent)

STRUCTURAL DESCRIPTION	Pre-tone –1 ˆ Tone 1+

b) Clauses

System network

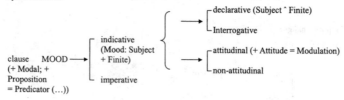

Clause *I would as soon live with a pair of unoiled garden shears*

SYSTEMIC DESCRIPTION	clause: finite: indicative: (declarative / attitudinal)

STRUCTURAL DESCRIPTION	Modal <Subject ˆ Finite ˆ Attitude> ˆ Propositional <Predicator>

Clause   *said her inamoratus*

Note: A clause having the features 'quoting / given' does not enter into the mood system. It is structured as Predicator ˆ Subject (optionally Subject ˆ Predicator if Subject is personal pronoun); the Predicator is a 'quoting' verb, finite, in simple past or present tense.

c) Verbal groups

System network

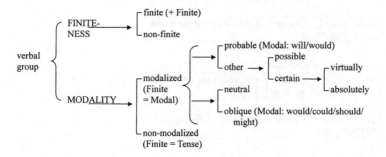

Verbal group *would live*

SYSTEMIC DESCRIPTION	verbal group: (finite: modalized: (probable / oblique))

STRUCTURAL DESCRIPTION	Finite=Modal + Predication

Verbal group *said*

SYSTEMIC DESCRIPTION	verbal group: (finite: non-modalized)

STRUCTURAL DESCRIPTION	Finite (=Tense) + Predication

d) Nominal groups

System network

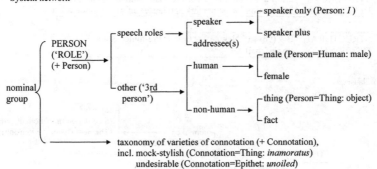

Nominal group *I*

SYSTEMIC DESCRIPTION	nominal group: speech role: speaker

STRUCTURAL DESCRIPTION	Person: speaker

73

Nominal group *a pair of unoiled garden shears*

SYSTEMIC DESCRIPTION	nominal group: ((other person: non-human: thing) / undesirable)

STRUCTURAL DESCRIPTION	Connotation (=Epithet) + Person: other

Nominal group *her inamoratus*

SYSTEMIC DESCRIPTION	nominal group: ((other person: human: male) / mock-stylish)

STRUCTURAL DESCRIPTION	Connotation (=Thing) = Person: other

e) Adverbial group: No interpersonal structure

f) Prepositional group: No interpersonal structure

D. Textual

a) Information unit

   System network

Information unit B: *I would as soon live with a pair of unoiled garden shears*
                     A: *said her inamoratus*

SYSTEMIC DESCRIPTION	information unit: unmarked (clause complex: quoting) information focus: unmarked (clause) information focus

STRUCTURAL DESCRIPTION	B = (Given ˆ New) ˆ A = Given; Pre-tonic ˆ Tonic (tonic ˆ 'tail')

b) Clauses

   System network

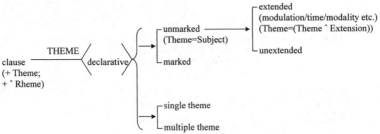

Clause *I would as soon live with a pair of unoiled garden shears*

SYSTEMIC DESCRIPTION	clause: ((unmarked (declarative) theme: extended: modulation) / single theme)

STRUCTURAL DESCRIPTION	Theme <Theme ˆ Extension> ˆ Rheme

Clause   *said her inamoratus*

Note: A clause having the features 'quoting/given' does not enter into the Theme system. It consists of a Rheme element only.

c) Verbal groups: No textual systems (see note at end)

d) Nominal groups

System network

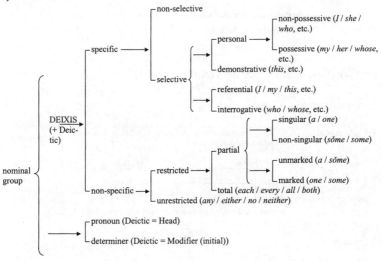

Nominal group   *I*

SYSTEMIC DESCRIPTION	nominal group: ((specific: selective: ((personal: non-possessive) / referential)) / pronoun)

STRUCTURAL DESCRIPTION	Deictic = Head: pronoun

75

Nominal group   *a pair of unoiled garden shears*

SYSTEMIC DESCRIPTION	nominal group: (non-specific: restricted: partial: (singular / unmarked) / determiner)

STRUCTURAL DESCRIPTION	Deictic = Modifier: determiner ˆ ...

Nominal group   *her inamoratus*

SYSTEMIC DESCRIPTION	nominal group: (specific: selective: ((personal: possessive) / referential) / determiner)

STRUCTURAL DESCRIPTION	Deictic = Modifier: determiner ˆ ...

    e) Adverbial group: no textual structure

    f) Prepositional group: no textual structure

5.2   *Generalized structural descriptions*

A. Generalized structures by rank

a) Clause complex

"*I would as soon live with a pair of unoiled garden shears*"	*said her inamoratus*

    Logical:

B: Quoted	A: Quoting

b) Information unit

// – 1+ˆ *I would as* / *soon* / *live with a pair of* / *unoiled* / *garden*	/ *s h e a r s*	| *said her i* / *namo* / *ratus* //

    Textual Information

Given ...	... New	| Given

    Interpersonal: key

Pretone -1	| Tone 1+	

c) Clause

I	| *would*	| *as soon*	| *live*	| *with*	*a pair of unoiled garden shears*
Experiential: transitivity; modulation					
Participant	Process				|Participant
Medium = Attribuend	Process: relation	| Modulation |			|Attribute
Interpersonal: mood					
Modal Subject	| Finite	| Propositional | Attitude |	Predicator		
Textual: theme					
Theme Theme	| Extension		Rheme		
Combined:					
Subject	| Predicator	| Adjunct (1) |		| Adjunct (2)	

d) Nominal group

	I
Logical: modification	α: Head
Experiential: taxonomy of participants	Thing: self
Interpersonal: person	Person: speaker
Textual: deixis	Deictic: pronoun

e) Verbal group

	would	*live*
Logical: modification	β: Modifier	α: Head
Experiential: taxonomy of processes; tense	Tense: present	Thing: process
Interpersonal: finiteness; modality	Finite=Modal	Predication

f) Adverbial group

	as	*soon*
Logical: modification	β: Modifier	α: Head
Exper.: taxonomy of circumstances	Comparative	Thing: circumstance

g) Propositional group

	with	*a pair of unoiled garden shears*
Exper.: taxonomy of circumstances	Process: circ.	Medium

h) Nominal group

	a	*pair*	*of*	*unoiled*	*garden*	*shears*
Logical:	β: Mod.	α: Head	α: Head	β: Modifier		
				γ: Modifier	β: Modifier	α: Head
Experiential:		Numerative: measure		Epithet	Classifier	Thing: common
Interpersonal:				Connotation		Person: other
Textual:	Deictic					

i) Clause

	(did)	*said*	*(say)*	*her inamoratus*
Experiential: transitivity	Process	Process: verbalization		Participant Medium = Speaker
Interpersonal: mood	Modal Finite		Propositional Predicator	Subject
Textual: theme	Rheme			

j) Verbal group *(said, =)*

	did	*say*
Logical: modification	β: Modifier	α: Head
Exper.: taxonomy of process; tense	Tense: past	Things: process
Interpersonal: finiteness	Finite	Predicator

k) Nominal group

	her	*inamoratus*
Logical: modification	β: Modifier	α: Head
Exper.: taxonomy of participants		Thing: common
Interpersonal: person, connotation		Person=Connotation
Textual: deixis	Deictic	

77

B. Generalized structure showing all ranks

	I	would	as soon	live	with [a pair of unoiled garden shears]	said	her inamoratus
LXGR:	||| I	would	as soon	live	with [a pair of unoiled garden shears]	|| said <did say>	her inamoratus |||
PHON:	//−1+ˏ I	would	as / soon /	live	with a pair of / unoiled / garden / s h e a r s	said	her i / namo / ratus //

Cl. comp.: LOG.	||| B: Quoted					|| A: Quoting	
Info. unit: INT.	// Pre-tone: −1				/Tone: 1+	// said <did say>	// her inamoratus //
'' TEXT.	// Given ...				... New		// Given

Clause ranks

	I	would	as soon	live	with [a pair of unoiled garden shears]	said	her inamoratus
Clause: EXP.	Medium	Process	Modulation		Attribute	Process	Medium
Clause: INT.	Modal	Propositional	Attitude			Modal | Prop^nl	
	Subject	Finite		Predicator		Finite | Predic.	Subject
Clause: TEXT.	Theme					Rheme	
	Theme	Extension	Rheme				
Clause: <combined>	Subject	Predicator	Adjunct (1)		Adjunct (2)	Predicator	Subject

Group ranks

	n.gp. I	v. gp. would live	adv. gp. as soon	prep. gp. with	n. gp. [a pair of unoiled garden shears]	v. gp. 'did say'	n. gp. her inamoratus
Group: LOG. (word compl.)		α: Head / β: Modifier ←α: Head	$\beta \longleftarrow \alpha$		$[\beta \rightarrow (\alpha\alpha \rightarrow \alpha\beta\ (\alpha\beta\gamma \rightarrow \alpha\beta\beta \leftarrow \alpha\beta\alpha))]$	$\beta \longleftarrow \alpha$	$\beta \longleftarrow \alpha$
Group: EXP.	Thing	Tense / Thing	Comp. Thing	Process	Medium [Numerative Epithet Classifier Thing]	Tense | Thing	Thing
Group: INT.	Person	Finite | Predic.			[Connotation Person]	Finite | Predic.	Connotation= Person
Group: TEXT.	Deictic				[Deictic]		Deictic

5.3   A note on the description

Systems in which this sentence does not select, or selects only unmarked options, are omitted from the networks. This includes sub-systems derived by further differentiation: nearly every network is open-ended to the right. The networks therefore give only a partial representation of the systems associated with each unit.

With a few exceptions (e.g. deixis in the nominal group), realizations are shown only for options selected by this sentence. They are shown in parentheses following the option in question. Realizations include insertion of elements, sub-categorization, ordering of elements, and pre-selection of options in systems of lower rank. An example of the last is the realization of modulation in the clause through selection in the modality system in the verbal group and the "manner" taxonomy in the adverbial group.

Vocabulary enters in as "most delicate grammar". Lexical selections are not distinct from grammatical ones; lexical items appear as one form of the realization of systemic options, typically as the last step in sub-categorization. Certain systems thus have the effect of specifying lexical taxonomies. Such taxonomies are like other sets of options in being functionally specific.

It follows from the functional organization of the grammar that the final "wording" (realization at the lexicogrammatical level) is the product of a large number of selections, simultaneous and ordered. For example, the words *I* and *would* each stands, as realization, at the intersection of a set of options from one or more than one functional component. The order of elements in the clause derives from a combination of options in the mood and theme systems, and so on.

We have stressed the functional organization of the system, and taken the functional components as dominating over the structural hierarchy, or "rank scale". This is because we are approaching the lexicogrammar from the semantic end, as the realization of meanings. In fact, the functional organization is clearly predominant in the clause; it is difficult to describe the clause other than as a composition of structural configurations each deriving from its own functional net-work. As one goes down the rank scale, the perspective changes. In the group structures, the functional components are less clearly distinct, and there is more interplay among them. For example, modality in the verbal group represents both modulation (experiential) and modality (interpersonal) in the clause; and modality and tense interact with each other and with polarity. So the verbal group is equally well, or perhaps better, represented as a single system network; likewise the other groups. Systems of the word (not discussed here) can be represented only in this way, except that the logical component of word structure remains distinct. Here we are concerned with text as semantic choice, and so have highlighted the semantic element in the organization of the grammatical system by using a functional interpretation of the structure throughout.

This is not to say that there are not elements of the different kinds of meaning in the makeup of the smaller units, but merely that these do not appear as independent systems and structures. For one thing, there are connotative choices in verbs and adverbs as well as in nouns; note the choice of *said* in contrast to *wuffled* or *gurbled* (not referred to because unmarked). Another example is one already noted in 2.2 above, the contribution of textual meaning to the structure of the group. In the clause, there is a choice of theme; any element, or combination of elements, can take on thematic value, realized by its being put first. But there is an unmarked choice, depending on the selection of mood: WH–element, finite verb, or subject; this being in each case the characteristic theme of such a clause, 'now this is the element I want supplied', and so on. In the group, there is no **choice** of theme; the order of elements is fixed. But it is the thematic principle that **determines** this fixed sequence, and explains why, in the verbal and nominal group, the element that has deictic value comes first: this is the element that relates to the "here and now". The thematic feature is present in the structure of the group, although not as an independent option in the way that it is in the clause.

'The Lover and His Lass' by James Thurber

1. An arrogant gray parrot and his arrogant mate listened, one African afternoon, in disdain and derision, to the lovemaking of a lover and his lass, who happened to be hippopotamuses.
2. "He calls her snooky-ookums," said Mrs. Gray.
3. "Can you believe that?"
4. "No," said Gray.
5. "I don't see how any male in his right mind could entertain affection for a female that has no more charm than a capsized bathtub."
6. "Capsized bathtub, indeed!" exclaimed Mrs. Gray.
7. "Both of them have the appeal of a coastwise fruit steamer with a cargo of waterlogged basketballs."

8. But it was spring, and the lover and his lass were young, and they were oblivious of the scornful comments of their sharp-tongued neighbors, and they continued to bump each other around in the water, happily pushing and pulling, backing and filling, and snorting and snaffling.

9. The tender things they said to each other during the monolithic give-and-take of their courtship sounded as lyric to them as flowers in bud or green things opening.

10. To the Grays, however, the bumbling romp of the lover and his lass was hard to comprehend and even harder to tolerate, and for a time they thought of calling the A.B.I., or African Bureau of Investigation, on the ground that monolithic lovemaking by enormous creatures who should have become decent fossils long ago was probably a threat to the security of the jungle.

11. But they decided instead to phone their friends and neighbors and gossip about the shameless pair, and describe them in mocking and monstrous metaphors involving skidding buses on icy streets and overturned moving vans.

12. Late that evening, the hippopotamus and the hippopotami were surprised and shocked to hear the Grays exchanging terms of endearment.

13. "Listen to those squawks," wuffled the male hippopotamus.

14. "What in the world can they see in each other?" gurbled the female hippopotamus.

15. "I would as soon live with a pair of unoiled garden shears," said her inamoratus.

16. They called up their friends and neighbors and discussed the incredible fact that a male gray parrot and a female gray parrot could possibly have any sex appeal.

17. It was long after midnight before the hippopotamuses stopped criticizing the Grays and fell asleep, and the Grays stopped maligning the hippopotamuses and retired to their beds.

18. Moral: *Laugh and the world laughs with you, love and you love alone.*

PART TWO

HIGHLY VALUED TEXTS
(NOVEL, DRAMA, SCIENCE IN POETRY,
POETRY IN SCIENCE)

EDITOR'S INTRODUCTION

Turning to 'highly valued texts', M. A. K. Halliday examines the works of the novelist, William Golding, whose prose offers 'a particular way of looking at experience'; J. B. Priestley, the dramatist, who creates a world of meaning through dialogue; Alfred Lord Tennyson, whose poetry constructs 'a semiotic universe at the intersection of science and poetry'; and Charles Darwin, the scientist, whose 450 pages of intense scientific argument has a unique place in the history of ideas. Whether prose or poetry, drama or scientific discourse, each is 'an "instantiation" of the linguistic system' and therefore may be studied as one would any kind of language, in terms of the linguistic resources that contribute to the realization of its 'meaning potential'.

The first paper in this part, 'Linguistic function and literary style: an inquiry into the language of William Golding's *The Inheritors*' appeared in 1971. Halliday begins by explaining how 'the total network of meaning potential is actually composed of a number of smaller networks, each one highly complex in itself but related to the others in a way that is relatively simple: rather like an elaborate piece of circuitry made up of two or three complex blocks of wiring with fairly simple interconnections.' Each block corresponds to one of the functions of language: ideational, interpersonal and textual. Each function defines a set of options or choices, all of which are meaningful, none meaningless, some of which will become more prominent than others. Halliday uses the term **prominence** 'as a general name for the phenomenon of linguistic highlighting, whereby some feature of the language of a text stands out in some way.' What stands out in Golding's *The Inheritors* are selections in transitivity. 'Transitivity,' as Halliday explains in this paper, 'is the set of options whereby the speaker encodes his experience of the processes of the external world, and of the internal world of his own consciousness, together with the participants in these processes and their attendant circumstances; and it embodies a very basic distinction of processes into two types, those that are regarded as due to an external cause, an agency other than the person or object involved, and those that are not ... Transitivity is really the cornerstone of the semantic organization of experience; and it is at one level what *The Inheritors* is about.'

J. B. Priestley is described by Halliday in 'The de-automatization of grammar: from Priestley's *An Inspector Calls*' (1982) as 'at once a novelist, dramatist, essayist, autobiographer, critic, and social historian.' The predominant themes in his plays include interdependence and social responsibility: 'no man is an island'; and time: 'time is not ticking our lives away'. Halliday acknowledges the much criticized 'flat and naturalistic' language spoken by Priestley's characters, and the declarative manner in which the themes are sometimes enunciated. However, in *An Inspector Calls*, the time theme is 'a motif that permeates the interaction of the participants, and is more or less covertly woven in to the dialogue.' Once the dramatist stops 'defining the nature of the world' and starts 'implying his world rather than presenting it', the language is likely to become 'de-automatized'. Halliday prefers Mukařovský's term 'de-automatization' to 'foregrounding' 'since what is in question is not simply prominence but rather the partial freeing of the lower-level systems from the control of the semantics so that they become domains of choice in their own right.' To 'de-automatize' means to 'try to interpret the grammar in terms that go beyond its direct realizational function'; 'to focus out the background, and let the words and structures speak for themselves'. In *An Inspector Calls* the complex interrelationship of themes related to obligation, personality and time are built from semantic systems of time, mood and polarity.

The last two papers in this part, 'Poetry as scientific discourse: the nuclear sections of Tennyson's *In Memoriam*' (1987) and 'The construction of knowledge and value in the grammar of scientific discourse: with reference to Charles Darwin's *The Origin of Species*' (1990) explore works that share a common birthright, both being 'constituted out of the impact between scientific and poetic forces of meaning.' While Tennyson's *In Memoriam* is science in poetry, Darwin's *The Origin of Species* is poetry in science. Halliday employs the same 'grammatics' to interpret and understand both. Halliday looks at the central passage in Tennyson's *In Memoriam* in terms of its logical structure, mood, and transitivity patterns, revealing a rhetorical and logical dynamic that celebrates the liberating power of knowledge. From his analysis of the final two paragraphs of Darwin's *The Origin of Species*, Halliday shows how 'the clauses are rather clearly organized, through their textual functions of Theme (in Theme–Rheme) and New (in Given–New), around a small number of distinct but interlocking motifs' culminating in a resounding lexicogrammatical cadence that 'brings the clause, the sentence, the paragraph, the chapter and the book to a crashing conclusion with a momentum to which I can think of no parallel elsewhere in literature.'

LINGUISTIC FUNCTION AND LITERARY STYLE: AN INQUIRY INTO THE LANGUAGE OF WILLIAM GOLDING'S *THE INHERITORS* (1971)

My main concern, in this paper, is with criteria of relevance. This, it seems to me, is one of the central problems in the study of "style in language": I mean the problem of distinguishing between mere linguistic regularity, which in itself is of no interest to literary studies, and regularity which is significant for the poem or prose work in which we find it. I remember an entertaining paper read to the Philological Society in Cambridge some years ago by Professor John Sinclair (1965), in which he drew our attention to some very striking linguistic patterns displayed in the poetry of William McGonagall, and invited us to say why, if this highly structured language was found in what we all agreed was such very trivial poetry, we should be interested in linguistic regularities at all. It is no new discovery to say that pattern in language does not by itself make literature, still less "good literature": nothing is more regular than the rhythm of *Three Blind Mice*, and if this is true of phonological regularities it is likely to be true also of syntactic ones. But we lack general criteria for determining whether any particular instance of linguistic prominence is likely to be stylistically relevant or not.

This is not a simple matter, and any discussion of it is bound to touch on more than one topic, or at the least to adopt more than one angle of vision. Moreover the line of approach will often, inevitably, be indirect, and the central concern may at times be lost sight of round some of the corners. It seems to me necessary, first of all, to discuss and to emphasize the place of semantics in the study of style; and this in

First published in *Literary Style: A Symposium*, edited by Seymour Chatman. London and New York: Oxford University Press, 1971, pp. 330–68.

turn will lead to a consideration of "functional" theories of language and their relevance for the student of literature. At the same time these general points need to be exemplified; and here I have allowed the illustration to take over the stage: when I re-examined for this purpose a novel I had first studied some four years ago, *The Inheritors* by William Golding, there seemed to be much that was of interest in its own right.[1] I do not think there is any antithesis between the "textual" and the "theoretical" in the study of language, so I hope the effect of this may be to strengthen rather than to weaken the general argument. The discussion of *The Inheritors* may be seen either in relation to just that one work or in relation to a general theory; I am not sure that it is possible to separate these two perspectives, either from each other or from various intermediate fields of attention such as an author, a genre, or a literary tradition.

The paper will fall into four parts: first, a discussion of a "functional theory of language"; second, a reference to various questions raised at the Style in Language Conference of 1958 and in other current writings; third, an examination of certain features of the language of *The Inheritors*; and fourth, a brief résumé of the question of stylistic relevance. Of these, the third part will be the longest.

1   The concept of "function" in language and linguistics

The term **function** is used, in two distinct though related senses, at two very different points in the description of language. First it is used in the sense of "grammatical" (or "syntactic") function, to refer to elements of linguistic structures such as actor and goal or subject and object or theme and rheme. These "functions" are the roles occupied by classes of words, phrases, and the like in the structure of higher units. Secondly, it is used to refer to the "functions" of language as a whole: for example in the well-known work of Karl Bühler (1934), in which he proposes a three-way division of language function into the representational, the conative and the expressive (see also Chapter 2 of Vachek 1966).

Here I am using "function" in the second sense, referring, however, not specifically to Bühler's theory, but to the generalized notion of "functions of language". By a functional theory of language I mean one which attempts to explain linguistic structure, and linguistic phenomena, by reference to the notion that language plays a certain part in our lives, that it is required to serve certain universal types of demand. I find this approach valuable in general for the insight it gives into the nature and use of language, but particularly so in the context of stylistic studies.

The demands that we make on language, as speakers and writers, listeners and readers, are indefinitely many and varied. They can be derived, ultimately, from a small number of very general headings; but what these headings are will depend on what questions we are asking. For example, if we were to take a broadly psychological viewpoint and consider the functions that language serves in the life of the individual, we might arrive at some such scheme as Bühler's, referred to above. If on the other hand we asked a more sociological type of question, concerning the functions that language serves in the life of the community, we should probably elaborate some framework such as Malinowski's (1935) distinction into a pragmatic and a magical function. Many others could be suggested besides.

These questions are extrinsic to language; and the categorizations of language function that depend on them are of interest because, and to the extent that, the questions themselves are of interest. Such categorizations therefore imply a strictly instrumental view of linguistic theory. Some would perhaps reject this on the grounds that it does not admit the autonomy of linguistics and linguistic investigations. I am not myself impressed by that argument, although I would stress that any one particular instrumental view is by itself inadequate as a general characterization of language. But a purely extrinsic theory of language functions does fail to take into account one thing, namely the fact that the multiplicity of function, if the idea is valid at all, is likely to be reflected somewhere in the internal organization of language itself. If language is, as it were, programmed to serve a variety of needs, then this should show up in some way in an investigation of linguistic structure.

In fact this functional plurality is very clearly built into the structure of language, and forms the basis of its semantic and "syntactic" (i.e. grammatical and lexical) organization. If we set up a functional framework that is neutral as to external emphasis, but designed to take into account the nature of the internal semantic and syntactic patterns of language, we arrive at something that is very suggestive for literary studies, because it represents a general characterization of semantic functions – of the meaning potential of the language system. Let me suggest here the framework that seems to me most helpful. It is a rather simple catalogue of three basic functions, one of which has two subheadings.

In the first place, language serves for the expression of content: it has a representational, or, as I would prefer to call it, an **ideational** function. (This is sometimes referred to as the expression of "cognitive meaning", though I find the term "cognitive" misleading; there is, after all, a cognitive element in all linguistic functions.) Two points need to be emphasized concerning this ideational function of language. The first is that it is through this function that the speaker or writer embodies in language his experience of the phenomena of the real world; and this includes his experience of the internal world of his own consciousness: his reactions, cognitions, and perceptions, and also his linguistic acts of speaking and understanding. We shall in no sense be adopting an extreme pseudo-Whorfian position (I say "pseudo-Whorfian" because Whorf himself never was extreme) if we add that, in serving this function, language lends structure to his experience and helps to determine his way of looking at things. The speaker can see through and around the settings of his semantic system; but he is aware that, in doing so, he is seeing reality in a new light, like Alice in Looking-Glass House. There is, however, and this is the second point, one component of ideational meaning which, while not unrelatable to experience, is nevertheless organized in language in a way which marks it off as distinct: this is the expression of certain fundamental logical relations such as are encoded in language in the form of co-ordination, apposition, modification, and the like. The notion of co-ordination, for example, as in *sun, moon, and stars*, can be derived from an aspect of the speaker's experience; but this and other such relations are realized through the medium of a particular type of structural mechanism (that of linear recursion) which takes them, linguistically, out of the domain of experience to form a functionally neutral, "logical" component in the total spectrum of meanings. Within the ideational function of language, therefore, we can recognize two sub-functions, the **experiential** and the **logical**; and the distinction is a significant one for our present purpose.

In the second place, language serves what we may call an **interpersonal** function. This is quite different from the expression of content. Here, the speaker is using language as the means of his own intrusion into the speech event: the expression of his comments, his attitudes, and evaluations, and also of the relationship that he sets up between himself and the listener – in particular, the communication role that he adopts, of informing, questioning, greeting, persuading, and the like. The interpersonal function thus subsumes both the expressive and the conative, which are not in fact distinct in the linguistic system: to give one example, the meanings 'I do not know'

91

(expressive) and 'you tell me' (conative) are combined in a single semantic feature, that of question, typically expressed in the grammar by an interrogative; the interrogative is both expressive and conative at the same time. The set of communication roles is unique among social relations in that it is brought into being and maintained solely through language. But the interpersonal element in language extends beyond what we might think of as its rhetorical functions. In the wider context, language is required to serve in the establishment and maintenance of all human relationships; it is the means whereby social groups are integrated and the individual is identified and reinforced. It is, I think, significant for certain forms of literature that, since personality is dependent on interaction which is in turn mediated through language, the "interpersonal" function in language is both interactional and personal: there is, in other words, a component in language which serves at one and the same time to express both the inner and the outer surfaces of the individual, as a single undifferentiated area of meaning potential that is personal in the broadest sense.[2]

These two functions, the ideational and the interpersonal, may seem sufficiently all-embracing; and in the context of an instrumental approach to language they are. But there is a third function which is in turn instrumental to these two, whereby language is, as it were, enabled to meet the demands that are made on it; I shall call this the **textual** function, since it is concerned with the creation of text. It is a function internal to language, and for this reason is not usually taken into account where the objects of investigation are extrinsic; but it came to be specifically associated with the term "functional" in the work of the Prague scholars who developed Bühler's ideas within the framework of a linguistic theory (cf. their terms "functional syntax", "functional sentence perspective"). It is through this function that language makes links with itself and with the situation; and discourse becomes possible, because the speaker or writer can produce a text and the listener or reader can recognize one. A **text** is an operational unit of language, as a sentence is a syntactic unit; it may be spoken or written, long or short; and it includes as a special instance a literary text, whether haiku or Homeric epic. It is the text and not some super-sentence that is the relevant unit for stylistic studies; this is a functional-semantic concept and is not definable by size. And therefore the "textual" function is not limited to the establishment of relations between sentences; it is concerned just as much with the internal organization of the sentence, with its meaning as a message both in itself and in relation to the context.

A tentative categorization of the principal elements of English syntax in terms of the above functions is given in Table 1. This table is intended to serve a twofold purpose. In the first place, it will help to make more concrete the present concept of a functional theory, by showing how the various functions are realized through the grammatical systems of the language, all of which are accounted for in this way. Not all the labels may be self-explanatory, nor is the framework so compartmental as in this bare outline it is made to seem: there is a high degree of indeterminacy in the fuller picture, representing the indeterminacy that is present throughout language, in its categories and its relations, its types and its tokens. Secondly it will bring out the fact that the syntax of a language is organized in such a way that it expresses as a whole the range of linguistic functions, but that the symptoms of functional diversity are not to be sought in single sentences or sentence types. In general, that is to say, we shall not find whole sentences or even smaller structures having just one function. Typically, each sentence embodies all functions, though one or another may be more prominent; and most constituents of sentences also embody more than one function, through their ability to combine two or more syntactic roles.

Let us introduce an example at this point. Here is a well-known passage from *Through the Looking-Glass, and What Alice Found There*:

"I don't understand you," said Alice. "It's dreadfully confusing!"

"That's the effect of living backwards," the Queen said kindly: "it always makes one a little giddy at first –"

"Living backwards!" Alice repeated in great astonishment. "I never heard of such a thing!"

"– but there's one great advantage in it, that one's memory works both ways."

"I'm sure *mine* only works one way," Alice remarked. "I can't remember things before they happen."

"It's a poor sort of memory that only works backwards," the Queen remarked.

"What sort of things do *you* remember best?" Alice ventured to ask.

"Oh, things that happened the week after next," the Queen replied in a careless tone.

To illustrate the last point first, namely that most constituents of sentences embody more than one function, by combining different syntactic roles: the constituent *what sort of things* occupies simultaneously the syntactic roles of Theme, of Phenomenon (that is, object of cognition, perception, etc.) and of Interrogation point. The theme represents a particular status in the message, and is thus an expression of "textual" function: it is the speaker's point of departure. If the

Table 1 Functions and ranks in the grammar of Modern English

COHESION ("above the sentence": non-structural relations)
reference; substitution & ellipsis; conjunction;
lexical cohesion

function: rank:	IDEATIONAL		INTERPERSONAL	TEXTUAL
	EXPERIENTIAL	LOGICAL		
CLAUSE	TRANSITIVITY types of process participants and circumstances (identity clauses) (things, facts, and reports)	condition addition report	MOOD types of speech function modality (the WH-function)	THEME types of message (identity as text relation) (identification, predication, reference, substitution)
Verbal GROUP	TENSE (verb classes)	POLARITY catenation secondary tense	PERSON ("marked" options)	VOICE ("contrastive" option)
Nominal GROUP	MODIFICATION epithet function enumeration (noun classes) (adjective classes)	classification sub-modification	ATTITUDE attitudinal modifiers intensifiers	DEIXIS determiners "phoric" elements (qualifiers) (definite article)
Adverbial (incl. prepositional) GROUP	"MINOR PROCESSES" prepositional relations (classes of circumstantial adjunct)	narrowing sub-modification	COMMENT (classes of comment adjunct)	CONJUNCTION (classes of discourse adjunct)
WORD (incl. lexical item)	LEXICAL "CONTENT" (taxonomic organization of vocabulary)	compounding derivation	LEXICAL "REGISTER" (expressive words) (stylistic organization of vocabulary)	COLLOCATION (collocational organization of vocabulary)
INFORMATION UNIT			TONE intonation systems	INFORMATION distribution & focus

PARATACTIC COMPLEXES (all ranks)
co-ordination
apposition

HYPOTACTIC COMPLEXES OF CAUSE, GROUP, AND WORD

speaker is asking a question he usually, in English, takes the request for information as his theme, expressing this by putting the question phrase first; here, therefore, the same element is both Theme and Interrogation point – the latter being an expression of "interpersonal" function since it defines the specific communication roles the speaker has chosen for himself and for the listener: the speaker is behaving as questioner. *What sort of thing* is the Phenomenon dependent on the mental process *remember*, and this concept of a mental phenomenon, as something that can be talked about, is an expression of the "ideational" function of language – of language as content, relatable to the speaker's and the listener's experience. It should be emphasized that it is not, in fact, the syntactic role in isolation, but the structure of which it forms a part that is semantically significant: it is not the theme, for example, but the total Theme–Rheme structure which contributes to the texture of the discourse.

Thus the constituents themselves tend to be multivalent; which is another way of saying that the very notion of a constituent is itself rather too concrete to be of much help in a functional context. A constituent is a particular word or phrase in a particular place; but functionally the choice of an item may have one meaning, its repetition another, and its location in structure yet another – or many others, as we have seen. So, in the Queen's remark *it's a poor sort of memory that only works backwards*, the word *poor* is a Modifier, and thus expresses a subclass of its head-word *memory* (ideational); while at the same time it is an Epithet expressing the Queen's attitude (interpersonal), and the choice of this word in this environment (as opposed to, say, *useful*) indicates more specifically that the attitude is one of disapproval. The words *it's . . . that* have here no reference at all outside the sentence, but they structure the message in a particular way (textual), which represents the Queen's opinion as if it was an Attribute (ideational), and defines one class of *memory* as exclusively possessing this undesirable quality (ideational). The lexical repetition in *memory that only works backwards* relates the Queen's remark (textual) to *mine only works one way*, in which *mine* refers anaphorically, by ellipsis, to *memory* in the preceding sentence (textual) and also to *I* in Alice's expression of her own judgement *I'm sure* (interpersonal). Thus ideational content and personal interaction are woven together with, and by means of, the textual structure to form a coherent whole.

Taking a somewhat broader perspective, we again find the same interplay of functions. The ideational meaning of the passage is enshrined in the phrase *living backwards*; we have a general characterization of the nature of experience, in which *things that happened the week after next* turns out to be an acceptable sentence. (I am not suggesting it is serious, or offering a deep literary interpretation; I am merely using it to illustrate the nature of language.) On the interpersonal level the language expresses, through a pattern of question (or exclamation) and response, a basic relationship of seeker and guide, in interplay with various other paired functions such as yours and mine, for and against, child and adult, wonderment and judgement. The texture is that of dialogue in narrative, within which the Queen's complex thematic structures (e.g. *there's one great advantage to it, that* . . .) contrast with the much simpler (i.e. linguistically unmarked) message patterns used by Alice.

A functional theory of language is a theory about meanings, not about words or constructions; we shall not attempt to assign a word or a construction directly to one function or another. Where then do we find the functions differentiated in language? They are differentiated semantically, as different areas of what I called the "meaning potential". Language is itself a potential: it is the totality of what the speaker can do. (By "speaker" I mean always the language user, whether as speaker, listener, writer, or reader: *homo grammaticus*, in fact.) We are considering, as it were, the dynamics of the semantic strategies that are available to him. If we represent the language system in this way, as networks of interrelated options which define, as a whole, the resources for what the speaker wants to say, we find empirically that these options fall into a small number of fairly distinct sets. In the last resort, every option in language is related to every other; there are no completely independent choices. But the total network of meaning potential is actually composed of a number of smaller networks, each one highly complex in itself but related to the others in a way that is relatively simple: rather like an elaborate piece of circuitry made up of two or three complex blocks of wiring with fairly simple interconnections. Each of these blocks corresponds to one of the functions of language.

In Table 1, where the columns represent our linguistic functions, each column is one "block" of options. These blocks are to be thought of as wired "in parallel". That is to say, the speaker does not first think of the content of what he wants to say and then go on to decide what kind of a message it is and where he himself comes into it – whether it will be statement or question, what modalities are involved and the like.[3] All these functions, the ideational, the interpersonal and the textual, are simultaneously embodied in his planning procedures. (If we pursue the metaphor, it is the rows of the table that are wired "in series": they represent the hierarchy of constituents in the grammar, where the different functions come together. Each row is one constituent type, and is a point of intersection of options from the different columns.)

The linguistic differentiation among the ideational, interpersonal and textual functions is thus to be found in the way in which choices in meaning are interrelated to one another. Each function defines a set of options that is relatively – though only relatively – independent of the other sets. Dependence here refers to the degree of mutual determination: one part of the content of what one says tends to exert a considerable effect on other parts of the content, whereas one's attitudes and speech roles are relatively undetermined by it: the speaker is, by and large, free to associate any interpersonal meanings with any content. What I wish to stress here is that all types of option, from whatever function they are derived, are meaningful. At every point the speaker is selecting among a range of possibilities that differ in meaning; and if we attempt to separate meaning from choice we are turning a valuable distinction (between linguistic functions) into an arbitrary dichotomy (between "meaningful" and "meaningless" choices). All options are embedded in the language system: the system **is** a network of options, deriving from all the various functions of language. If we take the useful functional distinction of "ideational" and "interpersonal" and rewrite it, under the labels "cognitive" and "expressive", in such a way as sharply to separate the two, equating cognitive with meaning and expressive with style, we not only fail to recognize the experiential basis of many of our own intuitions about works of literature and their impact – style as the expression of what the thing is about, at some level[4] (my own illustration in this paper is one example of this) – but we also attach the contrasting status of "non-cognitive" (whatever this may mean) to precisely these options that seem best to embody our conception of a work of literature, those whereby the writer gives form to the discourse and expresses his own individuality.[5] Even if we are on our guard against the implication that the regions of language in which style resides are the ones which are linguistically non-significant, we are still drawing the wrong line. There are no regions of language in which style does not reside.

We should not in fact be drawing lines at all; the boundaries on our map consist only in shading and overlapping. Nevertheless they are there; and provided we are not forced into seeking an unreal distinction between the "what" and the "how", we can show, by reference to the generalized notion of linguistic functions, how such real contrasts as that of denotation and connotation relate to the functional map of language as a whole, and thus how they may be incorporated into the linguistic study of style. It is through this chain of reasoning that we may hope to establish criteria of relevance, and to demonstrate the connection between the syntactic observations which we make about a text and the nature of the impact which that text has upon us. If we can relate the linguistic patterns (grammatical, lexical, and even phonological) to the underlying functions of language, we have a criterion for eliminating what is trivial and for distinguishing true foregrounding from mere prominence of a statistical or an absolute kind.

Foregrounding, as I understand it, is prominence that is motivated. It is not difficult to find patterns of prominence in a poem or prose text, regularities in the sounds or words or structures that stand out in some way, or may be brought out by careful reading; and one may often be led in this way towards a new insight, through finding that such prominence contributes to the writer's total meaning. But unless it does, it will seem to lack motivation; a feature that is brought into prominence will be "foregrounded" only if it relates to the meaning of the text as a whole. This relationship is a functional one: if a particular feature of the language contributes, by its prominence, to the total meaning of the work, it does so by virtue of and through the medium of its own value in the language – through the linguistic function from which its meaning is derived. Where that function is relevant to our interpretation of the work, the prominence will appear as motivated. I shall try to illustrate this by reference to *The Inheritors*. First, however, a few remarks about some points raised at the 1958 Style in Language Conference and in subsequent discussions, which I hope will make slightly more explicit the context within which Golding's work is being examined.

2   Questions of prominence (from *Style in Language*, 1960)

There are three questions I should like to touch on: Is prominence to be regarded as a departure from or as the attainment of a norm? To what extent is prominence a quantitative effect, to be uncovered or at least stated by means of statistics? How real is the distinction between prominence that is due to subject–matter and prominence that is due to something else? All three questions are very familiar, and my justification for bringing them up once more is not that what I have to say about them is new but rather that some partial answers are needed if we are attempting an integrated approach to language and style, and that these answers will be pertinent to a consideration of our main question, which is that of criteria of relevance.

I have used the term "prominence" as a general name for the phenomenon of linguistic highlighting, whereby some feature of the language of a text stands out in some way. In choosing this term I hoped to avoid the assumption that a linguistic feature which is brought under attention will always be seen as a departure. It is quite natural to characterize such prominence as departure from a norm, since this explains why it is remarkable, especially if one is stressing the subjective nature of the highlighting effect; thus Leech, discussing what he refers to as "schemes" ("foregrounded patterns . . . in grammar or phonology"), writes "It is ultimately a matter of subjective judgement whether . . . the regularity seems remarkable enough to constitute a definite departure from the normal functions of language" (1965, p. 70). But at the same time it is often objected, not unreasonably, that the "departure" view puts too high a value on oddness, and suggests that normal forms are of no interest in the study of style. Thus Wellek: "The danger of linguistic stylistics is its focus on deviations from, and distortions of, the linguistic norm. We get a kind of counter-grammar, a science of discards. Normal stylistics is abandoned to the grammarian, and deviational stylistics is reserved for the student of literature. But often the most commonplace, the most normal, linguistic elements are the constituents of literary structure."[6]

Two kinds of answer have been given to this objection. One is that there are two types of prominence, only one of which is negative, a departure from a norm; the other is positive, and is the attainment or the establishment of a norm. The second is that departure may in any case be merely statistical: we are concerned not only with deviations, ungrammatical forms, but also with what we may call "deflections", departures from some expected pattern of frequency.

The distinction between negative and positive prominence, or departures and regularities, is drawn by Leech, who contrasts foregrounding in the form of "motivated deviation from linguistic, or other socially accepted norms" with foregrounding applied to "the opposite circumstance, in which a writer temporarily renounces his permitted freedom of choice, introducing uniformity where there would normally be diversity" (1965, p. 69). Strictly speaking this is not an "opposite circumstance", since if diversity is normal, then uniformity is a deviation. But where there is uniformity there is regularity; and this can be treated as a positive feature, as the establishment of a norm. Thus, to quote Hymes, ". . . in some sources, especially poets, style may not be deviation from but achievement of a norm."[7]

However, this is not a distinction between two types of prominence; it is a distinction between two ways of looking at prominence, depending on the standpoint of the observer. There is no single universally relevant norm, no one set of expectancies to which all instances may be referred. On the one hand, there are differences of perspective. The text may be seen as "part" of a larger "whole", such as the author's complete works, or the tradition to which it belongs, so that what is globally a departure may be locally a norm. The expectancies may lie in "the language as a whole", in a diatypic variety or register[8] characteristic of some situation type (Osgood's "situational norms"[9]), in a genre or literary form, or in some special institution such as the Queen's Christmas message; we always have the choice of saying either "this departs from a pattern" or "this forms a pattern". On the other hand, there are differences of attention. The text may be seen as "this" in contrast with "that", with another poem or another novel; stylistic studies are essentially comparative in nature, and either may be taken as the point of departure. As Hymes says, there are egalitarian universes, comprising sets of norms, and "it would be arbitrary to choose one norm as a standard from which the others depart".[10] It may be more helpful to look at a given instance of prominence in one way rather than in another, sometimes as departure from a norm and sometimes as the attainment of a norm; but there is only one type of phenomenon here, not two.

There is perhaps a limiting case, the presence of one ungrammatical sentence in an entire poem or novel; presumably this could be viewed only as a departure. But in itself it would be unlikely to be of any interest. Deviation, the use of ungrammatical forms, has received a great deal of attention, and seems to be regarded, at times, as prominence *par excellence*. This is probably because it is a deterministic concept. Deviant forms are actually prohibited by the rules of whatever is taken to be the norm; or, to express it positively, the norm that is established by a set of deviant forms excludes all texts but the one in which they occur. But for this very reason deviation is of very limited interest in stylistics. It is rarely found; and when it is found, it is often not relevant. On the contrary, if we follow McIntosh (who finds it "a chastening thought"), ". . . quite often . . . the impact of an entire work may be enormous, yet word by word, phrase by phrase, clause by clause, sentence by sentence, there may seem to be nothing very unusual or arresting, in grammar or in vocabulary. . . ."[11]

Hence the very reasonable supposition that prominence may be of a probabilistic kind, defined by Bloch as "frequency distributions and

Table 2 Frequency of transitivity clause types

A Process:	ACTION intransitive movement	intransitive other	ACTION transitive movement	transitive other	location/possession	mental process	attribution	other (equation, event)	TOTAL
human { people	9		1	1	1	12			24
human { tribe	2		1			1			4
part of body	2				1	3	2		8
inanimate	4		1		12		3		20
	17		3	1	14	16	5		56
B (i)									
human { people	4		1	3*	2	1			11
human { tribe	5		1	1	2				9
part of body									
inanimate	13	1	2		5			2	23
	22	1	4	4	9	1		2	43
B (ii)									
human { people	13	2	1		2	4			22
human { tribe									
part of body	3				1		2		6
inanimate	3	1	1	2	4		6	2	19
	19	3	2	2	7	4	8	2	47
C									
human { people	1		1	2		4			8
human { tribe	3	2	5	11	3	11	3	2	40
part of body	2	1					5		8
inanimate	2	1			3		4	1	11
	8	4	6	13	6	15	12	3	67

* including two passives, which are also negative and in which the actor is not explicit: *The tree would not be cajoled or persuaded.*

transitional probabilities [which] differ from those . . . in the language as a whole".[12] This is what we have referred to above as "deflection". It too may be viewed either as departure from a norm or as its attainment. If, for example, we meet seven occurrences of a rather specific grammatical pattern, such as that cited by Leech "*my* + noun + *you* + verb" (1965, p. 70), a norm has been set up and there is, or may be, a strong local expectancy that an eighth will follow; the probability of finding this pattern repeated in eight successive clauses is infinitesimally small, so that the same phenomenon constitutes a departure. It is fairly easy to see that the one always implies the other; the contravention of one expectation is, at the same time, the fulfillment of a different one. Either way, whether the prominence is said to consist in law-breaking or in law-making, we are dealing with a type of phenomenon that is expressible in quantitative terms, to which statistical concepts may be applied.

In the context of stylistic investigations, the term "statistical" may refer to anything from a highly detailed measurement of the reactions of subjects to sets of linguistic variables, to the parenthetical insertion of figures of occurrences designed to explain why a particular feature is being singled out for discussion. What is common to all these is the assumption that numerical data on language may be stylistically significant; whatever subsequent operations are performed, there has nearly always been some counting of linguistic elements in the text, whether of phonological units or words or grammatical patterns, and the figures obtained are potentially an indication of prominence. The notion that prominence may be defined statistically is still not always accepted; there seem to be two main counterarguments, but whatever substance these may have as stated they are not, I think, valid objections to the point at issue. The first is essentially that, since style is a manifestation of the individual, it cannot be reduced to counting. This is true, but, as has often been said before, it misses the point. If there is such a thing as a recognizable style, whether of a work, an author, or an entire period or literary tradition, its distinctive quality can in the last analysis be stated in terms of relative frequencies, although the linguistic features that show significant variation may be simple and obvious or extremely subtle and complex. An example of how period styles may be revealed in this way will be found in Josephine Miles' "Eras in English poetry" in which she shows that different periods are characterized by a distinction in the dominant type of sentence structure, that between "the sort which emphasizes substantial elements – the phrasal and co-ordinative modifications of subject and object – and the sort which emphasizes clausal co-ordination and complication of the predicate".[13]

The second objection is that numbers of occurrences must be irrelevant to style because we are not aware of frequency in language and therefore cannot respond to it. This is almost certainly not true. We are probably rather sensitive to the relative frequency of different grammatical and lexical patterns, which is an aspect of "meaning potential"; and our expectancies, as readers, are in part based on our awareness of the probabilities inherent in the language. This is what enables us to grasp the new probabilities of the text as local norm; our ability to perceive a statistical departure and restructure it as a norm is itself evidence of the essentially probabilistic nature of the language system. Our concern here, in any case, is not with psychological problems of the response to literature but with the linguistic options selected by the writer and their relation to the total meaning of the work. If in the selections he has made there is an unexpected pattern of frequency distributions, and this turns out to be motivated, it seems pointless to argue that such a phenomenon could not possibly be significant.

What cannot be expressed statistically is foregrounding: figures do not tell us whether a particular pattern has or has not "value in the game".[14] For this we need to know the rules. A distinctive frequency distribution is in itself no guarantee of stylistic relevance, as can be seen from authorship studies, where the diagnostic features are often, from a literary stand point, very trivial ones.[15] Conversely, a linguistic feature that is stylistically very relevant may display a much less striking frequency pattern. But there is likely to be some quantitative turbulence, if a particular feature is felt to be prominent; and a few figures may be very suggestive. Counting, as Miller remarked, has many positive virtues. Ullmann offers a balanced view of these when he writes "Yet even those who feel that detailed statistics are both unnecessary and unreliable [in a sphere where quality and context, aesthetic effects and suggestive overtones are of supreme importance] would probably agree that a rough indication of frequencies would often be helpful" (1965, p. 22). A rough indication of frequencies is often just what is needed: enough to suggest why we should accept the analyst's assertion that some feature is prominent in the text, and to allow us to check his statements. The figures, obviously, do not alone constitute an analysis, interpretation, or evaluation of the style.

But this is not, be it noted, a limitation on quantitative patterns as such; it is a limitation on the significance of prominence of any kind. Deviation is no more fundamental a phenomenon than statistical deflection: in fact there is no very clear line between the two, and in any given instance the most qualitatively deviant items may be among the least relevant. Thus if style cannot be reduced to counting, this is because it cannot be reduced to a simple question of prominence. An adequate characterization of an author's style is much more than an inventory of linguistic highlights. This is why linguists were so often reluctant to take up questions of criticism and evaluation, and tended to disclaim any contribution to the appraisal of what they were describing: they were very aware that statements about linguistic prominence by themselves offer no criterion of literary value. Nevertheless some values, or some aspects of value, must be expressed in linguistic terms. This is true, for example, of metrical patterns, which linguists have always considered their proper concern. The question is how far it is also true of patterns that are more directly related to meaning: what factors govern the relevance of "effects" in grammar and vocabulary? The significance of rhythmic regularity has to be formulated linguistically, since it is a phonological phenomenon, although the ultimate value to which it relates is not "given" by the language – that the sonnet is a highly valued pattern is not a linguistic fact, but the sonnet itself is (Levin 1971). The sonnet form defines the relevance of certain types of phonological pattern. There may likewise be some linguistic factor involved in determining whether a syntactic or a lexical pattern is stylistically relevant or not.

Certainly there is no magic in unexpectedness; and one line of approach has been to attempt to state conditions under which the unexpected is **not** relevant – namely when it is not really unexpected. Prominence, in this view, is not significant if the linguistically unpredicted configuration is predictable on other grounds; specifically, by reference to subject–matter, the implication being that it would have been predicted if we had known beforehand what the passage was about. So, for example, Ullmann warns of the danger in the search for statistically defined key-words: "One must carefully avoid what have been called contextual words whose frequency is due to the subject-matter rather than to any deep-seated stylistic or psychological tendency" (1965, p. 27). Ullmann's concern here is with words that serve as indices of a particular author, and he goes on to discuss the significance of recurrent imagery for style and personality, citing as an example the prominence of insect vocabulary in the writings of Sartre (Ullmann 1965, p. 29; see also 1964, pp. 186–8); in this context we can see that, by contrast, the prevalence of such words in a treatise on entomology would be irrelevant. But it is less easy to see how this can be generalized, even in the realm of vocabulary; is lexical foregrounding entirely dependent on imagery?

Can we in fact dismiss, as irrelevant, prominence that is due to subject-matter? Can we even claim to identify it? This was the third and final question I asked earlier, and it is one which relates very closely to an interpretation of the style of *The Inheritors*. In *The Inheritors*, the features that come to our attention are largely syntactic, and we are in the realm of syntactic imagery, where the syntax, in Ohmann's words, "serves [a] vision of things. . . . since there are innumerable kinds of deviance, we should expect that the ones elected by a poem or poet spring from particular semantic impulses, particular ways of looking at experience" (1967, p. 237). Ohmann is concerned primarily with "syntactic irregularities", but syntax need not be deviant in order to serve a vision of things; a foregrounded selection of everyday syntactic options may be just as visionary, and perhaps more effective. The vision provides the motivation for their prominence; it makes them relevant, however ordinary they may be. The style of *The Inheritors* rests very much on foregrounding of this kind.

The prominence, in other words, is often due to the vision. But "vision" and "subject-matter" are merely the different levels of meaning which we expect to find in a literary work; and each of these, the inner as well as the outer, and any as it were intermediate layers, finds expression in the syntax. In Ruqaiya Hasan's words, "Each utterance has a thesis: what it is talking about uniquely and instantially; and in addition to this, each utterance has a function in the internal organization of the text: in combination with other utterances of the text it realizes the theme, structure and other aspects. . . ." (1967, pp. 109–10; 1971). Patterns of syntactic prominence may reflect thesis or theme or "other aspects" of the meaning of the work; every level is a potential source of motivation, a kind of semantic "situational norm". And since the role of syntax in language is to weave into a single fabric the different threads of meaning that derive from the variety of linguistic functions, one and the same syntactic feature is very likely to have at once both a deeper and a more immediate significance, like the participial structures in Milton as Chatman has interpreted them (1968, pp. 1386–99).

Thus we cannot really discount "prominence due to subject-matter", at least as far as syntactic prominence is concerned; especially where vision and subject-matter are themselves as closely interwoven as they are in *The Inheritors*. Rather, perhaps, we might think of the choice of subject-matter as being itself a stylistic choice, in the sense that the subject-matter may be more or less relevant to the underlying themes of the work. To the extent that the subject-matter is an integral element in the total meaning – in the artistic unity, if you will – to that extent, prominence that is felt to be partly or wholly "due to" the subject-matter, far from being irrelevant to the style, will turn out to be very clearly foregrounded.

To cite a small example that I have used elsewhere, the prominence of finite verbs in simple past tense in the well-known "Return of Excalibur" lines in Tennyson's *Morte d'Arthur* relates immediately to the subject-matter: the passage is a direct narrative. But the choice of a story as subject-matter is itself related to the deeper preoccupations of the work – with heroism and, beyond that, with the *res gestae*, with deeds as the realization of the true spirit of a people, and with history and historicalism; the narrative register is an appropriate form of

105

expression, one that is congruent with the total meaning, and so the verb forms that are characteristically associated with it are motivated at every level. Similarly, it is not irrelevant to the **style** of an entomological monograph (although we may not be very interested in its style) that it contains a lot of words for insects, if in fact it does. In stylistics we are concerned with language in relation to all the various levels of meaning that a work may have.

But while a given instance of syntactic or lexical prominence may be said to be "motivated" either by the subject-matter or by some other level of the meaning, in the sense of deriving its relevance therefrom, it cannot really be said to be "due to" it. Neither thesis nor theme imposes linguistic patterns. They may set up local expectancies, but these are by no means always fulfilled; there might actually be very few insect words in the work on entomology – and there are very few in Kafka.[16] There is always choice. In *The Inheritors*, Golding is offering a "particular way of looking at experience", a vision of things which he ascribes to Neanderthal man; and he conveys this by syntactic prominence, by the frequency with which he selects certain key syntactic options. It is their frequency which establishes the clause types in question as prominent; but, as Ullmann has remarked, in stylistics we have **both** to count things **and** to look at them, one by one, and when we do this we find that the foregrounding effect is the product of two apparently opposed conditions of use. The foregrounded elements are certain clause types which display particular patterns of transitivity, as described in the next section; and in some instances the syntactic pattern is "expected" in that it is the typical form of expression for the subject-matter – for the process, participants, and circumstances that make up the thesis of the clause. Elsewhere, however, the same syntactic elements are found precisely where they would not be expected, there being other, more likely ways of "saying the same thing".

Here we might be inclined to talk of semantic choice and syntactic choice: what the author chooses to say, and how he chooses to say it. But this is a misleading distinction; not only because it is unrealistic in application (most distinctions in language leave indeterminate instances, although here there would be suspiciously many) but more because the combined effect is cumulative: the one does not weaken or cut across the other but reinforces it. We have to do here with an interaction, not of meaning and form, but of two levels of meaning, both of which find expression in form, and through the same syntactic features. The immediate thesis and the underlying theme come together in the syntax; the choice of subject-matter is motivated by the deeper meaning, and the transitivity patterns realize both. This is the explanation of their powerful impact.

The foregrounding of certain patterns in syntax as the expression of an underlying theme is what we understand by "syntactic imagery", and we assume that its effect will be striking. But in *The Inheritors* these same syntactic patterns also figure prominently in their "literal" sense, as the expression of subject-matter; and their prominence here is doubly relevant, since the literal use not only is motivated in itself but also provides a context for the metaphorical – we accept the syntactic vision of things more readily because we can see that it coincides with, and is an extension of, the reality. *The Inheritors* provides a remarkable illustration of how grammar can convey levels of meaning in literature; and this relates closely to the notion of linguistic functions which I discussed at the beginning. The foregrounded patterns, in this instance, are ideational ones, whose meaning resides in the representation of experience; as such they express not only the content of the narrative but also the abstract structure of the reality through which that content is interpreted. Sometimes the interpretation matches our own, and at other times, as in the drawing of the bow in Passage A below, it conflicts with it; these are the "opposed conditions of use" referred to earlier. Yet each tells a part of the story. Language, because of the multiplicity of its functions, has a fugue-like quality in which a number of themes unfold simultaneously; each of these themes is apprehended in various settings, or perspectives, and each melodic line in the syntactic sequence has more than one value in the whole.

3 Some features of the grammar of *The Inheritors*

The Inheritors[17] is prefaced by a quotation from H. G. Wells' *Outline of History*:

> We know very little of the appearance of the Neanderthal man, but this
> . . . seems to suggest an extreme hairiness, an ugliness, or a repulsive
> strangeness in his appearance over and above his low forehead, his beetle
> brows, his ape neck, and his inferior stature. . . . Says Sir Harry Johnston,
> in a survey of the rise of modern man in his *Views and Reviews*: "The
> dim racial remembrance of such gorilla-like monsters, with cunning
> brains, shambling gait, hairy bodies, strong teeth, and possibly cannibal-
> istic tendencies, may be the germ of the ogre in folklore."

The book is, in my opinion, a highly successful piece of imaginative prose writing; in the words of Kinkead-Weekes and Gregor (1967), in their penetrating critical study, it is a "reaching out through the imagination into the unknown". The persons of the story are a small band of Neanderthal people, initially eight strong, who refer to themselves as "the people"; their world is then invaded by a group of more advanced stock, a fragment of a tribe, whom they call at first "others" and later "the new people". This casual impact – casual, that is, from the tribe's point of view – proves to be the end of the people's world, and of the people themselves. At first, and for more than nine-tenths of the book (pp. 1–216), we share the life of the people and their view of the world, and also their view of the tribe: for a long passage (pp. 137–80) the principal character, Lok, is hidden in a tree watching the tribe in their work, their ritual and their play, and the account of their doings is confined within the limits of Lok's under-standing, requiring at times a considerable effort of "interpretation". At the very end (pp. 216–38) the stand point shifts to that of the tribe, the inheritors, and the world becomes recognizable as our own, or something very like it. I propose to examine an aspect of the linguistic resources as they are used first to characterize the people's world and then to effect the shift of world-view.

For this purpose I shall look closely at three passages taken from different parts of the book; these are reproduced below (pp. 121–4). Passage A is representative of the first, and longest, section, the narrative of the people; it is taken from the long account of Lok's vigil in the tree. Passage C is taken from the short final section, concerned with the tribe; while Passage B spans the transition, the shift of stand point occurring at the paragraph division within this passage. Linguistically, A and C differ in rather significant ways, while B is in certain respects transitional between them.

The clauses of Passage A [56][18] are mainly clauses of action [21], location (including possession) [14], or mental process [16]; the remain-der [5] are attributive.[19] Usually the process is expressed by a finite verb in simple past tense [46]. Almost all of the action clauses [19] describe simple movements (*turn, rise, hold, reach, throw forward,* etc.); and of these the majority [15] are intransitive; the exceptions are *the man was holding the stick, as though someone had clapped a hand over her mouth, he threw himself forward,* and *the echo of Liku's voice in his head sent him trembling at this perilous way of bushes towards the island.* The typical pattern is exemplified by the first two clauses, *the bushes twitched again* and *Lok steadied by the tree,* and there is no clear line, here, between action and location: both types have some reference in space, and both have one participant only. The clauses of movement usually [16] also specify location, e.g. *the man turned sideways in the bushes, he rushed to the edge of the water*; and on the other hand, in addition to what is clearly movement, as in *a stick rose upright*, and what is clearly location, as in *there were hooks in the bone*, there is an intermediate type exemplified by [*the bushes*] *waded out*, where the verb is of the movement type but the subject is immobile.

The picture is one in which people act, but they do not act on things; they move, but they move only themselves, not other objects. Even such normally transitive verbs as *grab* occur intransitively: *he grabbed at the branches* is just another clause of movement (cf. *he smelled along the shaft of the twig*). Moreover a high proportion [exactly half] of the subjects are not people; they are either parts of the body [8] or inanimate objects [20], and of the human subjects half again [14] are found in clauses which are not clauses of action. Even among the four transitive action clauses, cited above, one has an inanimate subject and one is reflexive. There is a stress set up, a kind of syntactic counterpoint, between verbs of movement in their most active and dynamic form, that of finite verb in independent clause,[20] in the simple past tense characteristic of the direct narrative of events in a time sequence, on the one hand, and on the other hand the preference for non-human subjects and the almost total absence of transitive clauses. It is particularly the lack of transitive clauses of action with human subjects (there are only two clauses in which a person acts on an external object) that creates an atmosphere of ineffectual activity: the scene is one of constant movement, but movement which is as much inanimate as human and in which only the mover is affected – nothing else changes. The syntactic tension expresses this combination of activity and helplessness.

No doubt this is a fair summary of the life of Neanderthal man. But Passage A is not a description of the people. The section from which it is taken is one in which Lok is observing and, to a certain extent, interacting with the tribe; they have captured one of the people, and it is for the most part their doings that are being described. And the tribe are not helpless. The transitivity patterns are not imposed by the subject-matter; they are the reflection of the underlying theme, or rather of one of the underlying themes – the inherent limitations of understanding, whether cultural or biological, of Lok and his people, and their consequent inability to survive when confronted with beings at a higher stage of development. In terms of the processes and events as we would interpret them, and encode them in our grammar, there is no immediate justification for the predominance of intransitives; this is the result of their being expressed through the medium of the semantic structure of Lok's universe. In our interpretation, a goal-directed process (or, as I shall suggest below, an externally caused process) took place: someone held up a bow and drew it. In Lok's interpretation, the process was undirected (or, again, self-caused): *a stick rose upright* and *began to grow shorter at both ends*. (I would differ slightly here from Kinkead-Weekes and Gregor, who suggest, I think, that the form of Lok's vision is perception and no more. There may be very little processing, but there surely is some; Lok has a theory – as he must have, because he has language.)

Thus it is the syntax as such, rather than the syntactic reflection of the subject-matter, to which we are responding. This would not emerge if we had no account of the activities of the tribe, since elsewhere – in the description of the people's own doings, or of natural phenomena – the intransitiveness of the syntax would have been no more than a feature of the events themselves, and of the people's ineffectual manipulation of their environment. For this reason the vigil of Lok is a central element in the novel. We find, in its syntax, both levels of meaning side by side: Lok is now actor, now interpreter, and it is his potential in both these roles that is realized by the overall patterns of prominence that we have observed, the intransitives, the non-human subjects, and the like. This is the dominant mode of expression. At the same time, in Passage A, among the clauses that have human subjects, there are just two in which the subject is acting on something external to himself, and in both these the subject is a member of the tribe; it is not Lok. There is no instance in which Lok's own actions extend beyond himself; but there is a brief hint that such extension is conceivable. The syntactic foregrounding, of which this passage provides a typical example, thus has a complex significance: the predominance of intransitives reflects, first, the limitations of the people's own actions; second, the people's world-view, which in general cannot transcend these limitations – but within which there may arise, thirdly, a dim apprehension of the superior powers of the "others", represented by the rare intrusion of a transitive clause such as *the man was holding the stick out to him*. Here the syntax leads us into a third level of meaning, Golding's concern with the nature of humanity; the intellectual and spiritual developments that contribute to the present human condition, and the conflicts that arise within it, are realized in the form of conflicts between the stages of that development – and, syntactically, between the types of transitivity.

Passage A is both text and sample. It is not only these particular sentences and their meanings that determine our response, but the fact that they are part of a general syntactic and semantic scheme. That this passage is representative in its transitivity patterns can be seen from comparison with other extracts.[21] It also exemplifies certain other relevant features of the language of this part of the book. We have seen that there is a strong preference for processes having only one participant: in general there is only one nominal element in the structure of the clause, which is therefore the Subject. But while there are very few Complements,[22] there is an abundance of Adjuncts [44]; and most of these [40] have some spatial reference. Specifically, they are (a) static [25], of which most [21] are place adjuncts consisting of preposition plus noun, the noun being either an inanimate object of the immediate natural environment (e.g. *bush*) or a part of the body, the remainder [4] being localizers (*at their farthest, at the end*, etc.); and (b) dynamic [15], of which the majority [10] are of direction or non-terminal motion (*sideways, [rose] upright, at the branches, towards the island*, etc.) and the remainder [5] perception, or at least circumstantial to some process that is not a physical one (e.g. *[looked at Lok] along his shoulder, [shouted] at the green drifts*). Thus with the dynamic type, either the movement is purely perceptual or, if physical, it never reaches a goal: the nearest thing to terminal motion is *he rushed to the edge of the water* (which is followed by *and came back!*).

The restriction to a single participant also applies to mental process clauses [16]. This category includes perception, cognition, and reaction, as well as the rather distinct sub-category of verbalization; and such clauses in English typically contain a Phenomenon, that which is seen, understood, liked, etc. Here, however, the Phenomenon is often [8] either not expressed at all (e.g. *[Lok] gazed*) or expressed indirectly through a preposition, as in *he smelled along the shaft of the twig*; and sometimes [3] the subject is not a human being but a sense organ (*his nose examined this stuff and did not like it*). There is the same reluctance to envisage the "whole man" (as distinct from a part of his body) participating in a process in which other entities are involved.

There is very little modification of nouns [10, out of about 100]; and all modifiers are non-defining (e.g. *green drifts, glittering water*) except where [2] the Modifier is the only semantically significant element in the nominal, the Head noun being a mere carrier demanded by the rules of English grammar (*white bone things, sticky brown stuff*). In terms of the immediate situation, things have defining attributes only if these attributes are their sole properties; at the more abstract level, in Lok's understanding the complex taxonomic ordering of natural phenomena that is implied by the use of defining modifiers is lacking, or is only rudimentary.

We can now formulate a description of a typical clause of what we may call "Language A", the language in which the major part of the book is written and of which Passage A is a sample, in terms of its process, participants and circumstances:

(1) There is one participant only, which is therefore subject; this is
    (a) actor in a non-directed action (action clauses are intransitive), or participant in a mental process (the one who perceives etc.), or simply the bearer of some attribute or some spatial property;
    (b) a person (*Lok, the man, he*, etc.), or a part of the body, or an inanimate object of the immediate and tangible natural environment (*bush, water, twig*, etc.);
    (c) unmodified, other than by a determiner which is either an anaphoric demonstrative (*this, that*) or, with parts of the body, a personal possessive (*his* etc.).

(2) The process is
    (a) action (which is always movement in space), or location-possession (including, e.g. *the man had white bone things above his eyes* = "above the man's eyes there were . . ."), or mental process (thinking and talking as well as seeing and feeling – a "cunning brain"! – but often with a part of the body as subject);
    (b) active, non-modalized, finite, in simple past tense (one of a linear sequence of mutually independent processes).

(3) There are often other elements which are adjuncts, i.e. treated as circumstances attendant on the process, not as participants in it; these are
    (a) static expressions of place (in the form of prepositional phrases), or, if dynamic, expressions of direction (adverbs only) or of non-terminal motion, or of directionality of perception (e.g. *peered at the stick*);
    (b) often obligatory, occurring in clauses which are purely locational (e.g. *there were hooks in the bone*).

A grammar of Language A would tell us not merely what clauses occurred in the text but also what clauses could occur in that language.[23] For example, as far as I know the clause *a branch curved downwards over the water* does not occur in the book; neither does *his hands felt along the base of the rock*. But both of them could have done. On the other hand, *he had very quickly broken off the lowest branches* breaks four rules: it has a human actor with a transitive verb, a tense other

112

than simple past, a defining modifier, and a non-spatial adjunct. This is not to say that it could not occur. Each of these features is improbable, and their combination is very improbable; but they are not impossible. They are improbable in that they occur with significantly lower frequency than in other varieties of English (such as, for example, the final section of *The Inheritors*).

Before leaving this passage, let us briefly reconsider the transitivity features in the light of a somewhat different analysis of transitivity in English. I have suggested elsewhere that the most generalized pattern of transitivity in Modern English, extending beyond action clauses to clauses of all types, those of mental process and those expressing attributive and other relations, is one that is based not on the notions of actor and goal but on those of cause and effect.[24] In any clause, there is one central and obligatory participant – let us call it the "affected" participant – which is inherently involved in the process. This corresponds to the actor in an intransitive clause of action, to the goal in a transitive clause of action, and to the one who perceives etc., in a clause of mental process; Lok has this function in all the following examples: *Lok turned away, Fa drew Lok away, Lok looked up at Fa, Lok was frightened, curiosity overcame Lok*. There may then be a second, optional participant, which is present only if the process is being regarded as brought about by some agency other than the participant affected by it: let us call this the "agent". This is the actor in a transitive clause of action and the initiator in the various types of causative; the function of *Tuami* in *Tuami waggled the paddle in the water* and *Tuami let the ivory drop from his hands*. As far as action clauses are concerned, an intransitive clause is one in which the roles of "affected" and "agent" are combined in the one participant; a transitive clause is one in which they are separated, the process being treated as one having an external cause.

In these terms, the entire transitivity structure of Language A can be summed up by saying that there is no cause and effect. More specifically: in this language, processes are seldom represented as resulting from an external cause; in those instances where they are, the "agent" is seldom a human being; and where it is a human being, it is seldom one of the people. Whatever the type of process, there tends to be only one participant; any other entities are involved only indirectly, as circumstantial elements (syntactically, through the mediation of a preposition). It is as if doing was as passive as seeing and things no more affected by actions than by perceptions: their role is as in clauses of mental process, where the object of perception is not in any sense "acted on" – it is in fact the perceiver that is the "affected" participant, not the thing perceived – and likewise tends to be expressed circumstantially (e.g. *Lok peered at the stick*). There is no effective relation between persons and objects: people do not bring about events in which anything other than they themselves, or parts of their bodies, are implicated.

There are, moreover, a great many, an excessive number, of these circumstantial elements; they are the objects in the natural environment, which as it were take the place of participants, and act as curbs and limitations on the process. People do not act on the things around them; they act within the limitations imposed by the things. The frustration of the struggle with the environment, of a life "poised . . . between the future and the past" (Kinkead-Weekes and Gregor 1967, p. 81), is embodied in the syntax: many of the intransitive clauses have potentially transitive verbs in them, but instead of a direct object there is a prepositional phrase. The feeling of frustration is perhaps further reinforced by the constant reference to complex mental activities of cognition and verbalization. Although there are very few abstract nouns, there are very many clauses of speaking, knowing and understanding (e.g. *Lok understood that the man was holding the stick out to him*); and a recurrent theme, an obsession almost, is the difficulty of communicating memories and images (*I cannot see this picture*) – of transmitting experience through language, the vital step towards that social learning which would be a precondition of their further advance.

Such are some of the characteristics of Language A, the language which tells the story of the people. There is no such thing as a "Language B". Passage B is simply the point of transition between the two parts of the book. There is a "Language C": this is the language of the last 16 pages of the novel, and it is exemplified by the extract shown as Passage C below. But Passage B is of interest because linguistically it is also to some extent transitional. There is no doubt that the first paragraph is basically in Language A and the second in Language C; moreover the switch is extremely sudden, being established in the first three words of B (ii), when Lok, with whom we have become closely identified, suddenly becomes *the red creature*. Nevertheless B (i) does provide some hints of the change to come.

There are a few instances [4] of a human "agent" (actor in a transitive clause); not many, but one of them is Lok, in *Lok . . . picked up Tanakil*. Here is Lok acting on his environment, and the object "affected" is a human being, and one of the tribe! There are some non-spatial adjuncts, such as *with an agonized squealing, like the legs of a giant.* There are abstract nominals: *demoniac activity, its weight of branches.* And there are perhaps more modifiers and complex verb forms than usual. None of these features is occurring for the first time; we have had forward-looking flashes throughout, e.g. (p. 191) *He had a picture of Liku looking up with soft and adoring eyes at Tanakil, guessed how Ha had gone with a kind of eager fearfulness to meet his sudden death* and (pp. 212–13) *"Why did you not snatch the new one?"* and *"We will take Tanakil. Then they will give back the new one"*, both spoken by the more intelligent Fa (when transitive action clauses do occur in Language A, they are often in the dialogue). But there is a greater concentration of them in B (i), a linguistic complexity that is also in harmony with the increased complexity of the events, which has been being built up ever since the tribe first impinged on the people with the mysterious disappearance of Ha (p. 65). The syntax expresses the climax of the gradual overwhelming of Lok's understanding by new things and events; and this coincides with the climax in the events themselves as, with the remainder of the people all killed or captured, Lok's last companion, Fa, is carried over the edge of the waterfall. Lok is alone; there are no more people, and the last trace of his humanity, his membership of a society, has gone. In that moment he belongs to the past.

Lok does not speak again, because there is no one to speak to. But for a while we follow him, as the tribe might have followed him, although they did not – or rather we follow *it*; there can be no *him* where there is no *you* and *me*. The language is now Language C, and the story is that of *homo sapiens*; but for a few paragraphs, beginning at B (ii), as we remain with Lok, the syntax harks back to the world of the people, just as in B (i) it was beginning to look forward. The transition has taken place; *it was a strange creature, smallish, and bowed* that we had come to know so well. But it is still the final, darkening traces of this creature's world that we are seeing, fleetingly as if in an escaping dream.

A brief sketch of B (ii): There are very few transitive clauses of action [4]; in only one of these is Lok the agent – and here the "affected" entity is a part of his own body: *it put up a hand.* The others have *the water* and *the river* as agent. Yet nearly half [22] the total number of clauses [47] have Lok as subject; here, apart from a few [4] mental process clauses, the verb is again one of simple movement or posture, and intransitive (*turn, move, crouch,* etc.; but including for the first time some with a connotation of attitude like *sidle* and *trot;* cf. *broke into a queer, loping run*). The remaining subjects are inanimate objects [19] and parts of the body [6]. But there are differences in these subjects. The horizons have widened; in addition to *water* and *river* we now have *sun* and *green sky* — a reminder that the new people walk upright; cf. (p. 143) *they did not look at the earth but straight ahead*; and there are now also human evidences and artifacts: *path, rollers, ropes*. And the parts of the body no longer see or feel; they are subjects only of intransitive verbs of movement (e.g. *its long arms swinging*), and mainly in non-finite clauses, expressing the dependent nature of the processes in which they participate. A majority [32] of the finite verbs are still in simple past tense; but there is more variation in the remainder, as well as more non-finite verbs [8], reflecting a slightly increased proportion of dependent clauses that is also a characteristic of Language C. And while in many clauses [21] we still find spatial adjuncts, these tend to be more varied and more complex (e.g. *down the rocks beyond the terrace from the melting ice in the mountains*).

This is the world of the tribe; but it is still inhabited, for a brief moment of time, by Lok. Once again the theme is enunciated by the syntax. Nature is no longer totally impenetrable; yet Lok remains powerless, master of nothing but his own body. In Passages A and B taken together, there are more than 50 clauses in which the subject is Lok; but only one of these has Lok as an agent acting on something external to himself, one that has already been mentioned: *Lok picked up Tanakil*. There is a double irony here. Of all the positive actions on his environment that Lok might have taken, the one he does take is the utterly improbable one of capturing a girl of the tribe — improbable in the event, at the level of subject-matter (let us call this "level one"), and improbable also in the deeper context ("level two"), since Lok's newly awakened power manifests itself as power over the one element in the environment that is "superior" to himself. It is at a still deeper "level three" that the meaning becomes clear. The action gets him nowhere; but it is a syntactic hint that his people have played their part in the long trek towards the human condition.

By the time we reach Passage C, the transition is complete. Here, for the first time, the majority of the clauses [48 out of 67] have a human subject; of these, more than half [25] are clauses of action, and most of these [19] are transitive. Leaving aside two in which the thing 'affected' is a part of the body, there is still a significant increase in the number of instances [17, contrasting with 5 in the whole of A and B together] in which a human agent is acting on an external object. The world of the inheritors is organized as ours is; or at least in a way that we can recognize. Among these are two clauses in which the subject is *they*, referring to the people ("the devils": e.g. *they have given me back a changeling*); in the tribe's scheme of things, the people are by no means powerless. There is a parallel here with the earlier part. In Passage A the actions of the tribe are encoded in terms of the world-view of the people, so that the predominance of intransitive clauses is interpreted at what we called "level two", although there is a partial reflection of "level one" in the fact that they are marginally less predominant when the subject-matter concerns the tribe. Similarly, in Passage C references to the people are encoded in terms of the world-view of the tribe, and transitive structures predominate; yet the only member of the people who is present − the only one to survive − is the captured baby, whose infant behaviour is described in largely intransitive terms (pp. 230–31). And the references to the people, in the dialogue, include such formulations as *"They cannot follow us, I tell you. They cannot pass over water"*, which is a "level-one" reassurance that, in a "level-two" world of cause and effect whose causes are often unseen and unknown, there are at least limits to the devils' power.

We can now see the full complementarity between the two "languages", but it is not easy to state. In Language A there is a level-two theme, that of powerlessness. The momentary hints of potency that we are given at level one represent an antithetic variation which, however, has a significance at level three: the power is ascribed to the tribe but signifies Lok's own incipient awareness, the people's nascent understanding of the human potential. This has become a level-two theme in Language C; and in like fashion the level-two theme of Language A becomes in Language C a level-one variation, but again with a level-three significance. The people may be powerless, but the tribe's demand for explanations of things, born of their own more advanced state, leads them, while still fearfully insisting on the people's weakness in action, to ascribe to them supernatural powers.

While there are still inanimate subjects in the clause [11], as there always are in English, there is no single instance in Passage C of an inanimate agent. In A and B we had *the echo of Liku's voice in his head sent him trembling . . .*, *the branches took her, the water had scooped a bowl out of the rock*; in C we have only *the sail glowed, the sun was sitting in it, the hills grow less*. Likewise all clauses with parts of the body as subject [8] are now intransitive, and none of them is a clause of mental process. Parts of the body no longer feel or perceive; they have attributes ascribed to them (e.g. *his teeth were wolf's teeth*) or they move (*the lips parted, the mouth was opening and shutting*). The limbs may move and posture, but only the whole man perceives and reacts to his

117

environment. Now, he also shapes his environment: his actions have become more varied – no longer simply movements; we find here *save, obey,* and *kiss* – and they produce results. Something, or someone, is affected by them.

Just as man's relation to his environment has altered, so his perception of it has changed; the environment has become enlarged. The objects in it are no longer the *twig, stick, bush, branch* of Language A, nor even the larger but still tangible *river, water, scars in the earth.* In Passage B (ii) we already had *air* and *sun* and *sky* and *wind;* in C we have *the mountain . . . full of golden light, the sun was blazing, the sand was swirling* (the last metaphorically); and also human artifacts: *the sail, the mast.* Nature is not tamed: the features of the natural environment may no longer be agents in the transitivity patterns, but neither are they direct objects. What has happened is that the horizons have broadened. Where the people were bounded by tree and river and rock, the tribe are bounded by sky and sea and mountain. Although they are not yet conquered, the features that surround them no longer circumscribe all action and all contemplation. Whereas Lok *rushed to the edge of the water and came back,* the new people *steer in towards the shore,* and *look across the water at the green hills.*

4   Final remarks on stylistic "relevance"

The Inheritors has provided a perspective for a linguistic inquiry of a kind whose relevance and significance is notoriously difficult to assess: an inquiry into the language of a full-length prose work. In this situation syntactic analysis is unlikely to offer anything in the way of new interpretations of particular sentences in terms of their subjectmatter; the language as a whole is not deviant, and the difficulties of understanding are at the level of interpretation – or rather perhaps, in the present instance, re-interpretation, as when we insist on translating *the stick began to grow shorter at both ends* as "the man drew the bow". I have not, in this study, emphasized the use of linguistic analysis as a key; I doubt whether it has this function. What it can do is to establish certain regular patterns, on a comparative basis, in the form of differences which appear significant over a broad canvas. In *The Inheritors* these appear as differences within the text itself, between what we have called "Language A" and "Language C". In terms of this novel, if either of these is to be regarded as a departure, it will be Language C, which appears only briefly at the very end; but in the context of Modern English as a whole it is Language A which constitutes the departure and Language C the norm. There is thus a double shift of stand point in the move from global to local norm, but one which brings us back to more or less where we started.

The focus of attention has been on language in general, on the language system and its relation to the meanings of a literary work. In the study of the text, we have examined instances where particular syntactic options have been selected with a greater than expected frequency, a selection that is partly but not wholly explained by reference to the subject-matter; and have suggested that, by considering how the meaning of these options, taken in the context of the ideational function of language as a whole, relates to an interpretation of the meaning of the work, one can show that they are relevant both as subject-matter and as underlying theme. Each sentence in the passages that were observed in detail is thus potentially of interest both in itself and as an instance of a general trend; and we have been able to ignore other differences, such as that between dialogue and narrative, although a study of these as subvarieties would almost certainly yield further points of interest. Within the present context, the prominence that we have observed can be said to be "motivated"; it is reasonable to talk of foregrounding, here, as an explanation of stylistic impact.

The establishment of a syntactic norm (for this is what it is) is thus a way of expressing one of the levels of meaning of the work: the fact that a particular pattern constitutes a norm **is** the meaning. The linguistic function of the pattern is therefore of some importance. The features that we have seen to be foregrounded in *The Inheritors* derive from the ideational component in the language system; hence they represent, at the level at which they constitute a norm, a world-view, a structuring of experience that is significant because there is no *a priori* reason why the experience should have been structured in this way rather than in another. More particularly, the foregrounded features were selections in transitivity. Transitivity is the set of options whereby the speaker encodes his experience of the processes of the external world, and of the internal world of his own consciousness, together with the participants in these processes and their attendant circumstances; and it embodies a very basic distinction of processes into two types, those that are regarded as due to an external cause, an agency other than the person or object involved, and those that are not. There are, in addition, many further categories and subtypes. Transitivity is really the cornerstone of the semantic organization of experience; and it is at one level what *The Inheritors* is about. The theme of the entire novel, in a sense, is transitivity: man's interpretation

119

of his experience of the world, his understanding of its processes and of his own participation in them. This is the motivation for Golding's syntactic originality; it is because of this that the syntax is effective as a "mode of meaning".[25] The particular transitivity patterns that stand out in the text contribute to the artistic whole through the functional significance, in the language system, of the semantic options which they express.

This is what we understand by "relevance" – the notion that a linguistic feature "belongs" in some way as part of the whole. The pursuit of prominence is not without significance for the understanding and evaluation of a literary work; but neither is it sufficient to be a rewarding activity in itself.[26] It has been said of phonological foregrounding that "there must be appropriateness to the nexus of sound and meaning";[27] and this is no less true of the syntactic and semantic levels, where, however, the relationship is not one of sound and meaning but one of meaning and meaning. Here "relevance" implies a congruence with our interpretation of what the work is about, and hence the criteria of belonging are semantic ones. We might be tempted to express the relevance of syntactic patterns, such as we find in *The Inheritors*, as a "unity of form and meaning", parallel to the "sound and meaning" formulation above; but this would, I think, be a false parallel. The syntactic categories are *per se* the realizations of semantic options, and the relevance is the relevance of one set of meanings to another – a relationship among the levels of meaning of the work itself.

In *The Inheritors*, the syntax is part of the story. As readers, we are reacting to the whole of the writer's creative use of "meaning potential"; and the nature of language is such that he can convey, in a line of print, a complex of simultaneous themes, reflecting the variety of functions that language is required to serve. And because the elements of the language, the words and phrases and syntactic structures, tend to have multiple values, any one theme may have more than one interpretation: in expressing some content, for example, the writer may invite us at the same time to interpret it in quite a different functional context – as a cry of despair, perhaps. It is the same property of language that enables us to react to hints, to take offence and do all the other things that display the rhetoric of everyday verbal interaction. A theme that is strongly foregrounded is especially likely to be interpreted at more than one level. In *The Inheritors* it is the linguistic representation of experience, through the syntactic resources of transitivity, that is especially brought into relief, although there may be other themes not mentioned here that stand out in the same way. Every work achieves a unique balance among the types and components of meaning, and embodies the writer's individual exploration of the functional diversity of language.

APPENDIX
Extracts from *The Inheritors*

A.   (pp. 106–7)

The bushes twitched again. Lok steadied by the tree and gazed. A head and a chest faced him, half-hidden. There were white bone things behind the leaves and hair. The man had white bone things above his eyes and under the mouth so that his face was longer than a face should be. The man turned sideways in the bushes and looked at Lok along his shoulder. A stick rose upright and there was a lump of bone in the middle. Lok peered at the stick and the lump of bone and the small eyes in the bone things over the face. Suddenly Lok understood that the man was holding the stick out to him but neither he nor Lok could reach across the river. He would have laughed if it were not for the echo of the screaming in his head. The stick began to grow shorter at both ends. Then it shot out to full length again.

The dead tree by Lok's ear acquired a voice.

"Clop!"

His ears twitched and he turned to the tree. By his face there had grown a twig: a twig that smelt of other, and of goose, and of the bitter berries that Lok's stomach told him he must not eat. This twig had a white bone at the end. There were hooks in the bone and sticky brown stuff hung in the crooks. His nose examined this stuff and did not like it. He smelled along the shaft of the twig. The leaves on the twig were red feathers and reminded him of goose. He was lost in a generalized astonishment and excitement. He shouted at the green drifts across the glittering water and heard Liku crying out in answer but could not catch the words. They were cut off suddenly as though someone had clapped a hand over her mouth. He rushed to the edge of the water and came back. On either side of the open bank the bushes grew thickly in the flood; they waded out until at their farthest some of the leaves were opening under water; and these bushes leaned over.

The echo of Liku's voice in his head sent him trembling at this perilous way of bushes towards the island. He dashed at them where normally they would have been rooted on dry land and his feet splashed. He threw himself forward and grabbed at the branches with hands and feet. He shouted:

"I am coming!"

B.   (pp. 215–17)

(i) Lok staggered to his feet, picked up Tanakil and ran after Fa along the terrace. There came a screaming from the figures by the hollow log and a loud bang from the jam. The tree began to move forward and the logs were lumbering about like the legs of a giant. The crumplefaced woman was struggling with Tuami on the rock by the hollow log; she burst free and came running towards Lok. There was movement everywhere, screaming, demoniac activity; the old man was coming across the tumbling logs. He threw something at Fa. Hunters were holding the hollow log against the terrace and the head of the tree with all its weight of branches and wet leaves was drawing along them. The fat woman was lying in the log, the crumpled woman was in it with Tanakil, the old man was tumbling into the back. The boughs crashed and drew along the rock with an agonized squealing. Fa was sitting by the water holding her head. The branches took her. She was moving with them out into the water and the hollow log was free of the rock and drawing away. The tree swung into the current with Fa sitting limply among the branches. Lok began to gibber again. He ran up and down on the terrace. The tree would not be cajoled or persuaded. It moved to the edge of the fall, it swung until it was lying along the lip. The water reared up over the trunk, pushing, the roots were over. The tree hung for a while with the head facing upstream. Slowly the root end sank and the head rose. Then it slid forward soundlessly and dropped over the fall.

(ii) The red creature stood on the edge of the terrace and did nothing. The hollow log was a dark spot on the water towards the place where the sun had gone down. The air in the gap was clear and blue and calm. There was no noise at all now except for the fall, for there was no wind and the green sky was clear. The red creature turned to the right and trotted slowly towards the far end of the terrace. Water was cascading down the rocks beyond the terrace from the melting ice in the mountains. The river was high and flat and drowned the edge of the terrace. There were long scars in the earth and rock where the branches of a tree had been dragged past by the water. The red creature came trotting back to a dark hollow in the side of the cliff where there was evidence of occupation. It looked at the other figure, dark now, that grinned down at it from the back of the hollow. Then it turned away and ran through the little passage that joined the terrace to the slope. It halted, peering down at the scars, the abandoned rollers and broken ropes. It turned again, sidled round a shoulder of rock and stood on an almost imperceptible path that ran along the sheer rocks. It began to sidle along the path, crouch, its long arms swinging, touching, almost as firm a support as the legs. It was peering down into the thunderous waters but there was nothing to be seen but the columns of glimmering haze where the water had scooped a bowl out of the rock. It moved faster, broke into a queer loping run that made the head bob up and down and the forearms alternate like the legs of a horse. It stopped at the end of the path and looked down at the long streamers of weed that were moving backwards and forwards under the water. It put up a hand and scratched under its chinless mouth.

C. (pp. 228–9)

The sail glowed red-brown. Tuami glanced back at the gap through the mountain and saw that it was full of golden light and the sun was sitting in it. As if they were obeying some signal the people began to stir, to sit up and look across the water at the green hills. Twal bent over Tanakil and kissed her and murmured to her. Tanakil's lips parted. Her voice was harsh and came from far away in the night.

"Liku!"

Tuami heard Marlan whisper to him from by the mast.

"That is the devil's name. Only she may speak it."

Now Vivani was really waking. They heard her huge, luxurious yawn and the bear skin was thrown off. She sat up, shook back her loose hair and looked first at Marlan then at Tuami. At once he was filled again with lust and hate. If she had been what she was, if Marlan, if her man, if she had saved her baby in the storm on the salt water –

"My breasts are paining me."

If she had not wanted the child as a plaything, if I had not saved the other as a joke –

He began to talk high and fast.

"There are plains beyond those hills, Marlan, for they grow less; and there will be herds for hunting. Let us steer in towards the shore. Have we water – but of course we have water! Did the women bring the food? Did you bring the food, Twal?"

Twal lifted her face towards him and it was twisted with grief and hate.

"What have I to do with food, master? You and he gave my child to the devils and they have given me back a changeling who does not see or speak."

The sand was swirling in Tuami's brain. He thought in panic: they have given me back a changed Tuami; what shall I do? Only Marlan is the same – smaller, weaker but the same. He peered forward to find the changeless one as something he could hold on to. The sun was blazing on the red sail and Marlan was red. His arms and legs were contracted, his hair stood out and his beard, his teeth were wolf's teeth and his eyes like blind stones. The mouth was opening and shutting.

"They cannot follow us, I tell you. They cannot pass over water."

Notes

1. The results were presented in a paper read to the Conference of University Teachers of English, London (Bedford College), April 1965.
2. Paul Zumthor suggests (private communication) that a particular literary tradition may be characterized by the emphasis and value placed on one particular function, a shift in emphasis being associated with a major break in the tradition. Cf. Zumthor (1971).
3. Nor the other way round, at least in the typical instances. There are certain linguistic activities in which one or other function is prescribed and the speaker required to supply the remainder: "language exercises" such as "Now ask your neighbour a question" (in foreign language classes) and "Write a sonnet" (in school).
4. Cf. the discussion by Tzvetan Todorov (1971).
5. Including those which specify types of communication role, or illocutionary force, which Richard Ohmann proposes to use in a definition of literature. See Ohmann (1971).
6. René Wellek, "Closing statement (retrospects and prospects from the viewpoint of literary criticism)", in T. A. Sebeok (1960, pp. 417–18).
7. Dell H. Hymes, "Phonological aspects of style: some English sonnets", in Seymour Chatman and Samuel Levin (1967, pp. 33–53, see pp. 33–4).
8. On diatypic variation see Michael Gregory (1967, pp. 177–98).
9. Charles E. Osgood, "Some effects of motivation on style of encoding", in Sebeok (1960, p. 293).
10. As n. 7.
11. Angus McIntosh, "Saying", *Review of English Literature*, 6 (April 1965), 19. It is worth quoting further from the same paragraph: "It is at least clear that any approach to this kind of problem which looks at anything less than the whole text as the ultimate unit has very little to contribute.

Whatever it may be in linguistic analysis, the sentence is not the proper unit here. If there are any possibilities of progress, they must, I think, be on the lines of the old recognition, e.g. by the rhetoricians, of elements or strands of something or other which permeate long stretches of text and produce a gradual build-up of effect."

12. Bernard Bloch, "Linguistic structure and linguistic analysis", in A. A. Hill (1953, pp. 40–44).

13. Josephine Miles, "Eras in English poetry", in S. Chatman and S. Levin (1967, pp. 175–6).

14. Cf. George A. Miller, "Closing statement (retrospects and prospects from the viewpoint of psychology)", in Sebeok (1960, p. 394).

15. See the paper by Louis Milic (1971), in which he suggests that the diagnostic features of an author's style are generally to be found among the "unconscious" elements.

16. "Metamorphosis" has, I believe, only two occurrences of an insect name, although *crawl* is frequent.

17. William Golding, *The Inheritors* (London, 1955; paperback edition, 1961). The pagination is the same in both editions.

18. Figures in square brackets show numbers of occurrences. The most important of these are summarized in Table 2.

19. For a discussion of clause types see M. A. K. Halliday, "Language structure and language function", in John Lyons (1970, pp. 140–65). Reprinted in Halliday (2002), pp. 173–95.

20. Cf. M. A. K. Halliday, "Descriptive linguistics in literary studies", in A. Duthie (1964, p. 29). Reprinted as part of Chapter 1 of this volume.

21. The other extracts examined for comparison were three passages of similar length: p. 61 from *He remembered the old woman*; pp. 102–3 from *Then there was nothing more*; p. 166 from *At that the old man rushed forward*.

22. By "complement" is understood all nominal elements other than the subject: direct object, indirect object, cognate object, and adjectival and nominal complement. "Adjuncts" are non-nominal elements (adverbs and prepositional phrases).

23. Cf. James Peter Thorne (1965, pp. 49–59).

24. For discussions of transitivity see Charles J. Fillmore, "The case for case", in Emmon Bach and Robert T. Harms (1968, pp. 1–88); M. A. K. Halliday, *Grammar, Society and the Noun* (1967a); M. A. K. Halliday, "Notes on transitivity and theme in English" (Parts I and II), (1967b, pp. 37–81; 1968, pp. 179–215).

25. See J. R. Firth, "Modes of meaning", *Essays and Studies* (English Association, 1951). Reprinted in J. R. Firth (1957, pp. 190–215).

26. Cf. Roger Fowler, "Linguistic theory and the study of literature", in Roger Fowler (1966, pp. 1–28).

27. As n. 7 (p. 53).

Chapter Four

THE DE-AUTOMATIZATION
OF GRAMMAR: FROM PRIESTLEY'S
AN INSPECTOR CALLS
(1982)

In evaluations of J. B. Priestley's work a number of themes stand out. It is said that he is an entertainer and a craftsman, one who values technique above content; hence as a playwright his achievements are theatrical rather than dramatic. He has a leaning towards the happy ending, a suspicious optimism ill-suited to an age that prides itself on its message of doom and gloom. He has little concern for the individual psyche, and cares more for the group than for the personalities of its members; hence he is out of step with the march of western individualism. His philosophy is too straightforward for intellectuals but too thought-demanding for the mentally lazy, occupying an unfashionable middle ground between the academic and the pop. And perhaps, as John Braine has remarked in a recent study (1979), he has simply been too successful, so that his very success has prevented his work from being taken more seriously.

Probably the most sustained criticism of Priestley's dramatic writing, however, concerns the language he gives to his characters. Gareth Lloyd Evans (1964) describes it as "flat naturalistic prose"; and while he sometimes treats this as a deliberate, if misguided, decision on Priestley's part, referring to his "wayward refusal to tax the imaginations of his audiences with language that matches the themes of the plays" (p. 43), at other times he sees it as a straightforward inability to rise up to the demands of the occasion. He cites David Hughes' (1958) remark that "once again Priestley is confronted with a language he cannot persuade to leave the ground", and refers to "his failure to discover a language

First published in *Language Form and Linguistic Variation: Papers Dedicated to Angus McIntosh*, edited by John M. Anderson. Amsterdam: John Benjamins, pp. 129–59.

which was flexible enough to withstand the sharp fluctuations of the play's movement and meaning" (p. 145). Priestley himself, as Evans points out, has explicitly defended his own choice of language on the grounds that he was working "within the tradition of English realism. Too much enrichment of speech would have destroyed this realism."

If Priestley's dramatic writing is so devoid of special effects that it even "does not give the effect of being attached to character" (p. 145) then presumably we should not expect to find in his plays any of the foregrounding of particular linguistic features that is often associated with a literary text and with the differences between one text and another. The implication is that we may not be able to characterize his language at all: it will be just a specimen, a kind of random sample of English, with its grammar and vocabulary fully "automatized". The words and structures will be functioning simply as the most neutral, or unmarked, expression of the meanings that lie behind them.

In line with the (European) structuralist approach to a text, described by Gerard Genette (1975–76) as a "recourse against the danger of [its] destruction", we treat the text as an object, having social value. This can lead to a separation between text and author, as if there was no particular connection between them; and this is something we may have to be on our guard against, because we cannot begin to interpret a text until we can say "I know what this text means", and knowing what a text means is achieved in the first place not by coming to it as a linguist, but rather by bringing to bear on it the whole of one's antecedent experience. To take an extreme case: in watching Priestley I cannot discount the fact that my family home was in Bradford, which is Priestley's home town; this community of origins means that I understand him more roundedly than I could expect to understand an author from Manchester, London, Scotland or the United States. In other words, to treat the text as an object does not imply that we detach it from its context of situation and culture. On the contrary; once so detached, it ceases to be accessible to objective interpretation.

If we follow the same line of thought as Michael Gregory (1978) in his "interpretative stylistics", by the fact of our knowing what the text means we are driven to ask of it two very general questions. The first one is: Why does the text mean what it does? The second, more ambitious one, is: Why is the text valued as it is? These two questions are what stylistics is largely about: the source of the meanings that inhere in the text, and of the value it is accorded in the culture. Naturally, having once begun to interpret the text in this way, we may find it means something more than, or other than, what we first thought – but not something totally different. The interpretative experience is likely to deepen the impact the text has on us; but the impact has already been felt, otherwise we should probably not have bothered to examine this particular text in the first place.

The stylistic interpretation of the text is not, however, a "close reading" or "explication de texte", because these undertakings, admirable though they are, fail to relate the text to the linguistic system. Without this perspective, in which the system and the text are in focus at the same time (as they are with Hjelmslev, almost alone among theoretical linguists), interpretation may become either another "new criticism", under the guise of pragmatics, or a new formalism on a more macroscopic scale. For the linguist, of course, any text is a window on to the system; but to adopt this angle is to treat the text just as an instrument, not as an object. A literary text by definition is one that we are not treating simply as an instrument, but one of which we are impelled to ask the question posed by Foucault: "How is it that this utterance appeared and not another in its place?" But there is no way of answering such a question unless it is recognized that the text would not be a text if it was not a product – an "instantiation" – of the linguistic system.

Priestley is at once novelist, dramatist, essayist, autobiographer, critic, and social historian. His self-image is that of an entertainer, a craftsman, a man of letters; and his output of text has been prodigious. There is no difficulty in finding dominant themes in his work. He is almost never obscure; he prefers straight talk, and we are not inveigled into massive debates about his underlying values or the nature of his symbolism. The themes that concern us here will be two that are clearly among the predominant ones in his work. One is interdependence and social responsibility: "no man is an island". The other is time: "time is not ticking our lives away". Beyond both of these, linking them with each other and with other Priestleian motifs (such as that of the illusion of the separate self), is Priestley's concern with the nature of reality, and with the relation of reality to its manifestation on the surface of things.

It has often been pointed out, in a somewhat disparaging vein, that Priestley now and again as it were walks out on to the stage and enunciates his theme for us. The most obvious instance in *An Inspector Calls* is the Inspector's final speech:

> We don't live alone. We are members of one body. We are responsible
> for each other. And I tell you that the time will soon come when, if

men will not learn that lesson, then they will be taught it in fire and blood and anguish.

Moreover this "lesson" is further thrown into relief by repeated references to the "every man for himself" burden of Mr. Birling's self-important sermonizing. Compare the various lines in *I Have Been Here Before* which are explicitly concerned with time, e.g. the following spoken by Dr. Görtler in Act III:

> We do not go round in a circle. That is an illusion, just as the circling of the planets and stars is an illusion. We move along a spiral track.

Characters such as Dr. Görtler and Inspector Goole, in their different roles as guru, the 'Great Detective', and the like, serve as natural spokesmen for the issues that are being raised.

But the themes are by no means always treated in this declarative way. The time theme in *An Inspector Calls*, while clearly present, is subdued and largely implicit. In this connection it seems worth stressing once again that it is wrong to treat Priestley's dramatic time theme as if it was some kind of a scientific theory. Priestley used to be criticized for a naive acceptance of currently popular time theories such as those of J. W. Dunne (1934) and P. D. Ouspensky (1931), and especially for the "recurrence and intervention" concept that he used in *I Have Been Here Before*, with its obvious contradictions if taken literally. But this was never meant by him to be held up as a theory and evaluated as true or false. It is, first, something to be explored for its dramatic potential (and many of his plays make use of it in one form or another); and secondly, something that gives a new dimension to human relationships. Hence it is significant not for its intellectual content, as something to be presented in the text, but as a motif that permeates the interaction of the participants, and is more or less covertly woven in to the dialogue. Thus in *An Inspector Calls* (Act III):

(1) We hardly ever told him anything he didn't know; did you notice that?
(2) I didn't notice you told *him* that it's every man for himself. – Is that when the Inspector came, just after Father had said that?

– and of course the very last lines of the play. Such manifestations are "more or less" covert; they are hardly buried deep, but they do not constitute a direct presentation of the theme, and unlike the examples cited earlier they are likely to be taken in by the audience subconsciously rather than consciously.

It is a general assumption of structuralism that the meanings of a work of literature are dispersed throughout the text not just at different places in the syntagm but also, and more significantly, at different levels within the code. This dispersal into what Firth called the various "modes of meaning", for which he used the analogy of the dispersal of light throughout the spectrum, is typically an unconscious feature of the writing process (cf. Mukařovský's (1977) observation that "aesthetic intentionality does not necessarily presuppose a conscious intent"), and is hidden from the reader/listener unless he digs for it. Eco (1976) compares a work of art to a language, saying that "there must be an underlying system of mutual correlations, and thus a semiotic design which cunningly gives the impression of non-semiosis". It is this that accounts for the paradox of "poetic language": there is no such thing, but we can all recognize it when we see it. To quote Mukařovský again: "poetic language is permanently characterized only by its function: however, function is not a property but a *mode of utilizing* the properties of a given phenomenon" (pp. 3–4). How much the more is this true of the language of prose works, where we do not even pretend there is such a thing as "prosaic language" (as is clear from the meaning this expression has acquired). McIntosh (1965) observed of prose fiction that

> . . . quite often where the impact of an entire work may be enormous, yet word by word, phrase by phrase, clause by clause, sentence by sentence, there may seem to be nothing very unusual or arresting, in grammar or in vocabulary . . .

The dramatist has to create a world of meaning, and his resource for doing so is dialogue. He depends on what Berger and Luckmann (1966) call the "reality-generating power of conversation", a power that is covert and implicit in its effects: "most conversation does not in so many words define the nature of the world . . . [it] implies a world *within which* . . . simple propositions make sense, [and so] confirms the subjective reality of this world". But whereas outside the theatre this conversational magic has a lifetime in which to work, the dramatist has three to four hours. He therefore stipulates that we are to bring with us from outside the theatre all those aspects of everyday subjective reality that his play does not force us to repudiate; and he will supply the rest. In order to do this, if the reality he is constructing is a rather different one, and differs in ways that are not obvious on the surface, he may have to resort from time to time to "defining the nature of the world"; and when the reality is being thus presented to us, the language is likely to be fully automatized, with the words and structures and sounds being there in their automatic function of real-izing the semantic selections in an unmarked way – getting on with expressing the meanings, without parading themselves in patterns of their own. But for the rest, he will draw on the casualness of conver-sation, implying his world rather than presenting it; and it is here that the language is likely to become "de-automatized" (to use Mukařovský's term).

To create a partially differing reality by conversational means within the space-time of a dramatic performance is almost bound to demand some de-automatization of the language, whereby the patterning of words and structures enables them to make their own distinct contri-bution to the meaning. Mukařovský's formulations are still relevant: "the choice of vocabulary in a literary work . . . necessarily becomes part of the artistic organization of the work", and "a grammatical category can acquire aesthetic effect by the accumulation of words belonging to it" (pp. 37, 35). Hence "even a theme is connected to language bilaterally: not only is linguistic expression governed by its theme, but the theme is also governed by its linguistic expression . . . Not even theme, therefore, eludes linguistic analysis" (p. 55). The term "de-automatization", though cumbersome, is more apt than "fore-grounding", since what is in question is not simply prominence but rather the partial freeing of the lower-level systems from the control of the semantics so that they become domains of choice in their own right. In terms of systemic theory the de-automatization of the grammar means that grammatical choices are not simply determined from above: there is selection as well as pre-selection. Hence the wording becomes a quasi-independent semiotic mode through which the meanings of the work can be projected.

The question that is being raised here, therefore, is whether a language that is "flat and naturalistic", that "never leaves the earth" and "fails to match the themes of his plays", as has been so often said of Priestley's, can ever become "de-automatized". Is there enough "play" in it to allow for the dispersal and flow of meaning along the different channels of the linguistic system? Or does the commitment to "realism" in language debar a writer from the "code-like regularity in the selection of language categories" that Ruqaiya Hasan (1975) regards as necessary to the effective "symbolic articulation" of his underlying themes?

The following extract (Passage A) is taken from Act II of *An Inspector Calls*. (Italics have been added to highlight wordings singled out for discussion.)

MRS BIRLING: *I think* we've just about come to an end of this wretched business – (1)

GERALD: *I don't think* so (2). Excuse me (3).

(He goes out. They watch him go in silence. We hear the front door slam.)

SHEILA: (to Inspector) You know, you never showed him that photograph of her (4).

INSPECTOR: No (5). *It wasn't necessary* (6). And *I thought* it *better* not to (7).

MRS BIRLING: You have a photograph of this girl (8)?

INSPECTOR: Yes (9). *I think you'd better* look at it (10).

MRS BIRLING: *I don't see* any particular reason why *I should* – (11).

INSPECTOR: *Probably not* (12). But *you'd better* look at it (13).

MRS BIRLING: Very well (14).

(He produces the photograph and she looks hard at it.)

INSPECTOR: (taking back the photograph) You recognize her (15)?

MRS BIRLING: No (16). Why *should* I (17)?

INSPECTOR: Of course she *might have* changed lately, but *I can't believe* she *could have* changed so much (18).

MRS BIRLING: I don't *understand* you, Inspector (19).

INSPECTOR: You *mean* you don't choose to do, Mrs Birling (20).

MRS BIRLING: (angrily) I *meant* what I said (21).

INSPECTOR: You're not *telling* me *the truth* (22).

MRS BIRLING: I beg your pardon (23)!

BIRLING: (angrily, to Inspector) Look here, I'm *not going to have* this, Inspector (24). You'll *apologize* at once (25).

INSPECTOR: *Apologize* for what – doing my *duty* (26)?

BIRLING: No, for being so *offensive* about it (27). I'm a public man – (28).

INSPECTOR: (massively) Public men, Mr Birling, have *responsibilities* as well as *privileges* (29).

BIRLING: *Possibly* (30). But you weren't asked to come here to talk to me about my *responsibilities* (31).

SHEILA: *Let's hope not* (32). Though I'm beginning to *wonder* (33).

MRS BIRLING: Does that *mean* anything, Sheila (34)?

SHEILA: It *means* that we've no excuse now for putting on airs and that if we've any sense we won't try (35). Father threw this girl out because she asked for decent wages (36). I went and pushed her further out, right into the street, just because I was angry and she was pretty (37). Gerald set her up as his mistress and then dropped her when it suited him (38). And now you're pretending *you don't* recognize her from that photograph (39). I admit *I don't know* why you *should*, but *I know* jolly well *you did* in fact recognize her, from the way you looked (40). And if *you're not telling the truth*, why *should* the Inspector *apologize* (41)? And *can't you see*, both of you, *you're* making it worse (42)?

(She turns away. We hear the front door slam again.)

This exchange, which occurs at what is more or less the middle point of the play, constitutes a small, self-contained enactment that revolves around a photograph. In the simplest terms it has a structure as shown in Figure 1:

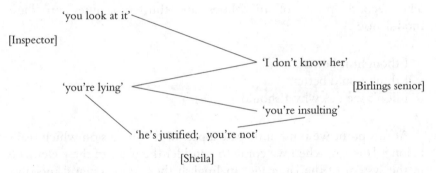

Figure 1 Dialogic progression in Passage A

Let us attempt to identify some of the linguistic features through which this structure is realized. In the first twelve speeches (sentences 1–18) we find the following expressions:

I think I don't think	'this business has ended'
I thought I think I don't see probably not	'the photograph should be looked at'
might have can't believe could have	'has she changed?'

These are expressions of modality; they represent the speaker's opinion – his judgement regarding the probabilities of the case. They cluster in this passage around three issues: the state of the inquiry (a transition from what has gone before), the examination of the photograph and the identification of the subject. The passage is also characterized by expressions of modulation, representing the speaker's assertion of the obligations inherent in the case; these relate to the second of the three issues just mentioned:

> it wasn't necessary
> it was better not to
> you'd better
> [any . . . reason why] I should
> you'd better
> [why] should I?

'(to) look at the photograph'

The second group of modalities are thus modalities on these modulations:

> I thought it better
> I think you'd better
> I don't see . . . why I should

At this point we must anticipate a part of the discussion which really belongs later on, when we come to consider the place of these elements in the system of the language. In English these two systems, modality and modulation, come together in the grammar: although the two can be expressed in different ways (*probably, I think*, etc. for modalities; *had better, are obliged to*, etc. for modulations), they also share a common means of expression in the form of the finite modal auxiliary verb:

	Modality/Modulation	*Modality*	*Modulation*
high	must (need, ought to)	certain	required
middle	will (would, shall, should)	probable	supposed
low	may (might, can, could)	possible	allowed

This overlap in expression reflects the fact that there is an overlap in the meanings. The semantic common ground between the two is to be seen in their orientation towards the speaker: modality is the

134

speaker's judgement of probability, modulation is the speaker's assessment of obligation. When expressed by a modal verb, the meaning is subjective; when it is expressed in other ways, the meaning is objectified – the speaker is claiming that the probabilities are inherent in the situation, or that the source of the obligations is elsewhere, as shown in Figure 2:

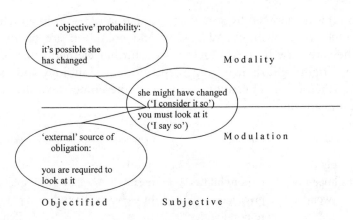

Figure 2 Orientation of probability and obligation

When the modality is expressed by a first person mental process clause, most typically 'I think', the meaning is likewise subjective; the difference is that now it is explicitly so. The Inspector uses the subjective mode in the expression of modality, not claiming for his opinions that they are anything other than just his opinions; and he stays in the middle range, where things are probable not certain. In expressing obligations, he uses the objective mode – but qualifies it by a subjective modality as he shifts the focus of attention (appropriately mediated through a photograph) from the last victim, Gerald, on to the next, Mrs. Birling (Figure 3):

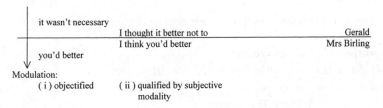

Figure 3 Orientation in Inspector's statements of obligation

There is then a little hinge passage (19–22), keyed in by expressions of cognition:

> understand
> mean
> mean
> tell the truth

and this is followed by a new confrontation (23–35) in which the three themes of probability, obligation and cognition are taken up again. They are now bonded together by a further element, that of interpersonal rights and their infringement – offence, apology and excuse; and the theme of obligation is now represented lexically instead of grammatically:

probability	*obligation*	*cognition*	*offence*
possibly	duty	mean	not . . . have this
let's hope not	responsibilities	mean	apologize
I . . . wonder	privileges	[if we've any] sense	apologize
	responsibilities		offensive
			weren't asked to
			excuse

Finally the dialogue is summarized by Sheila, who has re-entered it with a modality (*I wonder*), in the form of a narrative of what has been revealed so far (36–8) followed by a restatement of the earlier themes (39–42):

obligation	*cognition*	*offence*
should	don't know	apologize
should	know	
	tell the truth	
	see	

By now the probabilities have been replaced by categoricalities:

> [you] don't [recognize her]
> [I] don't [know] / [do know jolly well]
> [you] did [. . . recognize her]
> [you] aren't [telling the truth]
> [you] are [making it worse]

(There is an important distinction between 'certainty', which is a high degree of probability as in *you must recognize her*, and 'categoricality' which admits no degree of probability at all, as in *you (do) recognize her.*) The thematic pattern of this sequence, which forms a microdrama set between two slammings of the door, may be summarized as follows (Figure 4):

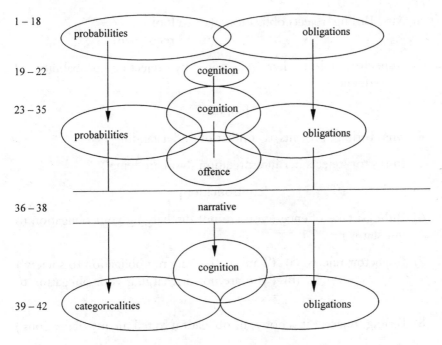

Figure 4 Thematic pattern in Passage A

When the grammar is interpreted in its purely "automatic" function as has been being done up to this point, we see how it realizes the semantic structure and in so doing engenders the movement of the text. The details of this movement, in the passage in question, could be tabulated schematically as follows:

[setting]

0) Mrs. Birling and Gerald: uncertainty building up (about ongoing process)

SLAM (i)

[challenge]

1) Inspector: obligations (a) Gerald need not see photograph (he will confess anyway)

                             (b) Mrs. Birling must see photograph (she is a tougher nut: modalized, then demodalized)

2) Mrs. Birling: rejects obligations (a) to look

                                      (b) to recognize

3) Inspector: rejects her rejection, by rejecting probability of consequences

[conflict]

4) Mrs. Birling: presents as conflict of understanding

5) Inspector: rejects her interpretation ('you are lying')

[confrontation]

6) Birlings: take offence ('you are not discharging your obligation to our status')

7) Inspector: rejects (a) ('I am discharging my obligation to society')

                          (b) ('you are not discharging your obligation to society')

8) Birling: rejects ('it is not your obligation to tell me my obligations')

9) Sheila: questions categoricality of this and affirms her understanding

[explanation]

10) Sheila: narrates events revealed so far

[summation]

11) Sheila: evaluates (a) ('you are categorical')

                     (b) ('I am uncertain')

                     (c) ('I am categorical that you are wrong')

                     (d) ('your understanding is at fault')

SLAM (ii)

Now let us "de-automatize", and try to interpret the grammar in terms that go beyond its direct realizational function. To do this is to distance the text, and respond to the language: to focus out the background, and let the words and structures speak for themselves. The photograph, which serves as a channel for the interactive events, disappears from view, leaving the concept of obligation foregrounded as a major theme of the play.

In the text, obligation is tied to judgements of probability: there are opinions relating to duties, and, as a minor motif, duties relating to opinions. The two themes are closely interwoven. We have already seen that this is a projection into the text of a relation that exists between them in the system. The scales of 'possible-certain' and 'allowed-required' both typically combine with a common semantic feature, that of 'subjective', in the sense of representing the speaker's judgement; and this is symbolized by the use of modal verbs as one form of the realization of both. We have referred to these as systems of modality and modulation. This particular semantic configuration is an essential element in the impact of the passage we have been considering. But to explain this more fully we need to take the interpretation of these systems one stage further, relating them to the very general semantic systems of mood and polarity. In the context of the language as a whole, 'possible-certain' and 'allowed-required' represent different scales of polarity, different forms of the indeterminacy of yes and no.

There are two scales of polarity in English, the indicative and the imperative. Indicative polarity is the scale from 'it is' to 'it isn't'; and the intermediate degrees are degrees of probability, 'it must be', 'it will be', 'it may be'. Imperative polarity is the scale from 'do!' to 'don't!'; the intermediate degrees are degrees of obligation, 'you must do', 'you should do', 'you may do'. The orientation towards the speaker that is characteristic of modality and modulation is thus a consequence of the speech function. The basic form of dialogue is that of exchange, which may be either exchange of information or exchange of goods-&-services; and this distinction is what lies behind the mood system, where indicative has evolved as the typical mode for the exchange of information and imperative for the exchange of goods-&-services.

If what is being exchanged is information, the speaker's subjective judgement relates to the likelihood or otherwise of the information being valid; hence the subjective scale of polarity is that of 'yes – maybe – no', where 'maybe' represents the indeterminacy of 'either yes or no' and encompasses various degrees of probability. If what is being exchanged is goods-&-services, the speaker's judgement relates to the desirability or otherwise of the goods-&-services being provided; hence the subjective scale of polarity is that of 'do! – you may do – don't!', where 'you may do' represents the indeterminacy of 'either do or don't' and encompasses various degrees of obligation. We can summarize this as in Figure 5:

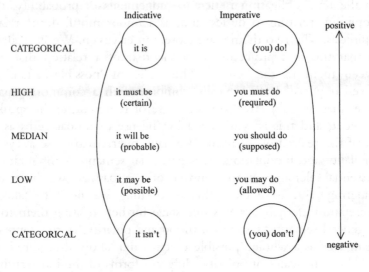

Figure 5   Degrees of modality and modulation

It is clear that the passage we have been considering encapsulates the theme of social responsibility not just as a topic but as an issue: as something that has to be accepted, but that also is associated with opinions, interpretations and conflicts. But what is foregrounded in this passage is not simply the issue of obligations and their central role as the focus of negotiation and dispute. It is also the nature of dialogue itself, the interactive process whereby such obligations are acted out and defined. They are not and cannot be functions of the individual, but come into being only in the course of, and as a necessary con-comitant of, the exchange of symbols; because the symbols themselves have a dual semiotic role, functioning both as instrument (**mediating in** the exchange of goods-&-services) and as object (**constituting** the exchange of information), the speaker's commitment to his part in the exchange is at the same time a commitment to the modes of validity enshrined in the social semiotic, the kinds of yes and no on which the social order ultimately rests.

140

The significance of the lexicogrammatical selections in the text can only be fully revealed by a consideration of their value in the semantic system. Textually, the passage under discussion centres around the scrutiny and recognition of a photograph. The words and structures which, in their automatic function as the "output" of semantic choices, carry forward the movement of the text, also become de-automatized and so take on a life of their own as engenderers of meaning. It is in this sense that "de-automatization" is more than prominence: prominence is achieved through an untypical distribution of symbols in their typical function in the text, whereas here we are referring to their appearance in a transcendent function, whereby a grammatical system as a whole directly encodes some higher-level semiotic, bypassing the semantic organization of the text.

This may be expected to be a feature of what are felt to be "key" passages; and although it would be a mistake to assume that every aspect of the meaning of a work will always be distinctively recognizable in some delimitable fragment or other – any given effect may be dispersed throughout the text – it is interesting to see whether we can find a similar display of any other underlying theme in the present play of Priestley's. Let us examine from this point of view another passage which immediately precedes the one we have just been considering.

An Inspector Calls, Act II: Passage B

INSPECTOR: I think she went away – to be alone, to be quiet, to *remember* all that had happened between you (1).

GERALD: How do you know that (2)?

INSPECTOR: She kept a rough sort of diary (3). And she said there that she had to go away and be quiet and *remember* "just to *make it last longer*" (4). She felt there'd *never* be anything as good *again* for her – so she had to *make it last longer* (5).

GERALD (gravely): I see (6). Well, I *never* saw her *again*, and that's all I can tell you (7).

INSPECTOR: It's all I want to know from you (8).

GERALD: In that case – as I'm rather more – upset – by this business than I probably appear to be – and – well, I'd like to be alone *for a little while* – I'd be glad if you'd let me go (9).

INSPECTOR: Go where (10)? Home (11)?

GERALD: No (12). I'll just go out – walk about – *for a while*, if you don't mind (13). I'll come back (14).

INSPECTOR: All right, Mr Croft (15).

SHEILA: But just in case you *forget* – or decide not to come back, Gerald, I think you'd better take this with you (16). (She hands him the ring.)

GERALD: I see (17). Well, I was *expecting* this (18).

SHEILA: I don't dislike you as I did *half an hour* ago, Gerald (19). In fact, in some odd way, I rather respect you more than I've *ever* done *before* (20). I knew anyhow you were lying about *those months last year* when you *hardly* came near me (21). I knew there was something fishy about *that time* (22). And *now* at least you've been honest (23). And I believe what you told us about the way you helped her *at first* (24). Just out of pity (25). And it was my fault really that she was so desperate when you first met her (26). But this has made a difference (27). You and I aren't the same people who sat down to dinner here (28). We'd have to start all over again, getting to know each other – (29)

BIRLING: Now, Sheila, I'm not defending him (30). But you must *understand* that a lot of young men – (31)

SHEILA: Don't interfere, please, Father (32). Gerald *knows what I mean*, and you apparently don't (33).

GERALD: Yes, I *know what you mean* (34). But I'm coming back – if I may (35).

SHEILA: All right (36).

MRS BIRLING: Well, really, I don't know. I think we've just about come to an end of this wretched business –

GERALD: I don't think so. Excuse me.

(He goes out. They watch him go in silence. We hear the front door slam.)

This piece of dialogue does not seem as thematically saturated as the last one. Nevertheless we can recognize in it a clearly marked semantic organization, related not in this instance to obligation and probability but to time. In general the 'time' theme, although strongly foregrounded in some of Priestley's plays (*I Have Been Here Before* is an obvious example), is more diffuse in *An Inspector Calls*; but it does emerge at least in this passage as a rather strongly foregrounded motif. Again we will look at the words and structures first in their "automatic" function, as the grammatical realization of ongoing semantic choices.

We can identify four elements in the semantics of time:

(1) *time passing*:

those months	for a while
last year	for a while
half an hour ago	that time

(2) *overcoming the passage of time*:
> to remember
> to remember
> to make it last
> to make it last
> [in case you] forget

(3) *sometimes, never*:
> never . . . again
> never . . . again
> more than ever
> hardly came near me

(4) *then and now*:

at first	[not . . . as . . . half an hour] ago
now	[more than . . .] before

"You and I aren't the same people who sat down to dinner here. We'd have to start all over again."

These are accompanied by a repetition of the themes of 'going away' and 'coming back'. Tracking them through the text we can summarize as follows:

(1) Eva Smith: remembers (a) makes time last
(b) feels it will never recur

(2) Gerald: distances past from present
(a) 'that event did never recur'
(b) 'I need a little while'
(c) 'I will come back'

(3) Sheila: distances 'us-then' from 'us-now'
(a) 'you will forget to come back'
(b) past | hour   'I never respected
| month   you: you hardly
                    came near'
▼ year

143

    (c) present: now 'I respect you:
        you . . .?'

    (d) past 'you and Eva'

    (e) 'present you and I $\neq$ past you and I'

(4) Gerald: tries to reconcile then and now: 'I'm coming back – if I may'

But in building up this pattern we have had to take account of another grammatical variable, that of tense. Here is the pattern of tense variation in Sheila's main speech (19–29) (Figure 6):

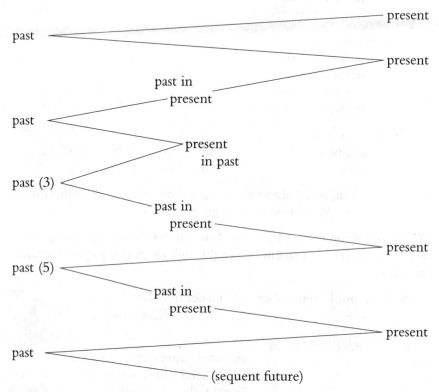

Figure 6   Movement of tense in Sheila's longest turn

ending up with "We'd have to start all over again" – perhaps hardly surprising in view of this somewhat disorientating oscillation of temporal focus.

Once again let us try and distance ourselves from the immediate textual environment in order to see the extent to which the expression of time has been de-automatized. To do this we need to refer to the

144

organization of time in the linguistic system; this is a potentially endless task, but we can perhaps isolate from the intricacies of the total picture, almost all of which would ultimately be relevant, two specific features that can be briefly characterized and displayed.

(1) Shifting time reference in the verb. The English verb incorporates primary tense, expressing deictic time (time relative to the 'now' of the act of meaning, e.g. *is, was, will be*), and secondary tense expressing serial time (time relative to the time referred to in the primary tense, e.g. present in past *was doing*, past in present *has done*). We see the interplay of these systems in the text in sequences such as the following (Figure 7):

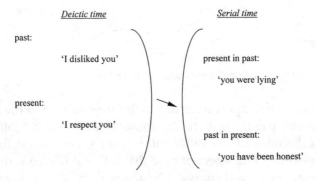

Figure 7   Deictic and serial time in English tenses

(2) Finiteness. What brings the process "down to earth", relating it to the here-&-now and so turning it into a proposition, into something that can be argued about, is the category of finiteness; and finiteness in English has two essential properties: (i) it is fused with polarity (positive/negative), and (ii) it is mediated through either primary tense (past/present/future) or modality/modulation (certain/probable/possible; required/supposed/allowed). We referred above to the fact that these two systems, which represent aspects of the speaker's judgement, constitute intermediate degrees of polarity lying between the positive and negative poles; and that in the indicative this indeterminacy takes the form of modality, the dimension of more or less probable. There is another dimension of polarity in the indicative mood: besides probability, which means 'either yes or no', there is the meaning 'both yes and no' which is the dimension of temporality. On the temporal dimension the middle term corresponding to 'probable' is 'usual', and the scale runs from 'sometimes' through

'usually' to 'always'. We can thus expand the left-hand side of Figure 5 to read as follows (Figure 8):

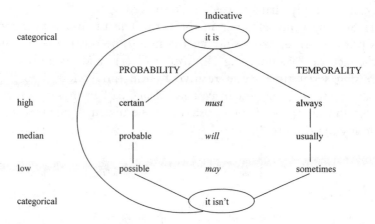

Figure 8   Degrees of probability and temporality

The system of temporality is not itself foregrounded in the text; it is present in this passage only in the forms *never, ever* and *hardly*, which are the realizations of the outer value (always/sometimes) fused with negative polarity. The aspect of time that is foregrounded is that of past and present, 'then' and 'now'. The temporality system is of interest because it provides another link between the themes of time and obligation, representing the speaker's judgement as a temporal indeterminacy ('at one time it is, at another time it is not'); and this is bound up, in the text, with the theme of then and now.

Thus the two themes of time and social obligation, which are so often associated in Priestley's plays, and are juxtaposed in the two passages we have been considering, turn out to be closely associated also in the linguistic system. The complex interplay between the two is a feature of the English language; it appears in its most highly coded form in the category of finiteness, realized through the auxiliary verbs that are sometimes aptly called "anomalous finites". It permeates these sequences of the text through the de-automatization of the words and structures that in their automatic function may express any one of the component elements involved.

The time theme as foregrounded here takes the form of an oscillation between past and present through the act of memory – remembering, 'making it last' – and, subsidiarily, through alternations in temporality in the sense described above. The mapping of these on to the axis of

146

then and now creates a characteristic Priestleian universe in which past and present co-exist. The author of these plays is entirely at home in the world in which today's children are growing up, reading accounts such as the following:

> Scientists once put a very accurate clock inside a space ship. Then they fired it into space. When the ship came back to earth they looked at the clock and gasped. For the clock on the space ship was showing a different time to the clocks on earth. The clock on the space ship had somehow *lost* time while it was out in space! But how can you lose time?
>
> Scientists say that when a space ship travels very fast, close to the speed of light, then time slows down in the space ship. It seems unbelievable, but it's true. Maybe it is a bit like reading a book. If you were one of the people in the book then time would be the same for everyone in the book. But if you were outside the book it would be different. You would be just someone reading that book. Then your time would be different. You could read about someone's whole lifetime in just a few hours. That's one way of looking at it. Maybe we are like characters in a book, trapped on earth. (Mark Oakey 1978)

In place of a linear progression through time, Priestley's drama calls rather for his own concept of "actualization", "the business of bringing events which already have their being in what I believe to be the more enduring and fundamental worlds of our feeling, imagination and will, into the world of material form". The theatre is thus being required to destroy the illusion on which it depends for its own success. Mukařovský points out that while the narrative mode is characterized by flow but no present, and the lyric by present but no flow, the essence of drama is that it has both: a temporal flow, the past–future axis, and a timeless present, the speaker–hearer axis. The finiteness of the dramatic mode is the same as the finiteness of the linguistic system, in which a syntagm becomes a speech event through having a "location" in time or a "validity" in the speaker's judgement; and the reference point of both of these is 'I-now'. But in Priestley's reality both the 'I' and the 'now' are illusory (his own comment on *Music at Night* is ". . . I was trying to show that personality, the separate self, is an illusion – a hopeless task in the theatre"). Each becomes real only through being projected outwards in some encompassing context: the self in family, social group, nation and human race, the present in another present where this one will be a moment in a book. The individual's social responsibilities are the actualization of the timeless fabric of existence which guarantees us and gives the 'I-now' such contingent reality as it has.

The "automatic" organization of lexicogrammatical patterns can present all this as theory or encapsulate it in the dramatic dialogue. But it is the de-automatization of the words and the grammatical structures that projects such ideological constructs into the microsemiotic encounters of the protagonists on the stage. In the present instance, this is achieved through the foregrounding of those elements of the linguistic system in which the complex interrelationships of obligation, personality and time are built in to the everyday give-and-take of dialogue, and so become part of what Berger and Luckmann refer to as the "ordinary, taken-for-granted world".

Chapter Five

POETRY AS SCIENTIFIC DISCOURSE: THE NUCLEAR SECTIONS OF TENNYSON'S *IN MEMORIAM* (1987)

1 Background

Linguists concerned with the study of texts, and particularly the study of highly-valued texts, the central domain of linguistic stylistics, have had to contend with two opposing traditions in the study of meaning. According to one persuasion, the meaning of a text is its referential content; meaning is displayed in the words and their construction; and if two texts have the same truth value they are held to be synonymous. According to the other, the meaning of a text is everything the particular critic can think of to say about it; meaning lurks in the void that is set "between the lines"; and no text is ever synonymous even with itself. The task for a linguistics of style has been to develop the positive features of both these images of language, both the leaner, classical one and the more fleshy, romantic one; to demonstrate that the meaning of a text is accessible – it is not some private figment of the critic's psychic powers – but that it encompasses a great deal more than the manifest propositional content.

Significant contributions to this task came from some of the great figures of the middle years of this century. Mukařovský made it clear that if a text was highly valued this was not because it was written in any special language evolved for the purpose (there is no such thing as a "literary register"), but because of the *functions* to which the language was addressed (1977). Mukařovský offered a rich multifunctional view of language, and from this he derived both a general theory of literary

First published in *Functions of Style*, edited by David Birch and Michael O'Toole. London: Pinter, 1987, pp. 31–44.

genres and an explanation for the semiotic efficacy of any particular text.

Firth's stylistic studies added another dimension to the rich interpretation of meaning: that of *levels*. Each level of linguistic organization, phonetic, phonological, morphological, syntactic, lexical, contributed its own "mode of meaning" to the text (1951). At a further level the text itself was contextualized: brought into relation with other, preceding texts, and with (the rest of) its context of situation – a context which might extend and modify through time, where a text had an extended history of its own.

Both these interpretations depended on explicit textual analysis of a "public" kind, for which the linguist could be called to account; and the basis for this was provided in Firth's own system-structure theory and in the functionalist theory of the Prague school. Two further essentials for the linguistic study of style came from the work of Hjelmslev and of Whorf. Hjelmslev clarified the theoretical status of a text, defining its relationship to the *system* of the language of which it is an instance (in Saussure this relationship of "instantiation" appears to be confused with that of "realization", the relationship among the levels of the system). Whorf introduced the notion of the "cryptotype", the semantic patterns that are submerged below the surface of the grammar but are accessible through a complex series of "reactances" and carry the main ideational and interpersonal motifs that inform the text.

2   General considerations

In the 1960s some important pioneering work was done in the linguistic study of literary texts based on this stratal-functional model of language (e.g. Gregory 1967, 1974; Hasan 1964, 1967; Leech 1965, 1969; McIntosh 1963, 1966; Sinclair, 1966). At the same time we were working towards an interpretation of the grammar of English that would serve the needs (inter alia) of stylistic research: that was itself multifunctional, multistratal, and abstract or "cryptotypic" in the Whorfian sense. Systemic grammar with its framework of levels and its metafunctional hypothesis was an attempt to meet this need (Halliday 1985a; cf. Kennedy 1982). The Hjelmslevian perspective has been sharpened by Martin's (1985) complementarity of synoptic and dynamic, and Lemke's work (1985) has greatly strengthened the theoretical foundations.

In the past five to seven years the field has been immensely enriched by combining the linguistic interpretation of texts in terms of grammar and discourse with the multiplicity of literary, sociopolitical and ideological perspectives that are loosely integrated under the name of semiotics. Some of the work which seems to me to have particularly broadened our horizons during the past ten years would include Kress on language and ideology – how grammar creates political realities; Fowler on the literary text in its social-historical context; Gregory's communication linguistics and the "phases" of a literary text; Hasan's perception of verbal art and the levels of literary semiosis; O'Toole's narrative analysis and his metafunctional interpretation of other semiotic systems; Carter on a literary text as a learning experience; Sinclair's perception of the intersection of the literary and the linguistic; Thibault's problematizing of the text as intersubjective process, and the subject as intertextual construct; Threadgold's multitextual interpretations drawing on all the discourses of semiotics; Butt on grammar in the construction of reality and the text in its place in the history of ideas (Butt 1984, 1988; Carter 1982; Fowler 1981; Gregory 1985; Hasan 1975, 1985; Kress and Hodge 1979; O'Toole 1982, 1994; Sinclair 1982; Thibault 1984, 1986; Threadgold 1986).

It seems to me that studies such as these have fashioned what starts out as a reasonably coherent account of language as system and process into a powerful tool for the interpretation of texts in their cultural or macrosemiotic environment. What I hope will emerge is a sense of the interdependence of all the parts. Let me try to express this in a series of interpretative steps; not implying by this an ordered methodological procedure, although I shall follow more or less this line of approach in the brief illustration that comes next.

We recognize that patterns in the grammar are ideational (either experiential, like transitivity; or logical, like expansion and projection), interpersonal (like mood and modality), or textual (like theme and information structure); and that any one of these **metafunctions** may be foregrounded in a given work, or part of a work. What we are establishing, however, is the metafunctional profile, or progression across the discourse; it is the intersection of these patterns in a unique combination that gives a text its characteristic flavour. Having separated the metafunctional components in order to understand why the text means what it does, we put them together again to explain why the text is valued as it is.

At the same time, secondly, we relate these patterns to patterns at other levels: both to the independently established lower-level patterns of phonology and so on, and also to the semantic patterns. These last are not, of course, established independently of the lexicogrammar –

151

they are **interpretations** of the lexicogrammar, especially the crypto-grammar – but they are related to it by more than one route: the grammar either functioning as realization, or "de-automatized" and so creating meanings of its own. This same dimension of *realization* enables us to enter the context of situation, the contextual configuration in terms of field, tenor and mode; and this in turn leads in to the context of culture, the socio-historical and ideological environment engendering, and engendered by, the text.

The relationship of "situation" to "culture" is one of *instantiation*; and this adds the third dimension to the analysis. At each level, the text instantiates the system; and this is also (like realization) a two-way process, since each instance disturbs the probabilities of the system and hence destroys and recreates it – almost identically, but not quite. One property of a highly valued text is its capacity to disturb the system beyond its simple quantitative function: the writer – or speaker – that we call innovative is one whose text causes perturbations greater than those associated with a single instance. Such texts often accumulate a layering of Firthian contexts. Our interpretation has to extend beyond the text to the system that creates and is created by it: otherwise, the text remains an island, something that no speaker could ever have constructed and no listener could ever have construed if they had.

But, fourthly, our own interpretative text so constituted is not a separate construction either. The interpretation is a complex semiotic act in which we as interpreters impinge on the meaning of the text we are interpreting: both by adding to its value and, usually, in more specific ways as well. A text brought into attention in this way becomes more than just another text; the discourse formed by its conjunction with other texts, including the analytic metatext, is something that is essentially new.

All this is obviously more than I can pretend to illustrate in one short essay. But to try and make some of these points more concrete I propose to discuss briefly one highly valued text fragment: one that in fact holds an important place in English semohistory, in the struggle to come to terms with the scientific ideology of the century following Newton. This is the central passage from Tennyson's *In Memoriam*: three sections (17 stanzas in all) falling more or less in the middle of the poem:

LIII.

OH yet we trust that somehow good
Will be the final goal of ill,

152

To pangs of nature, sins of will,
Defects of doubt, and taints of blood;

That nothing walks with aimless feet;
 That not one life shall be destroy'd,
 Or cast as rubbish to the void,
When God hath made the pile complete;

That not a worm is cloven in vain;
 That not a moth with vain desire
 Is shrivel'd in a fruitless fire,
Or but subserves another's gain.

Behold, we know not anything;
 I can but trust that good shall fall
 At last – far off – at last, to all,
And every winter change to spring.

So runs my dream: but what am I?
 An infant crying in the night:
 An infant crying for the light:
And with no language but a cry.

LIV.

THE wish, that of the living whole
 No life may fail beyond the grave;
 Derives it not from what we have
The likest God within the soul?

Are God and Nature then at strife,
 That Nature lends such evil dreams?
 So careful of the type she seems,
So careless of the single life;

That I, considering everywhere
 Her secret meaning in her deeds,
 And finding that of fifty seeds
She often brings but one to bear;

I falter where I firmly trod,
 And falling with my weight of cares
 Upon the great world's altar-stairs
That slope thro' darkness up to God;

I stretch lame hands of faith, and grope,
 And gather dust and chaff, and call
 To what I feel is Lord of all,
And faintly trust the larger hope.

LV.

"SO careful of the type?" but no.
　From scarped cliff and quarried stone
　She cries "a thousand types are gone:
I care for nothing, all shall go.

Thou makest thine appeal to me:
　I bring to life, I bring to death:
　The spirit does but mean the breath:
I know no more." And he, shall he,

Man, her last work, who seem'd so fair,
　Such splendid purpose in his eyes,
　Who roll'd the psalm to wintry skies,
Who built him fanes of fruitless prayer,

Who trusted God was love indeed
　And love Creation's final law —
　Tho' Nature, red in tooth and claw
With ravine, shriek'd against his creed —

Who loved, who suffer'd countless ills,
　Who battled for the True, the Just,
　Be blown about the desert dust,
Or seal'd within the iron hills?

No more? A monster then, a dream,
　A discord. Dragons of the prime,
　That tare each other in their slime,
Were mellow music match'd with him.

O life as futile, then, as frail!
　O for thy voice to soothe and bless!
　What hope of answer, or redress?
Behind the veil, behind the veil.

The remainder of the paper will be on the interpretation of this text.

3 Some metafunctional patterns in the lexicogrammar

(i) Logical: the clause complex
More than half of this passage is taken up by three very long clause
complexes. The first (stanzas 1–3 of section 53) is controlled by a
projection: *we trust that ...*, and is of the form

α　　'β1　　β+2　　β+31　　β3+2α　　b32ˣβ　　β+4　　β+51　　β5+2

This is followed, after the intervening *Behold, we know not anything*; by a shorter projection introduced by *I can but trust that . . .*, with just three clauses

$$\alpha \qquad \text{`}\beta1 \qquad \beta+2$$

Alan Sinfield, in his excellent study of the language of *In Memoriam*, pointed out this "analogical syntax", the "repeated constructions" that he found to be characteristic of the poem – these are the paratactic extensions shown up as +2, +3, +4, +5 in the analysis, and I shall return to these below. In the second of the long clause complexes (section 54, stanza 2 line 3 to the end of the section), the controlling logical structure is now **expansion**:

$$\alpha1 \qquad \alpha+2 \qquad \text{`}\beta\alpha1\alpha \qquad << \beta\text{`}\beta1 \qquad \beta\beta2\alpha \qquad \beta\beta2\text{`}\beta. >> \qquad \beta\alpha\text{`}\beta$$

$$\beta\alpha+2\text{`}\beta\alpha \qquad \beta\alpha2\beta=\beta \qquad \beta\alpha2\alpha1 \qquad \beta\alpha2\alpha+2 \qquad \beta\alpha2\alpha+3$$

$$\beta\alpha2\alpha+4 \qquad \beta\alpha2\alpha+5$$

This is a complicated one, with more hypotaxis than parataxis, but with another long paratactic sequence at the end, of the same extending type. In section 55, after a shorter clause complex based on paratactic projection (*she [Nature] cries*), there is a third long one, beginning with an expansion of the elaborating kind ("non-defining relative") and again containing one of Sinfield's "analogical" sequences:

$$\alpha1 \qquad <<=\beta1\alpha \qquad \beta1\text{`}\beta \qquad \beta+2 \qquad \beta+3 \qquad \beta+4\alpha\alpha \qquad \beta4\alpha\text{`}\beta1 \qquad \beta4\alpha\beta+2$$

$$\beta4\text{`}\beta\alpha \qquad \beta4\beta=\beta \qquad \beta+5 \qquad \beta+6 \qquad \beta+7 >> \qquad \alpha+2$$

Note that in all three instances this sequence occurs in a **dependent** environment: reported (*we trust that . . .*), enhancing (*so careless that . . .*) or elaborating (*man, her last work, who . . .*); (see further Section 5 below).

(ii) Interpersonal: mood
Throughout these three sections, the mood oscillates between declarative and non-declarative, the non-declaratives being interrogative or moodless. The pattern emerges as in Table 1. Rhetorically this alternation carries a pattern of assertion and challenge, terminating in an apostrophic coda where the clauses are exclamatory in function.

Table 1 Patterns of mood in the 17 stanzas

Inter-personal phase	Mood	Passage	Clause nuclei
phase 1	declarative	§ 53 st.1, 1.1 – st. 5, 1.1.	we trust we know not I can but trust so runs my dream
phase 2	interrogative/ moodless	§ 53 st. 5, 1.1 – § 54 st. 2, 1.2.	what am I? – an infant the wish: derives it not? are God and Nature at strife?
phase 3	declarative	§ 54 st. 2, 1.3 – § 55 st. 2, 1.4.	she seems she cries
phase 4	interrogative/ moodless	§ 55 st. 2, 1.4 – st. 6.	shall man be blown about or seal'd? no more? a monster a discord
phase 5	moodless	§ 55 st. 7	o life! o for thy voice! what hope of answer? behind the veil!

(iii) Experiential: transitivity

In § 53, and the first stanza of § 54, the process types are predominantly material: creative: destructive (with one constructive and one transformative): *destroy, cast, cleave, shrivel, fail; make (complete); change, derive*. The Medium in the destructive (mainly Goal, since they are largely passive) is a living creature – but always negated: *nothing, not one life, not a moth, not one worm, no life*. The next motif to emerge clearly is that of material: dispositive: motive, in § 54, stanzas 4 and 5: *falter, fall, stretch, grope*, with Medium (here Actor, since these are middle) *I*. There is a negative element in the Process (*falter* etc.; even *gather dust and chaff* is superventive (involuntary)). The third motif is found in § 55, stanzas 3–5, where the processes are semiotic ones, mental or

156

verbal: *love, trust, suffer*, the Medium being *man*; elsewhere the Process is material but there is a semiotic Range or circumstance: *roll the psalm, build fanes of prayer, battle for the True*. There is a minor motif of attribution: *be careful/careless*, with Medium *Nature*; *be at strife*, Medium *God and Nature*; and the contrasting pair *man seemed fair [but] dragons were mellow music match'd with him*. The transitivity patterns are in phase with the logical ones, so we can identify a second dimension of structure having an ideationally based phasal organization:

Table 2   Patterns of transitivity in the 17 stanzas

Ideational phase	Transitivity	Clause complex	Passage	Medium
phase A	material: destructive	projection: report/ idea	§ 53 – § 54 st. 1.	I, we
phase B	material: dispositive	expansion: enhancing	§ 54 sts. 2–5.	[Nature→] I
phase C	mental; verbal	projection: quote/ locution	§ 55 st. 1 – st. 2, 1.4.	Nature
phase D	mental; verbal	expansion; elaborating	§ 55 st. 2, 1.4 – st. 5.	man
phase E	(relational: attributive)		§ 55 sts. 6, 7.	

A comparison of the two will show that this is slightly, but not randomly, out of phase with the pattern set up by the interpersonal structure.

It may be helpful to note the major lexical chains deriving from the transitivity selections:

know	faith	trust	doubt	hope	wish	dream
goal	purpose	final	fruitless	vain	rubbish	futile
good	ill	evil	careful	careless		
soul	spirit	breath	life	death	grave	
falter	fall	lame	grope	secret	veil	

In addition to the foregrounded antonymies we may notice the range of certainty to uncertainty traversed by the first set, from *know* to *dream*.

4 Combination and interpretation

Let us put these together and interpret them in semantic terms. The overlapping Phase I/A is *declarative* in mood, *projecting* (*we trust*), with the projections either in *future* tense (*will be the final goal, shall be destroyed, shall fall, shall change*) or *present* with a Manner circumstantial of a teleological kind (*walks with aimless feet, is cloven in vain, is shrivelled in a fruitless fire*, etc.). Our trust is in ultimate goals: either good will happen, or if evil then for a good reason. The projection is a proposition: 'we believe' – or is it? *trust* is ambiguous, and the alternative interpretation 'we hope', with the projection as a proposal (as in *I trust you are not angry with me*), is gradually made to supersede: first by *we know not anything*, and finally when it becomes a wish. A wish is very far from a belief; it sends us back to reinterpret *trust* as '(vain) hope' (see below on the negatives), and this then explains the *somehow* – we really cannot see how all this could be. The wish, moreover, is in Phase 2, the challenge: 'look closely, and you will see where these vain hopes arise from'.

The challenge then sets off the dialogue with Nature: 'if the hopes are vain, here is the explanation'. We now pass to Phase B, where the assertion (Phase 3) is again *declarative*; but now *enhancing* (*so careless . . . that . . .*), with the expansions in *present* tense. We have moved from the unreal (projected future) to the real (non-projected present): abandoning the original hope, and clinging tenuously to the larger one (*faintly trust*). This is immediately dashed, in Phase C, by Nature's uncompromising assertion *all shall go*: no *indirect idea*, but a *direct locution*, and written in stone – the rockhard evidence of the fossils. And there is no appeal, because the "soul" is itself an illusion (I return to this below).

There is then a coincidence of Phase D with Phase 4: the controlling clause is now *interrogative*, the logical relation is *elaborating* (*man . . ., who . . .*) and the expansions are in *past* tense: 'who did all these things'. But these *who . . .* clauses are in this context concessive; and the 'doings' were largely acts of faith. What begins as 'trust in' the future is destroyed by present revelations, so that the trust itself is now a thing of the past; yet despite this faith-full past we ourselves have no future – there is no soul in a fossil.

This pattern of movement in the text is carried along by the two interlocking phasal structures. We could summarize it as in Table 3.

Table 3 Text movement shown by dominant selections in interpersonal and ideational systems

		PHASES 1 – 5: INTERPERSONAL		PHASES A – E: IDEATIONAL
	1	**1**		**A**
	2	(1) declarative		(a) material : destructive
53	3	(2) future		Medium = *we (I)*
	4	(1) interrogative; moodless	**2**	(b) projection : report/idea
	5	(2) present		
	1			
	2			Transitional
54	3	(1) declarative	**3**	**B**
				(a) material : dispositive
				Medium = I
	4	(2) present		(b) expansion : enhancing
	5			
	1			(a) mental ; verbal **C**
				Medium = *Nature*
	2			(b) projection : quote/locution
	3	(1) interrogative; moodless	**4**	(a) mental ; verbal **D**
55	4	(2) past		Medium = *man*
				(b) expansion : elaborating
	5			
	6			(a) relational : attributive **E**
	7	(1) moodless	**5**	(b) none
		(2) tenseless		

(1)	=	mood	(a) transitivity
(2)	=	primary (deictic) tense	(b) clause complex

5   The dynamics of the clause complex

The grammar of this passage is that of spoken rather than of written language. This is seen most clearly in the clause complexes; also in the transitivity patterns, where there is little nominalization or other grammatical metaphor and much of the lexical content is in the verbs. There is an excellent discussion of this in a little paper by Walker Gibson, written in 1958 (in the course of which he remarks "I submit, then, that Tennyson's 'poetic imagination' can sometimes be examined in terms of his grammar").

The significant feature of the clause complexes is not simply their great length, nor their combination of parataxis and hypotaxis, but their dynamic, **choreographic** nature: you cannot foresee the ending from the beginning, nor recover the beginning by looking at the end. They are not constructions, as are the clause complexes of written discourse. So, for example, if we chart the passage from *So careful of the type she seems* to *and (I) faintly trust the larger hope*, we see how many and various are the steps that have been taken in between, each moving off from the point where the last one landed. We have already noted the occurrence in them of long *paratactic* chains, an "accumulation of clauses with the same function" as Sinfield expresses it (1971, p. 99). But each of the dominant clause complexes in this passage has an identical structure (one also found elsewhere in the poem) whereby the paratactic sequence is launched by an initial *hypotaxis*; and in each case the hypotaxis undermines the whole effect, giving the entire sequence the status of a lost cause. 'We trust that (all this will happen − but we know it won't)'; 'Nature seems such that (I lose faith)'; 'shall man (though he trusted) end up as dust and fossil?' And this 'lost cause' effect is heightened by the transitivity patterns: the contrasts of affection plus positive ('we hope for everything') with cognition plus negative ('we know nothing'), of nature's acting with my faltering, and of man's past of 'doing' with his future of 'being done to' (*blown about the desert dust*).

This admission of defeat is plainly signalled by the grammar of the groups and phrases in Phase A. In its automated function, as realization of the semantics, the grammar here is positive: in *nothing walks with aimless feet, not a worm is cloven in vain* the negatives cancel out; everything has a purpose (so we trust). But in the de-automatized grammar, the meanings that are created by the grammar outside the control of the semantics, the negatives pile up, and the effect (*not a worm, aimless, nothing, in vain, no life*, etc.) is one of total defeat.

So while Sinfield is right in seeing the parataxis as the repeated piling up of the argument ("the most promising way [for Tennyson] of seeking truth" (1971 : 102)), in these critical passages the argument is admitted to have failed. The lexicogrammatical context is one in which the cause is already lost. This effect is perhaps further heightened by the 'unconvincing' motif which introduces all three of these clause complexes:

somehow good will be the final goal of ill
so careful of the type she seems
man her last work who seemed so fair.

6   Tennyson and the scientific imagination

There is no place here to discuss Sinfield's interpretation in further detail; Tennyson's belief in progress, his faith in mankind, and the meaningfulness to him of current developments in science are all closely examined through the study of the language (passim; and see Chapter XI for his conclusions). Sinfield remarks that science "forced itself upon" Tennyson, who "was just able to absorb the discoveries of the geologists" (1971, pp. 116, 206). Let us explore this point a little further.

Tennyson may be fighting a rearguard action in these lines; but he is aware that this is what he is doing, and he is not distressed by it. Both the rhetorical and the logical dynamic of the passage, as revealed by the interpersonal and ideational analyses, suggest this very strongly; and it is inescapable when the two are put together. Mankind may still be an infant, with no language but a cry (or only a protolanguage!); but he has now, it seems, once again found a place in nature. One of Nature's lines, in her part of the dialogue, tells how:

The spirit does but mean the breath:
I know no more.

In other words: the soul is dead; you have no more need of that hypothesis.

Nature, interpreted by science, has shown how man arose from the rest of creation. At first sight, this seems threatening; we are no longer protected by being uniquely the children of God. Individuals perish; and Tennyson's personal grief at the loss of a loved friend provokes what at level one is a rage against nature's indifference: her carelessness of the single life, casually abandoned and destroyed. But at level two the scientific enquiry takes over and the interest is in the type. Species perish too; many are there in the fossil library, that no longer exist. And the human species will also become extinct: mankind is not privileged – there is no immortality, even of the soul.

You appeal to me, says Nature, and your soul goes puff! This "spirit", the fiction of ancient Greek and Hebrew philosophy, is simply a puff of breath: a dressed-up pneuma and psyche – the breathing in and out, the painted deities of Heng and Ha that guard a Taoist temple. This is how the whole fancy started: – *I know no more.* McKellar (1985) provides an illuminating, fully documented account of the history of the concept of psycho–physical duality in western thinking.

It is clearly threatening to find one is no longer immortal. But, while **what we know** from science may be disturbing, **the fact that we have come to know it** is exhilarating; and it is the liberating power of knowledge that Tennyson is celebrating here. As Gibson points out (1958, p. 67), despite the protestation of ignorance in the final stanza of § 55 (*Behind the veil, behind the veil*), "[Tennyson's] dramatic stance has actually taken him a long way from any such humble position". He has read Sir Charles Lyell's *Principles of Geology*; and while there is no suggestion that he had read any work of Darwin (and he could not have read *The Origin of Species*, which appeared nearly ten years after *In Memoriam*), he was clearly and indeed explicitly aware of the current of evolutionary theory that was gathering momentum in biology. The entire dynamic of the text – the rhetorical structure (Phases 1–5), the dialogue with Nature, the movement created by the clause complexes (§ 4 above), the grammar's construction of blind trust as a lost cause – is both a **presentation** of what Gibson calls "the disquieting new world of science" and a **celebration** of it as something that increases rather than diminishes the stature of mankind.

These stanzas thus fall within the tradition of the scientific imagination: the works of the great poet-scientists from Lucretius onwards whose poetic text displays in a unique form the grammatical construction of reality. And this leads to one final question: what is the role of texts of this kind in the **long-term** dialogue with Nature, that which Prigogine and Stengers refer to (and use as sub-title) in their book *Order out of Chaos*? (Prigogine and Stengers 1985: esp. the Preface, pp. xxvii–xxxi). Is there a wider context, a further level of the social semiotic, in which this passage has to be interpreted?

7 Poetry in the dialogue with nature

Here is an extract from *The Origin of Species*:

As natural selection acts only by the accumulation of slight modifications of structure or instinct, each profitable to the individual under its
conditions of life, it may reasonably be asked, how a long and gradu-
ated succession of modified architectural instincts, all tending towards
the present perfect plan of construction, could have profited the pro-
genitors of the hive-bee? I think the answer is not difficult: it is known
that bees are often hard pressed to get sufficient nectar; and I am
informed by Mr. Tegetmeier that it has been experimentally found that
no less than from twelve to fifteen pounds of dry sugar are consumed
by a hive of bees for the secretion of each pound of wax: so that a
prodigious quantity of fluid nectar must be collected and consumed by
the bees in a hive for the secretion of the wax necessary for the construction of their combs. Moreover, many bees have to remain idle for
many days during the process of secretion. A large store of honey is
indispensable to support a large stock of bees during the winter; and the
security of the hive is known mainly to depend on a large number of
bees being supported. Hence the saving of wax by largely saving honey
must be a most important element of success in any family of bees. Of
course the success of any species of bee may be dependent on the
number of its parasites or other enemies, or on quite distinct causes, and
so be altogether independent of the quantity of honey which the bees
could collect. But let us suppose that this latter circumstance determined,
as it probably often does determine, the numbers of a humble-bee
which could exist in a country; and let us further suppose that the
community lived throughout the winter, and consequently required a
store of honey: there can in this case be no doubt that it would be an
advantage to our humble-bee, if a slight modification of her instinct led
her to make her waxen cells near together, so as to intersect a little; for
a wall in common even to two adjoining cells, would save some little
wax. Hence it would continually be more and more advantageous to
our humble-bee, if she were to make her cells more and more regular,
nearer together, and aggregated into a mass, like the cells of the
Melipona; for in this case a large part of the bounding surface of each
cell would serve to bound other cells, and much wax would be saved.
Again, from the same cause, it would be advantageous to the Melipona,
if she were to make her cells closer together, and more regular in every
way than at present; for then, as we have seen, the spherical surfaces
would wholly disappear, and would all be replaced by plane surfaces;
and the Melipona would make a comb as perfect as that of the hive-
bee. Beyond this stage of perfection in architecture, natural selection

could not lead; for the comb of the hive-bee, as far as we can see, is absolutely perfect in economising wax.

Thus, as I believe, the most wonderful of all known instincts, that of the hive-bee, can be explained by natural selection having taken advantage of numerous, successive, slight modifications of simpler instincts; natural selection having by slow degrees, more and more perfectly, led the bees to sweep equal spheres at a given distance from each other in a double layer, and to build up and excavate the wax along the planes of intersection. The bees, of course, no more knowing that they swept their spheres at one particular distance from each other, than they know what are the several angles of the hexagonal prisms and of the basal rhombic plates. The motive power of the process of natural selection having been economy of wax; that individual swarm which wasted least honey in the secretion of wax, having succeeded best, and having transmitted by inheritance its newly acquired economical instinct to new swarms, which in their turn will have had the best chance of succeeding in the struggle for existence.

Darwin is writing in the language of science. Behind this lie some four centuries of scientific English, from Chaucer onwards; and 150 years of continuous development from the English texts of Isaac Newton's works.

It is, obviously, very different from the language of Tennyson. Darwin's text is characterized by very simple clause complexes: the favoured structural pattern is one of embedding rather than taxis (hypotaxis or parataxis). There is a higher lexical density (lexical words per ranking clause), much more nominalization and a greater use of grammatical metaphor. (For these concepts, see Halliday 1985a; for these features as characteristic of written English, see Halliday 1987; for the relation between lexical density and grammatical metaphor, see Ravelli 1985.)

Where did this language evolve? It evolved as the language of physics – physicists led the way in creating the discourse of science. The model for

Hence the saving of wax by largely saving honey must be a most important element of success in any family of bees.

(which exemplifies all the features enumerated above) may be found in texts such as

Hence increase of temperature, at the same time as on one account it increases the absolute quantity of heat in an elastic fluid, diminishes the quantity on another account by an increase of pressure . . .

from Dalton's *A New System of Chemical Philosophy* (1827, p. 287).

164

But already in the eighteenth century the discourse of physics had come to be seen as alienating. Prigogine and Stengers observe (1985, p. 77):

> for nearly two centuries Laplace's demon has plagued our imagination, bringing a nightmare in which all things are insignificant. If it were really true that the world is such that a demon – a being that is, after all, like us, possessing the same science, but endowed with sharper senses and greater powers of calculation – could, starting from the observation of an instantaneous state, calculate its future and past, if nothing qualitatively differentiates the simple systems we can describe from the more complex ones for which a demon is needed, then the world is nothing but an immense tautology.

Where is the place of man in such a scheme of things? He is there only as an outsider:

> . . . in the mechanistic world view, the scientific description of nature will have its counterpart in man as an automaton endowed with a soul and thereby alien to nature.

(Prigogine and Stengers 1985, p. 83). This was the major preoccupation of the French Enlightenment; McKellar has described (1985: Chapter VII, esp. pp. 542 ff.) the rejection of this psycho-physical dualism, especially La Mettrie's attempt to demystify the psyche through the concept of the semiotic man-machine. Somehow, mankind had to re-enter the world of nature.

This was the significance of the new evolutionary theories, first in geology and then in the biological sciences: man once again became part of nature. But there was a price: he had to give up his godhead. Evolution could restore the "vital principle" – but only if man was first dethroned. Darwin finds it necessary to defend his theory by urging "that there is grandeur in this view of life" (459) (cf. Chapter 6 below):

> When I view all beings not as special creations, but as the lineal descendants of some few beings which lived long before the first bed of the Silurian system was deposited, they seem to me to become ennobled. (458)

In using this value-laden discourse Darwin was of course arming himself against the aggression and the ridicule he knew he was going to receive. But in ennobling man – and his fellow-creatures – in this way, Darwin was also re-ennobling science: bringing back the arrow of time, the sense of irreversible development towards increasingly complex forms of organization for which there was no place in the established physics of the period (Prigogine and Stengers 1985, pp. 128–9).

165

It is easy to scoff at Tennyson's acceptance of these ideas as being simply another manifestation of facile Victorian optimism. But that is surely to miss the point – which is that of the role of the poet-scientist in the semiotic processes of the culture. Tennyson was not bound by the tradition of scientific discourse; he was free to use the syntactically intricate, dynamic, non-metaphorical lexicogrammar of the everyday spoken language, and to create within it a form of discourse that could realize his own poetic imagination. In doing this he lessened the distance between scientific knowledge and everyday knowledge, so making science human once again – for the dehumanization of science had been a function of scientific **discourse**, whose grammar increasingly turned all happening into things and then set up abstruse relations between these things that only the initiate could comprehend.

When we reach this level of interpretation, we can see that the grammar, in these few sections of *In Memoriam*, has created an intricate semiotic helix, which we could gloss – in deplorably crude parody – as in Figure 1:

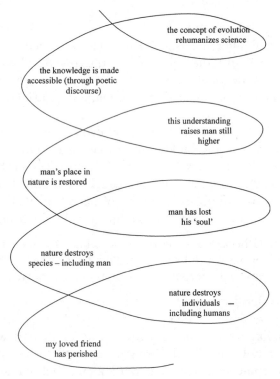

the concept of evolution rehumanizes science

the knowledge is made accessible (through poetic discourse)

this understanding raises man still higher

man's place in nature is restored

man has lost his 'soul'

nature destroys species – including man

nature destroys individuals – including humans

my loved friend has perished

Figure 1 Spiralling progression in the 17 stanzas, as suggested by the grammar

166

In the last analysis it is the meaning of Tennyson's choice of this way of meaning that has to be taken into account: the "function of the structure of functions", in the old Pragensian terminology. What this is telling us is that the knowledge that is made accessible through this poetic, non-technical discourse – the poeticization of science – is the very knowledge that is bringing science back into humanity. We are not alien to nature – because nature will turn out to be, essentially, like ourselves.

In putting it this way we have of course recontextualized the poem in the context of our own times. To quote Prigogine and Stengers again (1985, pp. xxviii; 208):

> *Science is rediscovering time* [their italics]. . . . history began by concentrating mainly on human societies, after which attention was given to the temporal dimensions of life and of geology. The incorporation of time into physics thus appears as the last stage of a progressive reinsertion of history into the natural and social sciences.

Obviously Tennyson was not describing, and could not describe, issues that were not yet formulated or apprehended by the scientists themselves. But that is irrelevant; in any case he was not describing anything – that is not how the grammar was being put into service. What he was doing with the grammar was something considerably more complex: constructing a semiotic universe at the intersection of science and poetry. The point is that he was doing this **with the grammar** (as always, in its systemic sense of "lexicogrammar"); so it is reasonable that we should use the study of grammar (our "grammatics", so to speak) as a means of trying to understand it.

Chapter Six

THE CONSTRUCTION OF KNOWLEDGE AND VALUE IN THE GRAMMAR OF SCIENTIFIC DISCOURSE: WITH REFERENCE TO CHARLES DARWIN'S *THE ORIGIN OF SPECIES*
(1990)

1 Theme and information in scientific discourse

The first part of this chapter will be a general discussion of certain features of the grammar of scientific English; in the second part I shall focus on one particular text, the final two paragraphs of Darwin's *The Origin of Species*. I shall assume the concept of **register**, or functional (diatypic) variation in language. It is convenient to talk of "a register", in the same way that one talks of "a dialect": in reality, of course, dialectal variation is typically continuous, along many dimensions (that is, with many features varying simultaneously), and what we call "a dialect" is a syndrome of variants that tend to co-occur. Those feature combinations that actually do occur – what we recognize as "the dialects of English", for example, or "the dialects of Italian" – are only a tiny fraction of the combinations that would be theoretically possible within the given language. Similarly, "a register" is a syndrome, or cluster of associated variants; and again only a small fraction of the theoretically possible combinations will actually be found to occur.[1]

What is the essential difference between dialectal variation and diatypic or register variation?[2] Prototypically, dialects differ in expression; our notion of them is that they are "different ways of saying the same thing". Of course, this is not without exception; dialectal variation arises from either geographical conditions (distance and physical barriers) or social-historical conditions (political, e.g. national

First published in *La rappresentazione verbale e iconica: valori estetici e funzionali. Atti del XI Congresso Nazionale dell'Associazzione Italiana di Anglistica, Bergamo, 24 e 25 Ottobre 1988*, edited by Clotilde de Stasio, Maurizio Gotti and Rossana Bonadei. Milan: Guerini Studio, 1990, pp 57–80.

boundaries; or hierarchical, e.g. class, caste, age, generation and sex), and as Hasan has shown[3] dialects that are primarily social in origin can and do differ also semantically. This is in fact what makes it possible for dialect variation to play such an important part in creating and maintaining (and also in transforming) these hierarchical structures. Nevertheless dialectal variation is primarily variation in expression: in phonology, and in the morphological formations of the grammar.

Registers, on the other hand, are not different ways of saying the same thing; they are ways of saying different things. Prototypically, therefore, they differ in content. The features that go together in a register go together for semantic reasons; they are meanings that typically co-occur. For this reason, we can translate different registers into a foreign language. We cannot translate different dialects; we can only mimic dialect variation.

Like dialects, registers are treated as realities by the members of the culture. We recognize "British English", "American English", "Australian English", "Yorkshire dialect", "Cockney", etc.; and likewise "journalese", "fairy tales", "business English", "scientific English" and so on. These are best thought of as spaces within which the speakers and writers are moving; spaces that may be defined with varying depth of focus (the dialect of a particular village versus the dialect of an entire region or nation; the register of high school physics textbooks versus the register of natural science), and whose boundaries are in any case permeable, hence constantly changing and evolving. A register persists through time because it achieves a contingent equilibrium, being held together by tension among different forces whose conflicting demands have to be met.[4] To give a brief example, grossly oversimplified but also highly typical: what we call "scientific English" has to reconcile the need to create new knowledge with the need to restrict access to that knowledge (that is, make access to it conditional on participating in the power structures and value systems within which it is located and defined).

In a recent short paper on the language of physical science I set out to identify, describe and explain a typical syndrome of grammatical features in the register of scientific English.[5] I cited a short paragraph from the *Scientific American* and focused particularly on the pattern represented in the following two clauses:

> The rate of crack growth depends . . . on the chemical environment.
> The development of a . . . model . . . requires an understanding of how stress accelerates the bond rupture reaction.

In their most general form, these clauses represent the two related motifs of '*a* causes/is caused by *x*', '*b* proves/is proved by *y*'. Let me cite another pair of examples taken from a different text:

> These results cannot be handled by purely structural models of laterality effects . . .   [*b* + prove + *y*]
> (if . . .) both word recognition and concurrent verbal memory produce more left than right hemisphere activation.   [*a* + cause + *x*]

Taken together: '*b* cannot be explained by *y* if *a* causes *x*'. At the level of the syntagm (sequence of classes), each of these consists of two nominal groups linked by a verbal group whose lexical verb is of the "relational" class, in this case *handle*, *produce*. Their analysis in systemic-functional grammar, taking account of just those features that are relevant to the present discussion, is as set out in Figure 1.[6]

In that paper I tried to show how and why this pattern evolved to become the dominant grammatical motif in modern scientific English. Historically the process is one of dialectic engagement between the nominal group and the clause. It is a continuous process, moving across the boundary between different languages: it began in ancient Greek, was continued in classical and then in medieval Latin, and then transmitted to Italian, English and the other languages of modern Europe. Table 1 is a summary of the relevant grammatical features that led up to this dominant motif, as they appear in two influential early scientific texts: Chaucer's *Treatise on the Astrolabe* (c. 1390) and Newton's *Opticks* from 300 years later.

What is not found in Chaucer's text, but is found in Newton, is this particular syndrome of clausal and nominal features: a clause of the type analysed in Figure 1, in which the nominal elements functioning as Token and Value are nominalizations of processes or properties; for example,

> The unusual Refraction is therefore perform'd by an original property of the Rays. [*Opticks*, p. 358]

This is still very much a minority type in Newton's writing; but it is available when the context demands. In order to see when the context does demand it, let me cite the immediately preceding text:

> . . . there is an original Difference in the Rays of Light, by means of which some Rays are . . . constantly refracted after the usual manner, and others constantly after the unusual manner. For if the difference be not original, but arises from new Modifications impress'd on the Rays at their first Refraction, it would be alter'd by new Modifications in the

three following Refractions; whereas it suffers no alteration, but is constant, . . . The unusual Refraction is therefore perform'd by an original property of the Rays.

Note in particular the sequence [*are*] *constantly* [*refracted*] *after the unusual manner . . . The unusual Refraction is therefore perform'd by . . .* Formulaically: "*a* happens . . . The happening of *a* is caused by . . .". The

	these results	cannot	be handled	by	purely structural models of laterality effects	
transitivity	Value / Identified	Process: relational / circumstantial: cause (internal)		Token / Identifier		

mood	Mood		Residue		
	Subject	Finite	Predicator	Adjunct	

theme	Theme	Rheme

information	Given	← · · · · · New

	both word recognition and concurrent verbal memory	produce		more left than right hemisphere activation	
transitivity	Token / Identified		Process: relational / circumstantial: cause (external)	Value / Identifier	

mood	Mood		Residue		
	Subject	Finite	Predicator	Complement	

theme	Theme	Rheme

information	Given	← · · · · · New

Figure 1 Transitivity (ideational), mood (interpersonal), and theme and information (textual) structures in the "favourite" clause type

nominalization *the unusual refraction* refers back to the earlier formulation *are refracted after the unusual manner,* in such a way as to make it the starting point for a new piece of information explaining how it is brought about.

Table 1 Some grammatical features in the scientific writings of Chaucer and Newton

	Grammatical features	**Typical contexts**
Chaucer: *Treatise on the Astrolabe*		
1: nominal	nouns:	technical terms:
	noun roots	technological (parts of instrument)
	nouns derived from verbs and adjectives	astronomical and mathematical
	nominal groups (with prepositional phrase and clause Qualifiers)	mathematical expressions
2: clausal	material and mental; imperative	instructions ('do this', 'observe/reckon that')
	relational ('be', 'be called'); indicative	observations; names and their explanations
Newton: *Opticks*		
1: nominal	nouns:	technical terms:
	noun roots	general concepts; experimental apparatus
	nouns derived from verbs and adjectives	physical and mathematical
	nominal groups (with prepositional phrase and clause Qualifiers)	mathematical expressions
	*nominalizations of processes & properties	logical argumentation; explanations and conclusions
2: clausal	material and mental; indicative	description of experiments ('I did this', 'I saw/ reasoned that')
	relational ('cause', 'prove'); indicative	logical argumentation; explanations and conclusions

* = not found in Chaucer's text

This grammatical pattern exploits the universal *metafunctional* principle of clause structure: that the clause, in every language, is a mapping of three distinct kinds of meaning – interpersonal, ideational and textual (clause as action, clause as reflection, clause as information). The structural mechanism for this mapping, as it is worked out in English, was shown in Figure 1. What concerns us here first and foremost is the textual component. In English the clause is organized textually into two simultaneous message lines, one of Theme + Rheme, and one of Given + New. The former presents the information from the speaker's angle: the Theme is 'what I am starting out from'. The latter presents the information from the listener's angle – still, of course, as constructed for him by the speaker: the New is 'what you are to attend to'. The two prominent functions, Theme and New, are realized in quite distinct ways: the Theme segmentally, by first position in the clause; the New prosodically, by greatest pitch movement in the tone group. Because of the different ways in which the two are constituted, it is possible for both to be mapped on to the same element. But the typical pattern is for the two to contrast, with tension set up between them, so that the clause enacts a dynamic progression from one to the other: from a speaker-Theme, which is also "given" (intelligence already shared by the listener), to a listener-New, which is also "rhematic" (a move away from the speaker's starting point). This pattern obviously provides a powerful resource for constructing and developing an argument.[7]

We could refer to this in Gestalt terminology as a move from "ground" to "figure", but that sets up too great a discontinuity between them and I shall prefer the "backgrounding – foregrounding" form of the metaphor since it suggests something more relative and continuous. The type of clause that is beginning to emerge in the Newtonian discourse, then, constructs a movement from a **backgrounded** element which summarizes what has gone before to a **foregrounded** element which moves on to a new plane. But there has to be a third component of the pattern, namely the relationship that is set up between the two; and it is this that provides the key to the potentiality of the whole, enabling the clause to function effectively in constructing knowledge and value. We have said that the relationship is typically one of cause or proof, as in the examples so far considered (*depends on, accelerates, produce, arises from, is performed by; requires an understanding of, cannot be handled by*). That was an oversimplification, and we now need to consider this relationship a little more closely.

The grammar of natural languages constructs a set of logical-semantic

Table 2 Common types of logical-semantic relation, with typical realization as conjunction and preposition

Expansion type	Category	Typical conjunction	Typical preposition
1 elaborating	expository	in other words; i.e.	namely
	exemplificatory	for example; e.g.	such as
2 extending	additive	and	besides
	alternative	or	instead of
	adversative	but	despite (in contrast)
3 enhancing	temporal	then (at that time)	after
	causal	so (for that reason)	because of
	conditional	then (in that case)	in the event of
	concessive	yet	despite (contrary to expectation)
	comparative	so (in that way)	like

relations: relations such as 'i.e.', 'e.g.', 'and', 'or', 'but', 'then', 'thus', 'so'. These are grammaticalized in various ways, typically (in English) by conjunctions and prepositions. There are many possible ways of categorizing these relations, depending on the criteria adopted; one schema that I find useful in applying the model of the grammar to discourse analysis is that shown in Table 2.[8]

In the type of clause that we are considering here, however, these relationships come to be lexicalized, as verbs; for example, the verbs *produce, arise from, depend on, lead to* as expressions of the causal relationship. Furthermore, this logical-semantic space is then crosscut along another dimension, according to whether the relationship is being set up in rebus or in verbis;[9] thus the causal relationship may be either (in rebus) '*a* causes *x*' or (in verbis) '*b* proves (= causes one to say) *y*'. Not all the logical-semantic relationships are lexicalized to the same extent; nor is this last distinction between relations in the events and relations in the discourse equally applicable to all. But the general pattern is as shown, with the experiential content entirely located within the two nominal groups and the verbal group setting up the relation between them. Table 3 lists some of the common verbs by which these logical-semantic relations are construed in lexical form.

Only a handful of these verbs occur in Newton's writings. The number has noticeably increased half a century later, in Joseph Priestley's *History and Present State of Electricity*; and by the time of James

Table 3 Examples of lexicalization of logical-semantic relations (as verbs)

Category	Examples of lexicalization (verbs)
expository	be represent constitute comprise signal reflect
exemplificatory	be exemplify illustrate
additive	accompany complement combine with
alternative	replace alternate with supplant
adversative	contrast with distinguish
temporal	follow precede anticipate co-occur with
causal	cause produce arise from lead to result in prove
conditional	correlate with be associated with apply to
concessive	contradict conflict with preclude
comparative	resemble compare with approximate to simulate

Note: Verbs in the same category are not, of course, synonymous, since they embody other features such as negative, causative. No distinction is shown here between "external" (in rebus) and "internal" (in verbis).

Clerk Maxwell's *An Elementary Treatise on Electricity*, after another 100 years, there are some hundreds of them in current use. My guess is that in modern scientific writing there are somewhere around 2,000, although in the early twentieth century a countertendency arose whereby the logical-semantic relationship is relexicalized, this time as a noun, and the verb is simply *be* or other lexical lightweight such as *have*, *bring*, *need*. The pattern is then '*a* is the cause of *x*', '*b* is the proof of *y*'; thus *is the cause of, is the result of, is a concomitant of, has as a consequence, is a representation of, is an alternative to; is the proof of, needs explanation as, is an illustration of, serves as evidence for*, etc. etc. Figure 2 displays some examples from a text in the *Scientific American*.

We can appreciate, I think, how such verbal representations are themselves also iconic. (1) There is a movement from a given Theme (background) to a rhematic New (foreground); this movement in time construes iconically the flow of information. (2) New semiotic entities are created by these nominal packages, like *rate of crack growth, left/right hemisphere activation, unusual refraction, resolution of the experimental difficulties*; the nominal expression in the grammar construes iconically an objectified entity in the real world. (3) The combination of (1) and (2) construes iconically the total reality in which we now live, a reality consisting of semiotic entities in a periodic flow of information – a flow that one might well say has now become a flood. The grammar constructs this world, as it has constructed (and continues to construct)

1 Theme	nominal group	the theoretical programme of devising models of atomic nuclei
Relation (extending: additive)	verbal group	has of course been ⟦complemented⟧ by
New	nominal group (noun: process)	experimental investigations
2 Theme	nominal group	the resulting energy level diagram
Relation (elaborating: expositive)	*be* + nominal group (noun: relation)	is in essence a ⟦representation⟧ of '*b* represents *γ*'
New	nominalization (rankshifted clause)	what nature allows the nucleus to do
3 Theme	nominal group (noun: process)	the resolution of the experimental difficulties
Relation (enhancing: causal)	*come* + nominal group (noun: relation)	came in the ⟦form⟧ of '*a* was resolved by *x*'
New	nominal group	an on-line isotope separation system

Figure 2 Examples showing logical-semantic relations lexicalized (1) as verb, (2) and (3) as noun (from J. H. Hamilton and J. A. Maruhn, "Exotic atomic nuclei", *Scientific American*, July 1986).

other worlds; and it does so, in this case, by this complex of semogenic strategies: "packaging" into extended nominal groups, nominalizing processes and properties, lexicalizing logical-semantic relations first as verbs and then as nouns, and constructing the whole into the sort of clause we meet with everywhere – not just in academic writing but in the newspapers, in the bureaucracy, and in our school textbooks – typified by the following from a primary school science text: *lung cancer death rates are clearly associated with increased smoking*. The grammar of a natural language is a theory of experience, a metalanguage of daily life; and the forms of verbal representation that evolved as part of modern science have penetrated into almost every domain of our semiotic practice.

★ ★ ★ ★ ★ ★ ★ ★ ★

2   The final paragraphs of *The Origin of Species*

Let me now move to the second part of the paper, which I realize will appear somewhat detached from the first, although I hope the overall direction will soon become clear. I am still taking as my "text" the language of science, but now contextualizing it within a more literary frame of reference. I said earlier that the concept of register, as functional variation in language, implies that our domain of inquiry is a text type rather than an individual text; we are interested in what is typical of this or that variety. In stylistics, on the other hand, we have traditionally been interested in the highly valued text as something that is unique, with the aim of showing precisely that it is not like any other texts. There are of course more or less codified genres of literature, text types showing similar text structures such as narrative fiction or lyric poetry; but there is no such thing as a literary register, or "literary English", as a functional variety of English.

Does this mean that we cannot have a highly valued text in some definable register such as the language of science? Clearly it does not. For one thing, we can treat any text as a unique semiotic object/event. If we take a piece of scientific writing and "read" it as a work of literature, we locate it in two value systems which intersect in a series of complementarities: (1) between the text as representing a register or type and the text as something unique; (2) between the traditional "two cultures", scientific and humanistic, the one privileging ideational meaning the other privileging interpersonal; (3) within the scientific, an analogous opposition between (in terms of eighteenth-century thought) the uniformity of the system and the diversity of natural processes, or (reinterpreted in modern terms) between order and chaos.[10]

But there are some texts which by their own birthright lie at the intersection of science and verbal art: which are not merely reconstituted in this dual mode by us as readers, but are themselves constituted out of the impact between scientific and poetic forces of meaning. I have written elsewhere about the crucial stanzas of Tennyson's *In Memoriam*, those which seem to me to lie at the epicentre of one such semiotic impact.[11] That is a text that would be categorized, in traditional terms, as elegiac poetry but containing certain passages with a scientific flavour or motif; and by studying its grammar we can get a sense of what that implies. In the text I am concerned with here, this relationship of "science" to "literature" is reversed: *The Origin of Species* will be classified in the library under "science", whereas in certain lights it appears as a highly poetic text. Interestingly, while in the Tennyson poem this impact is most strongly felt at a point more or less halfway through the text, here it is most striking at the very end – in the final two paragraphs, according to my own reading of the book. Text 1 (see Appendix) reproduces the two paragraphs in question.

Here Darwin not only sums up the position for which he has been arguing (over some 450 pages, in my edition)[12] but also defends it against the opposition and ridicule which he knew it was bound to evoke. The initial clause in the last sentence of all, *There is grandeur in this view of life*, presents a defiant, if perhaps rather forlorn, challenge to those whose only after-image of the text would be (as he foresaw) the humiliation of finding that they were descended from the apes.

I shall offer a very partial grammatical analysis of these paragraphs, taking account just of the two features discussed above: the "textual" organization of the clause in terms (1) of Theme–Rheme and (2) of Given–New. In embarking on this analysis, I was interested in finding out what rhetorical or discursive strategies Darwin was using, as he summed up his case and worked up to the resounding climax of that final clause: *from so simple a beginning endless forms most beautiful and most wonderful have been, and are being, evolved.* The patterning is not at all obvious; to me, at least, it did not stand out on the surface of the text. On the contrary, perhaps; one thing that makes this passage so effective may be that the reader is not presented with any explicit signal that 'this is the nature of my argument'.

Why then did I think that the clause-by-clause analysis of Theme and of New would be likely to reveal anything of interest? In general, these features of the clause grammar play a significant part in constructing the flow of the discourse. We have seen above, first, how they give texture to a single clause and, secondly, how they construe a pair of clauses into a coherent logical sequence, interacting with referential and lexical cohesion. In addition to this, the ongoing selection of elements functioning as Theme, and elements functioning as New, throughout a portion of a text is a major source of continuity and discursive power. In a seminal article written some ten years ago, on the status of Theme in discourse, Peter Fries showed that it was possible to relate Theme in the clause to the concepts of "method of development" and "main point" in composition theory.[13] Any motif that figured regularly as clause Theme could be seen to function as "method of development" in the text, while any motif that figured regularly as Rheme was likely to be functioning as "main point". Fries was concerned specifically with the category of Theme and so based his interpretation on the straightforward division of each clause into two parts, the Theme and the Rheme, treating the Rheme as equal in prominence with the Theme. This has the advantage with a written text that one does not need to give it the "implication of utterance", as is necessary if one wants to identify the element that is New. But the category of New is more appropriate, since it identifies prominence that is of a different kind and would therefore be expected to have a distinct function in the discourse; it is also more constraining, since not everything that is outside the Theme will fall within the New.[14] Here therefore I shall take it that what constitutes the "main point" of the discourse is any motif that figures regularly as New. The third reason for analysing this aspect of the grammar of the text, then, is that the analysis reveals a great deal about the organization of the discourse. All these considerations would of course apply to any text. But in many texts these patterns are near the surface, and emerge very quickly once one begins to read them carefully; whereas here they come to light only when one consciously attends to the grammatical structure.

Text 2 (see Appendix) shows the Theme in each ranking clause throughout the text.[15]

The grouping of these into motifs is set out in diagrammatic form in Figure 3. The first motif that emerges (numbered I in Figure 3) is very clearly that of authority, beginning with the Theme of the first clause *authors of the highest eminence*. This, when followed by *seem to be fully satisfied*, becomes solidary with a passage in the final paragraph of an earlier chapter where, mentioning a number of authorities who have (contra Darwin) *maintained the immutability of species*, he then goes on: *But I have reason to believe that one great authority, Sir Charles Lyell, from further reflexion entertains grave doubts on this subject.*[16] The motif of authority is thus already given, constructed out of the morphological relationship of *authors = authorities*. Darwin now extends it in a sequence of clause Themes as follows:

authors of the highest eminence – the Creator [to my mind] – I – we

By this thematic progression Darwin establishes his own claim to authority, wherewith to dispute and override these authors of the highest eminence. He first appeals to the Creator – but being careful to precede this with the interpersonal Theme *to my mind*, which both protects him against the arrogance of claiming to know the Creator's purposes and, by a neat metafunctional slip (from interpersonal "me" to ideational "me"),[17] leads naturally from his role as interpreter of the Creator's design to his position as an authority in his own right. This *I*

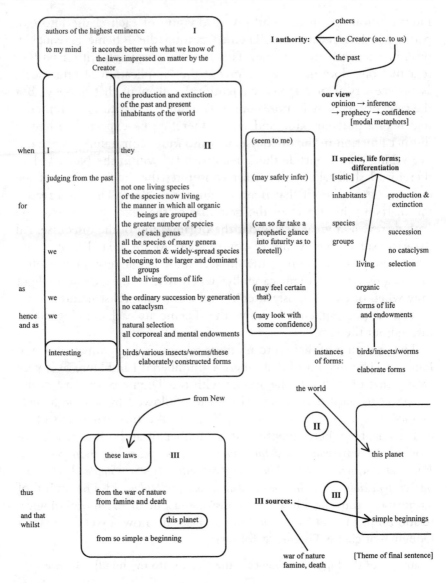

Figure 3 Motifs constructed as theme

is then modulated to *we*, in *we can so far take a prophetic glance into futurity*; preceded by a hypotactic clause (also thematic) *judging from the past*, which – without saying who or what is doing the judging (since it is non-finite and so needs no Subject) – justifies the assumption that "I" am in fact speaking on behalf of us all. Thus the clause Themes

180

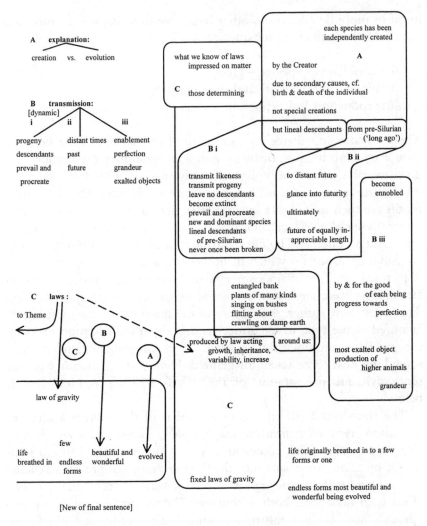

Figure 4 Motifs constructed as new

have by this point securely underpinned Darwin's own status as an authority; and this thematic motif is now abandoned.

Meanwhile, it has begun to be overtaken by another motif (numbered II), that of species, life forms, and their differentiation; first introduced as *the production and extinction of the past and present inhabitants of the world*. Since this is the principal motif of the whole book (as embodied in the title), it is natural for it to be set up by the grammar as one of the Themes of these final paragraphs. If we focus on this motif in more detail, on the other hand, we find that it is constructed out of three interlocking sub-motifs:

(i)   inhabitants – species – groups
(ii) living – forms of life and their endowments
(iii) production and extinction – succession – selection

These are developed side by side in the form of fairly long nominal groups which bring out, through their lexicogrammar, the number and diversity of species, the collocation of 'species' with 'life', and the steady, irreversible forward progression through time; the three sub-motifs are then united in a specific reference to *birds, various insects* and *worms (these elaborately constructed forms)*, which is the final appearance of this motif as Theme. The effect is one of a massive and powerful life-engendering process – which is, however, presented synoptically as an objectified 'state of affairs', since words representing processes are in fact nominalized: *production, extinction, succession, (no) cataclysm, selection*. This, as we saw earlier, is a feature of the grammar of the most highly favoured clause type in scientific writing: the nominalization picks up the preceding argument and presents it in this "objectified" form as something now to be taken for granted. Here it also contrasts with the more dynamic presentation of the motifs figuring as New (see B below).

The third motif (III in Figure 3) is that of the sources leading to speciation: *these laws; from the war of nature, famine and death; from so simple a beginning*. This comes in almost at the end; and Darwin leads into it by taking over *laws* into the Theme from the previous Rheme (*. . . produced by laws acting around us. These laws . . .*; cf. C below). The effect is to juxtapose, both within the Theme (and hence, being also "given", both to be construed as something already established), the two conflicting principles in nature – its lawfulness, and its lawlessness – which together by their dialectic interaction account for the origin of species.

I shall return below to the extraordinary final sentence of the text. Meanwhile let us consider the motifs that constitute the "main point" of the argument, as these appear clause by clause with the grammatical function of the New.[18] These are shown in Text 3 (see Appendix) and set out diagrammatically in Figure 4.

The first such motif (lettered A in Figure 4) is that of alternative explanations: specifically, creation versus evolution. It may be helpful to set the wordings out in a list:

182

> has been independently created
> due to secondary causes
> those [causes] determining the birth and death of the individual
> not as special creation (but as . . .)
> the lineal descendants
> long before the first bed of the Silurian system was deposited

The final one of these is the last appearance of this motif until the very last words of the text (. . . *have been, and are being, evolved*); meanwhile, via the two semantic features of generation (*lineal descendants*) and antiquity (*long before the first bed . . .*), it leads us in to the second of the "new" motifs, that of transmission – or better, transmitting, since the way the grammar constructs it is at least as much clausal as nominal.[19]

Like the second of the thematic motifs, this second motif within the New (B in Figure 4) is also constructed out of three sub-motifs:

   (i) progeny: (leave) descendants – (become) extinct – (procreate) new and dominant species
  (ii) time: remote past – distant futurity (*a secure future of inappreciable length*)
 (iii) ennoblement: (become) ennobled – (progress) towards perfection – most exalted object – the production of higher animals

The first two of these co-occur; the third is introduced at the beginning of this motif (*become ennobled*), then left aside and taken up again after the sub-motifs of progeny and time have been established. The message line is that descendancy across the ages equals ennoblement, and that this process will continue in the future as it has done in the past. The effect of associating the 'evolutionary' motifs of progeny and time with this one of ennoblement is to collocate evolution with positively loaded interpersonal expressions like *by and for the good of each being, towards perfection* and so on; this might serve to make such an unpalatable concept slightly less threatening and more acceptable.

There is then a short, transitional motif comprised of the environment in which the diversity of species (the birds, insects, etc. of II above) can be appreciated: *an entangled bank, plants of many kinds, (singing) on bushes, flitting about, (crawling) through the damp earth.* This could perhaps be seen as an appendage to B above, illustrating the progress towards perfection; but it is also transitional, via the search for explanation (*have all been produced by*), to the final motif (lettered C in Figure 4) which is broached as *laws acting around us.* These laws are then enumerated, as a long list of nominal groups, all with embedded

Table 4 Summary of motifs constructing Theme and New of ranking clauses in final two paragraphs of *The Origin of Species*

Theme ("method of development")   *New* ("main point")

I	authorities	A		explanation
II	the phenomenon of species:	B		the process of evolution:
	(i) inhabitants & groups		(i)	transmission & procreation
	(ii) life form & endowments		(ii)	time: past – future
	(iii) variation		(iii)	ennoblement
III	sources (law/war of nature)	C		law (natural selection)

phrases and/or clauses in them and all functioning as the final element in the one ranking clause – a clause which is (anomalously) non-finite, despite being the main and only clause in the sentence.[20]

Up to this point, then (that is, up to the final sentence of the final paragraph), the clauses are rather clearly organized, through their textual functions of Theme (in Theme–Rheme) and New (in Given–New), around a small number of distinct but interlocking motifs. We could summarize this pattern as in Table 4 above. Then, in the final sentence, the motifs of II, III, B and C are all brought together: and in an extremely complex pattern. The sentence begins with *There is grandeur in this view of life* ... Here *grandeur*, which relates to B(iii), is unusual in being at the same time both Theme and New; hence it is doubly prominent.[21] On a first reading, *in this view of life* seems to complete the clause; and since it is anaphorically cohesive (by reference *this*, and by lexical repetition of *life*) it is read as not only Rheme but also Given. It then turns out that Darwin has misled us with a grammatical pun, and that *life* actually begins a new clause, *life ... having been originally breathed into a few forms or into one*, all of which is a projected Qualifier to *view* ('the view that life was originally breathed ...'). This makes *life* thematic, and (since no longer anaphoric) a continuation of the motif of life forms in II(ii); this motif is then carried on into the New, in *(breathed) into a few forms or into one*. The next clause turns out to be another projected Qualifier to *view*, paratactically related to the last yet finite where the other was non-finite; furthermore it is a hypotactic clause complex in which the dependent clause comes first. The dependent clause has as Theme *this planet*, relating cohesively to *the world* at the very beginning of II(i): and as New (*has gone cycling on*) *according to the fixed law of gravity*, where *law of gravity* derives from motif C (natural laws) but shifts the attention from the temporally organized world of biology to the timeless universe of physics. The final clause, the culmination of the projected *view* in which there is *grandeur*, has the Theme from III (*from so simple a beginning*, with anaphoric *so*); the Rheme takes up the motifs of II, *endless forms*, and B(iii), *most beautiful and most wonderful*, leading to the final New element, the verbal group *have been, and are being, evolved*.

This resounding lexicogrammatical cadence brings the clause, the sentence, the paragraph, the chapter and the book to a crashing conclusion with a momentum to which I can think of no parallel elsewhere in literature – perhaps only Beethoven has produced comparable effects, and that in another medium altogether. Phonologically, the coordination of *have been, and are being*, forces a break in the rhythm (further reinforced by the surrounding commas) that directs maximum bodyweight on to the final word *evolved*. Grammatically, the word *evolved* has to resolve the expectation set up by the ellipsis in the uncompleted verbal group *have been*. Semantically, *evolved* has to resolve the conflict between *so simple a beginning* and *endless forms most beautiful and most wonderful*. All that is only what the word is expected to achieve within its own clause. In addition, within the projected clause complex, it has to complete the complex proportion between physical and biological processes:

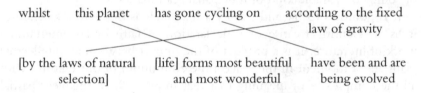

whilst   this planet   has gone cycling on   according to the fixed law of gravity

[by the laws of natural selection]   [life] forms most beautiful and most wonderful   have been and are being evolved

as well as another one set up with the preceding clause:

life   having been originally breathed   into a few forms or into one

from so simple a beginning   endless forms   have been . . . evolved

Within the sentence, the word *evolved* has to carry a culminative prominence to match the initiating prominence carried by *grandeur* (as Theme / New) at the beginning. Within these two paragraphs, it has to pick up the thematic motif of explanation, and to secure total commitment to one explanation and rejection of the other. It is here that the selection of voice becomes important: since the verbal group is passive, the responsibility for evolution is clearly lodged with the Creator (there is an external agency at hand; it is not . . . *have been, and are, evolving*). Yet all this load of work is hardly worth mentioning beside the major responsibility the word *evolved* has to bear, along with the verbal group of which it is a part: that of sustaining the climax of 450 pages of intense scientific argument. This is the culmination towards which the entire text has been building up. It would be hard to find anywhere in English a sentence, or a clause, or a group, or a word that has been made to carry such an awesome semiotic load.

I do not know how long it took Darwin to compose these two paragraphs, or whether he reflected consciously on their construction as he was doing it – I imagine not. I certainly had no idea, when starting the analysis, of what I was going to find. I had the sense of a remarkable and powerful piece of writing, as the climax to a remarkable and powerful book; and it struck me that something of the effect of these two paragraphs might lie in the patterning of the Theme and of the New – that is, in the textual component within the grammar of the clause. It is important to stress that that is in fact all that I have been looking at in this paper; I have said almost nothing about cohesion or transitivity or mood or the clause complex or any of the other lexicogrammatical systems / processes that go into the makeup of a text. Some, at least, of these other features would undoubtedly show interesting and significant patterns if we were to analyse them with this or some comparable kind of functional grammatics.

It is pointless to try and classify a text such as this – to ask whether it 'is' a scientific treatise or a declaration of faith or an entertaining work of literature. It is a product of the impact between an intellectual giant and a moment in the space-time continuum of our culture, with all the complexity of meaning that that implies. With this very partial analysis – a fragment of the grammar of a fragment of the text – I have tried to suggest something of how this text takes its place in semo-history. Some of the thematic patterning here is like that which I described in the first part of the paper, which evolved primarily (I think) in the context of scientific endeavour; we can recognize instances where Darwin is backgrounding some point already covered, so getting it taken for granted, and moving on from it, by a logical-semantic "process", to a foregrounded next stage; e.g. *from the war of nature . . . the production of the higher animals directly follows.* (There are more of this type in the more strictly "scientific" passages; for example the account of the honeycomb in Chapter 7, pp. 255–6.) But the pattern has rather a different value here from that which it typically has in the context in which it evolved; Darwin's strategy is that of accumulating masses of evidence rather than moving forward logically one step at a time. And particularly at critical moments he moves into a more monumental mode, that of a writer producing a text which he knows is unique and will have a unique place in the history of ideas. What is important is that we should be able to use the same theory and method of linguistic analysis – the same "grammatics" – whatever kind of text (or subtext) we are trying to interpret, whether Tennyson or Darwin, Mother Goose or the *Scientific American*. Otherwise, if we simply approach each text with an *ad hoc* do-it-yourself kit of private commentary, we have no way of explaining their similarities and their differences – the aesthetic and functional values that differentiate one text from another, or one voice from another within the frontiers of the same text.

Notes

1. That is, there are many "disjunctions"; see J. L. Lemke, *Semiotics and Education*, (1984) Toronto: Victoria University (Toronto Semiotic Circle, Monographs, Working Papers and Prepublications), 1984; especially pp. 132 ff. Dialectal disjunctions are mainly phonetic; cf. the Prague School's concept of functional equilibrium in phonology.
2. The term "diatypic" is taken from Michael Gregory, "Aspects of varieties differentiation", *Journal of Linguistics* 3, 1967. The term "register" was first used in this sense by T. B. W. Reid in "Linguistics, structuralism, philology", Archivum Linguisticum 8, 1956; cf. M. A. K. Halliday, Angus McIntosh and Peter Strevens, 1964.
3. See Ruqaiya Hasan, "Semantic variation and sociolinguistics", *Australian Journal of Linguistics* (1989).
4. The concept of register should therefore be defined so as to make explicit the dimension of power, as pointed out by Gunther Kress, "Textual matters: the social effectiveness of style", and Norman Fairclough, "Register, power and socio-semantic change", both in David Birch and Michael O'Toole (1988).
5. See M. A. K. Halliday, "On the language of physical science", in Mohsen Ghadessy (1999).
6. For this and other aspects of the systemic-functional grammar referred to throughout this paper see M. A. K. Halliday (1985a).
7. The Given + New structure is not, in fact, a structure of the clause; it constructs a separate unit (the "information unit") realized by intonation as a tone group. In spoken English the typical (unmarked) discourse pattern is that where one information unit is mapped on to one clause; further semantic contrasts are then created by departure from this unmarked mapping. In written English there are of course no direct signals of the information unit; while the unmarked mapping may be

taken as the typical pattern, a great deal of systematic variation will show up if the text is read aloud.

8. This is, obviously, a very sketchy and selective account. See Halliday (1985a, Chapters 7 and 9; and Table 9(3), pp. 306–7).

9. For this distinction see M. A. K. Halliday and Ruqaiya Hasan (1976, Chapter 5, "Conjunction", especially pp. 240–44). Here we refer to "external" (in rebus) and "internal" (in verbis) conjunctive relations.

10. We do not of course transcend these oppositions; the nearest we get to a position of neutrality, in the sense of being able to accommodate the complementarities on a higher stratum, is in the discourse of mathematics and of linguistics – as thematic rather than disciplinary discourses (perhaps now computer science and semiotics).

11. "Poetry as scientific discourse: the nuclear sections of Tennyson's *In Memoriam*", in David Birch and Michael O'Toole (1988). [See also Chapter 5, this volume.]

12. Charles Darwin, *The Origin of Species by Means of Natural Selection*, with a new foreword by Patricia Horan, New York: Avenel Books, 1979.

13. See Peter H. Fries, "On the status of Theme in English: arguments from discourse", *Forum Linguisticum* 6, 1981. For more recent discussions by the same author see Peter H. Fries (1994, 1995, 1996, 1997).

14. The boundary between Given and New is in any case fairly indeterminate. What is clearly marked by the intonation contour is the information focus: that is, the culmination of the New (signalled by tonic prominence). There is some prosodic indication where the New element begins, but it is much less clear (hence the move from Given to New is often regarded as continuous). See also note 19 below.

15. Ranking clauses are those which are not embedded (rankshifted); they enter as clauses (either alone, or in paratactic or hypotactic relation with others) into clause complexes (sentences). Embedded clauses are not considered, because they do not enter into clause complexes but function inside the structure of a nominal group, and present little choice of textual (thematic or informational) organization; thus their Theme–Rheme and Given–New structure has no significance for the overall patterning of the discourse.

16. Chapter 9, "Imperfection of the geological record".

17. In *to my mind* the "me" has no role in the transitivity structure (no ideational function). In *when I view . . .*, the same "me" has been transformed into a thinker, with a highly significant role in transitivity – as Senser in a mental process; note here also the lexical slip from *view* = "observe", suggested by *when I view all beings*, to *view* = "opine", a reinterpretation forced on the reader by the subsequent *as*.

18. Based on my own reading of the text: on the construction into information units and location of information focus.

19. This option is not available to a motif functioning as Theme, since

(almost) all thematic elements are nominals (any clause functioning as Theme has first to be nominalized). Instances such as *transmit likeness, transmit progeny, have left no descendants*, etc., illustrate the point made in note 14 above; in my reading the New could be heard as beginning with the verb in each case. I have used the more cautious interpretation, restricting it in most instances to the final (culminative) element.

20. I have treated all these as falling within the New, rather than attempting to analyse them further; a list tends to have special rhythmic and tonal properties of its own.

21. That is, it clearly represents a "marked" mapping of information structure on to thematic structure, characteristic of such existential clauses.

APPENDIX
Text 1

From Charles Darwin, *The Origin of Species by Means of Natural Selection*, London: J. Murray, 1859

Authors of the highest eminence seem to be fully satisfied with the view that each species has been independently created. To my mind it accords better with what we know of the laws impressed on matter by the Creator, that the production and extinction of the past and present inhabitants of the world should have been due to secondary causes, like those determining the birth and death of the individual. When I view all beings not as special creations, but as the lineal descendants of some few beings which lived long before the first bed of the Silurian system was deposited, they seem to me to become ennobled. Judging from the past, we may safely infer that not one living species will transmit its unaltered likeness to a distant futurity. And of the species now living very few will transmit progeny of any kind to a far distant futurity; for the manner in which all organic beings are grouped, shows that the greater number of species of each genus, and all the species of many genera, have left no descendants, but have become utterly extinct. We can so far take a prophetic glance into futurity as to fortell that it will be the common and widely-spread species, belonging to the larger and dominant groups, which will ultimately prevail and procreate new and dominant species. As all the living forms of life are the lineal descendants of those which lived long before the Silurian epoch, we may feel certain that the ordinary succession by generation has never once been broken, and that no cataclysm has desolated the whole world. Hence we may look with some confidence to a secure future of equally inappreciable length. And as natural selection works solely by and for the good of each being, all corporeal and mental endowments will tend to progress towards perfection.

It is interesting to contemplate an entangled bank, clothed with many plants of many kinds, with birds singing on the bushes, with various insects flitting about, and with worms crawling through the damp earth, and to reflect that these elaborately constructed forms, so different from each other, and dependent on each other in so complex a manner, have all been produced by laws acting around us. These laws, taken in the largest sense, being Growth with Reproduction; Inheritance which is almost implied by reproduction; Variability from the indirect and direct action of the external conditions of life, and from use and disuse; a Ratio of Increase so high as to lead to a Struggle for Life, and as a consequence to Natural Selection, entailing Divergence of Character and the Extinction of less-improved forms. Thus, from the war of nature, from famine and death, the most exalted object which we are capable of conceiving, namely, the production of the higher animals, directly follows. There is grandeur in this view of life, with its several powers, having been originally breathed into a few forms or into one; and that, whilst this planet has gone cycling on according to the fixed law of gravity, from so simple a beginning endless forms most beautiful and most wonderful have been, and are being, evolved.

Text 2

The text showing Theme–Rheme structure (Theme underlined)

Authors of the highest eminence seem to be fully satisfied with the view that each species has been independently created. To my mind it accords better with what we know of the laws impressed on matter by the Creator, that the production and extinction of the past and present inhabitants of the world should have been due to secondary causes, like those determining the birth and death of the individual. When I view all beings not as special creations, but as the lineal descendants of some few beings which lived long before the first bed of the Silurian system was deposited, they seem to me to become ennobled. Judging from the past, we may safely infer that not one living species will transmit its unaltered likeness to a distant futurity. And of the species now living very few will transmit progeny of any kind to a far distant futurity; for the manner in which all organic beings are grouped, shows that the greater number of species of each genus, and all the species of many genera, have left no descendants, but have become utterly extinct. <u>We can so far take a prophetic glance into futurity as to fortell that it will be the common and widely-spread species, belonging to the larger and dominant groups</u>, which will ultimately prevail and procreate new and dominant species. <u>As all the living forms of life</u> are the lineal descendants of those which lived long before the Silurian epoch, <u>we</u> may feel certain <u>that the ordinary succession by generation</u> has never once been broken, and <u>that no cataclysm</u> has desolated the whole world. <u>Hence</u> we may look with some confidence to a secure future of equally inappreciable length. <u>And as natural selection</u> works solely by and for the good of each being, <u>all corporeal and mental endowments</u> will tend to progress towards perfection.

<u>It is interesting</u> to contemplate an entangled bank, clothed with many plants of many kinds, with <u>birds</u> singing on the bushes, with <u>various insects</u> flitting about, and with <u>worms</u> crawling through the damp earth, and to reflect <u>that these elaborately constructed forms</u>, so different from each other, and dependent on each other in so complex a manner, have all been produced by laws acting around us. <u>These laws</u>, taken in the largest sense, being Growth with Reproduction; Inheritance which is almost implied by reproduction; Variability from the indirect and direct action of the external conditions of life, and from use and disuse; a Ratio of Increase so high as to lead to a Struggle for Life, and as a consequence to Natural Selection, entailing Divergence of Character and the Extinction of less-improved forms. <u>Thus, from the war of nature, from famine and death</u>, the most exalted object which we are capable of conceiving, namely, the production of the higher animals, directly follows. <u>There is grandeur</u> in this view <u>of life</u>, with its several powers, having been originally breathed into a few forms or into one; <u>and that, whilst this planet</u> has gone cycling on according to the fixed law of gravity, <u>from so simple a beginning</u> endless forms most beautiful and most wonderful have been, and are being, evolved.

Text 3

The text showing Given–New structure (New underlined)

Authors of the highest eminence seem to be fully satisfied with the view that each species <u>has been independently created</u>. To my mind it accords better with <u>what we know of the laws impressed on matter by the Creator</u>, that the production and extinction of the past and present inhabitants of the world should have been <u>due to secondary causes</u>, like those determining the birth and death of the individual. When I view all beings not as special creations, but as the lineal descendants of some few beings which lived long before the first bed of the Silurian system was deposited, they seem to me to become ennobled. Judging from the past, we may safely infer that not one living species will transmit its unaltered likeness to a distant futurity. And of the species now living very few will transmit progeny of any kind to a far distant futurity; for the manner in which all organic beings are grouped, shows that the greater number of species of each genus, and all the species of many genera, have left no descendants, but have become utterly extinct. We can so far take a prophetic glance into futurity as to fortell that it will be the common and widely-spread species, belonging to the larger and dominant groups, which will ultimately prevail and procreate new and dominant species. As all the living forms of life are the lineal descendants of those which lived long before the Silurian epoch, we may feel certain that the ordinary succession by generation has never once been broken, and that no cataclysm has desolated the whole world. Hence we may look with some confidence to a secure future of equally inappreciable length. And as natural selection works solely by and for the good of each being, all corporeal and mental endowments will tend to progress towards perfection.

It is interesting to contemplate an entangled bank, clothed with many plants of many kinds, with birds singing on the bushes, with various insects flitting about, and with worms crawling through the damp earth, and to reflect that these elaborately constructed forms, so different from each other, and dependent on each other in so complex a manner, have all been produced by laws acting around us. These laws, taken in the largest sense, being Growth with Reproduction; Inheritance which is almost implied by reproduction; Variability from the indirect and direct action of the external conditions of life, and from use and disuse; a Ratio of Increase so high as to lead to a Struggle for Life, and as a consequence to Natural Selection, entailing Divergence of Character and the Extinction of less-improved forms. Thus, from the war of nature, from famine and death, the most exalted object which we are capable of conceiving, namely, the production of the higher animals, directly follows. There is grandeur in this view of life, with its several powers, having been originally breathed into a few forms or into one, and that, whilst this planet has gone cycling on according to the fixed law of gravity, from so simple a beginning endless forms most beautiful and most wonderful have been, and are being, evolved.

PART THREE

EVERYDAY TEXTS
(WRITTEN, SPOKEN)

EDITOR'S INTRODUCTION

Presented here are the analyses of two examples of what may be referred to as 'everyday texts'. The first is a written text, the ZPG (Zero Population Growth) text; the second is a spoken text, taken from the culminative phase of a dissertation defence. Halliday approaches both as a grammarian, bringing them under grammatical scrutiny, attempting to show 'the grammar at work creating meaning'. Not only are the analyses interesting for what they reveal about the texts under investigation, but also instructive in the practice and methods of systemic grammar analysis. In both cases, Halliday stresses the fact that the analysis is by no means complete. As he points out, 'a rich interpretation of the grammar of any text would itself constitute a text of vastly greater length than the original.' Rather, he focuses on those systems that relate clearly to the functions of the text in its particular context of culture.

'Some lexicogrammatical features of the *Zero Population Growth* text' first appeared in 1991 in a collection of papers showing different analytical approaches applied by various authors to the same text, the ZPG text, which is an instance of a fund-raising letter. Halliday refers to his analysis as a 'partial interpretation', covering theme; information structure; mood and modality; transitivity; clause complexes; lexical cohesion; nominalization and grammatical metaphor. In terms of theme, Halliday notes how 'The thematic movement of the text clearly bears out Fries' interpretation of clause Theme in terms of the rhetorical concept of "method of development" (Fries 1981).' Based on the tonics of the text arrived at through reading the text aloud, Halliday attempts to establish the information structure emerging from the text. Looking next at mood and modality, including the writer's use of tense, and mood type – whether declarative or imperative, Halliday notes the single modalization occurring in the text, i.e. *may be*, and observes how this expression of probability 'has added a feature of tentativeness to the argument that your support now is critical (this may be our best opportunity, but it is important not to be too definite about that because we may want to ask for your support again later on.)' While for the most part, Halliday steers away from making evaluative comments about the text, still occasionally his findings prompt him to do so. As when, for example, doing the transitivity analysis, Halliday observed no clear pattern of movement from one kind of process to another, leading him to conclude 'that the text lacked direction in its chosen field; it seemed not to be "going anywhere", not even round in a circle.' Halliday's strategy for exploring the writer's use of grammatical metaphor is particularly noteworthy. To arrive at a more congruent form of the text, he reworded the text along the lines of 'how would I say this to a 12-year-old?' Halliday describes it as 'an intuitive venture at making the text more accessible'. The rewording of the text brings to the fore the following three features of the original text: clichés, ambiguities, and grammatical metaphors, each of which Halliday examines in turn.

In 'So you say "pass" . . . thank you three muchly' (1994) Halliday analyses the designated "core" passage from a dissertation defence. The subtext being investigated amounts to approximately 12.5 minutes of spoken text, and begins with one of the speakers saying, "So you say 'pass'", and ends with the same speaker's closing, "thank you three muchly". Halliday presents 'a clause-by-clause analysis of the subtext in respect of the systems of theme, information, transitivity, mood, modality and key; and an analysis of each clause complex by interdependency and expansion/projection.' His focus is 'on the wording: on patterns of selection at the lexicogrammatical level.' The dissertation defence is described as 'a lexicogrammatical event', one which exemplifies 'the power of discourse to change the environment that engendered it'. Explaining, Halliday states, 'We might want to think of the entire text as a kind of expanded performative: "We dub thee PhD." But this would obscure a more fundamental point, which is that *every* text is performative in this sense. There can be no semiotic act that leaves the world exactly as it was before.'

Chapter Seven

SOME LEXICOGRAMMATICAL
FEATURES OF THE
ZERO POPULATION GROWTH TEXT
(1992)

Introduction

This paper presents a partial interpretation of the ZPG text (see Appendix 3, p. 287) using systemic grammar. It consists of seven sections: (1) Theme; (2) Information structure; (3) Mood and modality; (4) Transitivity; (5) Clause complexes; (6) Lexical cohesion; (7) Nominalization and grammatical metaphor.[1]

I have used the suggested numbering of the portions of the text, in 30 segments. Of these 30, Segments 1–3 and 24–28 (a total of 8), while they have distinct functions in the structure and format of a letter, have almost none of the features of a clause; they are "clausettes" in the terminology of the Nigel grammar (Matthiessen 1985, pp. 102–3).

(1–3)   Title ▲ Date ▲ Address;
(24–28)   Valediction ▲ Signature ▲ Signatory ▲ Status ▲ Coda-signal

Four of them (24–27) could be regarded as forming a clausette complex, of structure xβ, α1, α=21, α2=2 (see Figure 1; for analysis and notation see Halliday 1985a, pp. 193–202).[2] Apart from occasional references to §3, I have ignored these segments in the present treatment.

First published in *Discourse Description: Diverse Linguistic Analyses of a Fund-raising Text*, edited by William C. Mann and Sandra A. Thompson. Amsterdam: John Benjamins, 1992, pp. 327–58.

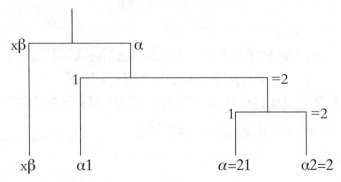

Figure 1   Segments 24–27 as "clausette complex"

This leaves 22 segments of the discourse. Of these, 13 consist of a single clause ("clause simplex"); the remainder are clause complexes, 4 with two and 5 with three clauses, as follows:

1 clause:	§§ 4 5 8 9 10 12 13 16 17 18 20 22 29	= 13
2 clauses:	§§ 11 14 15 23	(2×4) = 8
3 clauses:	§§ 6 7 19 21 30	(3×5) = 15
		Total = 36

giving a total of 36 clauses in all. Note that these are ranking clauses; embedded clauses, which are rankshifted to become constituents of nominal groups (there are 19 of these), do not participate in the clause-complex structure of the text. Where there is more than one ranking clause within a segment these will be indicated with capital letters A, B, C in the order in which they occur. In § 11, clause B is enclosed inside clause A; in § 14, for simplicity, the initial *but* is assigned to the clause *but to use it well*, which therefore becomes clause A. The analysis of the clause complexes is presented in Section 5; embedded clauses are also listed in that section.

As always in text grammar, alternative interpretations are possible at numerous points. Ideally, all should be offered and discussed; but this takes too long. Instead, one or two instances have been referred to, so as to suggest the kinds of consideration that apply.

1   Theme

Table 1 shows the Theme of each ranking clause, including textual, interpersonal and topical (experiential) Theme. Whatever is not shown

Table 1 Themes of ranking clauses

Clause no.	Theme: textual	Inter-personal	Topical	marked / unmarked
4			at 7 a.m. on October 25	marked
5			calls	unmarked
6A			staffers	unmarked
B			—	
C			—	unmarked
7A	when		we	unmarked
B			we	unmarked
C			we	unmarked
8			media and public reaction	unmarked
9	at first		the deluge of calls	unmarked
10	now		we	unmarked
11A			ZPG's 1985 Urban Stress Test	unmarked
B			—	
12			it	unmarked
13			the Urban Stress Test	unmarked
14A	but		—	
B			we	unmarked
15A			our small staff	unmarked
B	and		our modest resources	unmarked
16			your support now	unmarked
17			ZPG's 1985 Urban Stress Test	unmarked
18			with your contribution	marked
19A	even though		our national government	unmarked
B			we	unmarked
C			—	
20			every day	marked
21A			—	
B			—	
C			both elected officials and the American public	unmarked
22		please	make	unmarked
23A			whatever you give – $25 or as much as you can	unmarked
B			—	
29			the results of ZPG's 1985 Urban Stress Test	unmarked
30A			I	unmarked
B			you	unmarked
C			—	

as Theme is the Rheme; clauses where no Theme is shown consist entirely of Rheme.

For Theme see Halliday 1985a, Chapter 3 passim. The Theme is realized by initial position in the clause; it includes the first element that has a function in transitivity (the "topical" Theme), together with any other elements that precede it; for example *well* + *then* + *surely* + *that* in *well then surely that's the end of the affair*.

As will be noted, almost all topical Themes are unmarked; that is, the Theme is conflated with Subject in declarative and with Predicator in imperative.[3] Hence the three that are marked stand out, and two of them have a significant function in the construction of the text. One of these is the Theme of the text-initiating clause (§ 4), *at 7 a.m. on October 25*, which sets the text plan – deceptively, as it turns out – to narrative, by looking like an Orientation; the other is *with your contribution* (§ 18), which finally disposes of the earlier one and reveals the nature of the text as a begging letter. The third of the marked Themes, *every day* (§ 20), introduces a subroutine of 'constantly', perhaps contrasting with the initial time-frame *at 7 a.m. on October 25* but also setting the scene for the intensified imperative Theme *please make* ('so do something') in § 22. So the marked Themes tell their own rather explicit story: 'here's what happened one day – now about your contribution – here's what happens every day – so please!'

Let us now consider the Themes of all ranking clauses, unmarked as well as marked. After the initial time-frame we find eight clauses (§ 5–10) having as Theme *calls, staffers/we, media/calls, we* – alternating between them and us, outsiders and insiders; these are followed by three clauses having the *Urban Stress Test* as Theme (§ 11–13). In other words, having first constructed the theme of 'our relations with the media and the public', the writer then goes on to thematize 'what we did (that brought this about)'. The Theme now returns to 'us' (§ 14–15); but now it is 'poor us' (*our small staff, our modest resources*), so that when it shifts over to 'you' (*your support now*, and the marked *with your contribution*, in § 16–18) it is clear in what role 'you' are being expected to take part.

There is then a brief digression, where the Theme shifts to *our national government* and then (after the marked *every day*) to *both elected officials and the American public*; this serves as the context for again returning to 'you' as Theme, in *please make* (which has the only interpersonal Theme in the text), followed by the long embedded clause thematizing 'your money' (§ 19–23). Interspersed with the 'you' Themes, the Urban Stress Test appears in § 17 immediately before *with your contribution*, and now in § 29 just before the final segment. In § 30, for the only time in the letter, the writer uses *I*; and the thematic move from 'I' to 'you' in *I hope you'll help* gives the required personal flavour to the carefully contrived little postscript.

The thematic movement of the text clearly bears out Fries' interpretation of clause Theme in terms of the rhetorical concept of "method of development" (Fries 1981, 1994, 1996, 1997). We could diagram this movement as in Figure 2.

2 Information structure (Given and New; information focus)

I read the text aloud, to make explicit its "implication of utterance" (Firth 1968, pp. 30–31). Below is the transcription, in systemic notation. (See Halliday 1967b. Note that the **bold** type identifies the information focus, which is the culmination of the New element – the part that is presented as "for the listener's attention".)

3 //1 dear / friend of / Z P / **G** //

4 //3 ˏ at / seven a / **m** on Oc //3 tober twenty / **fifth** our //1 **phones** / started to / ring //

5 //1 calls / jammed our / switchboard / all / **day** //

6 //1 staffers stayed / late into the / **night** //3 answering / **questions** and //3 talking with re/**porters** from //3 **newspapers** //3 **radio** stations //3 **wire** services and T//1 **V** stations in //1 every / part of the / **country** //

7 //4 when we re/leased the re/sults of / ZPG's / nineteen eighty five / Urban / **Stress** / Test we had //1 no i/**dea** we'd get //1 such an over/ whelming re/**sponse** //

8 //3 media and / public re/**action** has been //1 nothing / short of in/**credible** //

9 //4 ˏ at / **first** the //4 deluge of / calls came / **mostly** from re/ /1 porters / eager to / tell the / public about / Urban / Stress Test re/**sults** //4 ˏ and from / outraged / public of/**ficials** who were //1 furious that we had / blown the / **whistle** on con//1 ditions in / their / **cities** //

10 //4 **now** we're / hearing from con//4 cerned / **citizens** in //3 all / parts of the / **country** who / want to know //3 what they can / **do** to hold //1 local of/ficials ac/**countable** for / tackling

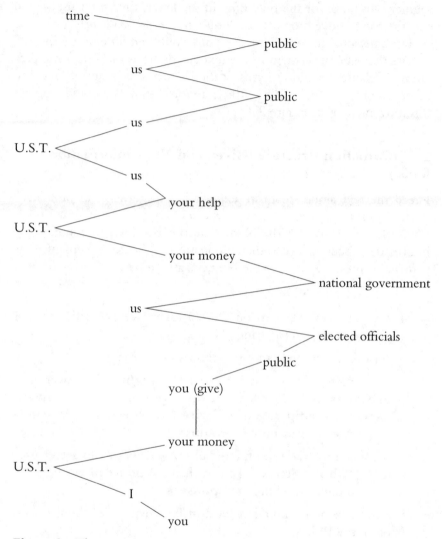

Figure 2 Thematic progression

//3 population re/lated / **problems** that //1 threaten / public /
health and / **well-being** //

11 //4 Z P / G's / nineteen eighty / five / Urban / **Stress** Test //
4 . cre/ated after / months of per/sistent and ex/haustive re/
search //3 . is the / nation's / first / **survey** of how //1
population / linked / pressures af/fect / U.S. / **cities** //

202

12 //3 ˏ it ranks a / hundred and / eighty-four / urban / **areas** on e//3 leven / different cri/**teria** ranging from //3 crowding and / **birth** rates to //1 air quality and / toxic / **wastes** //

13 //4 ˏ the / Urban / **Stress** Test / translates //4 complex / technical / **data** into an //1 easy to / use / **action** / tool for con//3 cerned / **citizens** e//3 lected of/**ficials** and o//1 **pinion** / leaders //

14 //4 ˏ but to / use it / **well** we //1 urgently / need your / **help** //

15 //13 ˏ our / small / staff is being / **swamped** with re/quests for / more infor/**mation** and our //4 modest re/**sources** are being //1 stretched to the / **limit** //

16 //1 your sup/port / now is / **critical** //

17 //4 Z P / G's / nineteen eighty / five / Urban / **Stress** Test may be our //4 best oppor/tunity / **ever** to //1 get the popu/ lation message / **heard** //

18 //3 ˏ with / your contri/**bution** //3 Z P / G can / arm our / growing / network of / local / **activists** with the ma//3 terials they / **need** to //3 warn com/munity / **leaders** about e//3 merging popu/lation linked / **stresses** be //1 fore they / reach / **crisis** / stage //

19 //4 even though our / **national** / government con/tinues to ig/ nore the / consequences of / uncontrolled / popu/lation / growth //4 **we** can / act to take //1 positive / action at the / **local** / level //

20 //3 every / **day** //3 ˏ de/cisions are being / **made** by //3 local of/**ficials** in //3 our com/**munities** that could //1 drastically af/ fect the / quality of our / **lives** //

21 //4 ˏ to make / **sound** / choices in / planning for / **people** //3 ˏ both e/lected of/**ficials** and the A//3 merican / **public** //1 need the popu/lation stresses / data re/vealed by our / **study** //

22 // 3 please make a / special contri/**bution** to /1 zero popu/ lation growth to/**day**//

23 //3 ˏ what/ever you / **give** //3 twenty five dollars / fifty dollars a / hundred dollars or as / much as you / **can** //1 ˏ will be / used im/**mediately** to //1 put the / Urban / Stress Test in the / hands of / those who / need it / **most** //

29 //4 , the re/sults of / Z P G's / nineteen eighty-five / Urban /
Stress Test were re //1 ported as a / top / **news** story by //1
hundreds of / newspapers and / TV and / **radio** stations from
//1 coast to / **coast** //

30 //4 , I / hope you'll / help us / **monitor** this re/markable /
media / coverage by com//1 pleting the en/closed re/**ply** form
//

The text was difficult to read aloud, and this turned out to be
because of its mixed characteristics: presented as a personal letter, and
hence in parts like spoken discourse (e.g. § 7), but in fact deliberately
composed and so often reaching a very high lexical density (e.g. § 13,
with 16 lexical words in one clause). The more spoken parts read
fluently with the tone group mapping generally on to the clause,
whereas the clauses in the more "written" sections were mostly broken
up into tone group sequences, with tones 3 3 3 . . . 1, such as are
typical of loud reading (for example in news bulletins).

Since obviously many other readings are possible I do not propose
to make too much of this analysis. But it bears importantly on the
previous section, because while (following Fries) the Theme carries the
method of development of the text, the New tends to correspond to
the rhetorical "main point". Fries, who is here treating only written
texts, discusses the issue entirely in thematic terms and identifies the
main point with the Rheme; and this is justifiable given that, especially
in writing, the information focus typically falls within the Rheme. But
the operative category is probably that of the New, so that we could
summarize Fries' findings as follows:

> Theme (typically falling within Given) represents "method of develop-
> ment"
> New (typically falling within Rheme) represents "main point"

The transcription shows what in one possible reading are the prominent
motifs within the New.

In this reading, most ranking clauses required more than one tone
group; this is predictable, since the text as a whole is clearly more like
writing than like speech. Where this effect was simply due to high
lexical density the pattern was the one mentioned above: a sequence
of tone 3 (low rising) followed by a final tone 1 (falling). Since tone
3, among its other functions, is also the listing tone in speech this
pattern also occurred where the clause incorporated a list (e.g. § 6).
In other contexts, where a segment consisted of more than one tone

group the pre-final tone was usually tone 4 (falling-rising); this is the characteristic tone where the Theme carries a separate tone group (as it often does, especially when a marked Theme), and also where there is a rising dependency in the clause complex (that is, β followed by α; these two are actually the same phenomenon, since where the β-clause does come first it is thereby marked as thematic in the clause complex).

So if we want to establish what it is that emerges as the overall information structure of this text, the motifs that make up the "main point" as it unfolds, we can examine two sets of instances: (a) the unmarked tonics (i.e. those which are clause-final – here mainly also final in the segment), which select tone 1; and (b) the tone 4 tonics, which are either marked (not clause-final) or on clauses that are not final in the segment. Those of type (a) will directly reveal the main point; while those of type (b) will express highlighted Themes, some-times involving a feature of contrast (e.g. national vs. local in § 19), against which the main point is explicitly foregrounded. We can ignore tonics on tone 3. (Tone 13, which occurs rarely here, can be treated as a variant of tone 1.)

The story told by the tone 1 tonics is that the text begins by taking the 'wow!' of publicity as its main point (§ 4–9). Note that the relevant unit is the whole element of clause structure on which the tonic falls; hence, in § 7, *such an overwhelming response*, and in § 8, *nothing short of incredible*. It then moves on to public health and the cities (§ 9–12), and from there to the sense of crisis and appeal for help (§ 14–18). The next five segments re-enact the two previous points with slightly different emphases: the quality of life on a more local level (§ 19–21), and the urgency of the appeal (§ 22–23; note tonics on *today, immediately, most*). Finally the postscript returns to publicity (§ 29) and then requests a reply (§ 30).

The tone 4 tonics, on the other hand, mainly highlight motifs that we have already identified as Themes: us, our data, our meagre resources, and our Urban Stress Test. Interestingly, the other Themes – you, and the general public – turned out not to be highlighted in this way. But, as already stressed, too much should not be derived from one reading; especially a reading by someone who is an outsider to this sub-culture.

3   Mood and modality

Table 2 gives the mood of each ranking clause in the text, and the modality if any; and enters the items functioning as Subject and as Finite (verbal operator). All ranking clauses are included, since all may have Subjects; but non-finite clauses do not select for mood, and finite dependent clauses are declarative by default (except for types of projection, which do not occur in this text).

Of the 23 clauses that select for mood (36 ranking clauses, minus four dependent finites and nine non-finites), all but one are declarative. Of the first six of these (§ 4–9), five have past as primary tense (*started, jammed, stayed, had, came*; cf. their dependents *released* and the sequent form *would* in *we'd*); the sixth has primary tense present but secondary past (*has been*, past in present). This reflects the narrative beginning of the text. The tense then shifts to present and remains so up to § 21 (*need*).

Then comes the one clause that is not declarative but imperative (§ 22: *please make . . .*); this brings about a sudden change in the relationship of writer to reader, the writer shifting to the goods-&-services mode of 'I'm asking you to do something'. On the way to this, however, there has been one modalization (§ 17, *may be*); this – the only expression of probability in the text – has added a feature of tentativeness to the argument that your support now is critical (this may be our best opportunity, but it is important not to be too definite about that because we may want to ask for your support again later on).

After the imperative clause the mood becomes declarative again; and the primary tense switches to future, then past, then future (§ 23, 29, 30): the first to tell you what we are going to do with your money, the second to return to the narrative left unfinished at the beginning, and the last to express another request, this time in the form of a declarative projection by a mental process (affect) verb, *I hope you will. . . .* This mildly metaphorical representation is preferred to a direct imperative for the final segment of the letter.

There are two modulated clauses, both of the 'ability' type expressed by *can* (§ 18, *ZPG can arm*; § 19, *we can act*); the Subject in both is 'ZPG'.

We saw in Section 1 that in almost all of the declarative clauses the Subject is also the Theme. Where the two are not conflated (in § 4, 18, 20), the Subjects are *our phones, ZPG* and *decisions*; no pattern there, of course, but it is interesting that the only time ZPG appears as a

Table 2 Subject, Finite and the selection of mood

Clause no.	Subject	Finite	Primary tense /modality	Mood
4	our phones	started	past	declarative
5	calls	jammed	past	declarative
6A	staffers	stayed	past	declarative
B	—			(non-finite)
C	—			(non-finite)
7A	we	released	past	declarative
B	we	had	past	declarative
C	we	would	future sequent	declarative
8	media and public reaction	has	present [past in]	declarative
9	the deluge of calls	came	past	declarative
10	we	are	present	declarative
11A	ZPG's 1985 Urban Stress Test	is	present	declarative
B	—			(non-finite)
12	it	ranks	present	declarative
13	the Urban Street Test	translates	present	declarative
14A	—			(non-finite)
B	we	need	present	declarative
15A	our small staff	is	present	declarative
B	our modest resources	are	present	declarative
16	your support now	is	present	declarative
17	ZPG's 1985 Urban Stress Test	may	probability/low	declarative
18	ZPG	can	ability/low	declarative
19A	our national government	continues	present	declarative
B	we	can	ability/low	declarative
C	—			(non-finite)
20	decisions	are	present	declarative
21A	—			(non-finite)
B				(non-finite)
C	both elected officials and the American public	need	present	declarative
22	—			imperative
23A	whatever you give – $25, $50, $100, or as much as you can	will	future	declarative
B	—			(non-finite)
29	the results of ZPG's 1985 Urban Stress Test	were	past	declarative
30A	I	hope	present	declarative
B	you	will	future	declarative
C	—			(non-finite)

participant (in the transitivity structure of the clause) it is Subject but not Theme. Otherwise, *ZPG* appears only as possessive Deictic, modifying *Urban Stress Test* (elsewhere it is replaced by *we*). So the movement of Subject in the text is similar to the movement of Theme; if anything, because of the instances where the two are dissociated the periodicity between 'us' and 'others' appears slightly more clearly with the Subject. We might recognize phases (as in Gregory 1985, pp. 194–8) as set out in Figure 3:

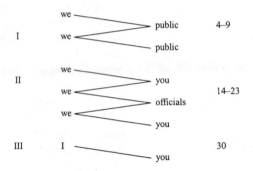

Figure 3   Phases based on Subject selection

– with the Urban Stress Test ("our" test) appearing from time to time as before. But the significance of Subject is rather different from that of Theme; the Subject is the element in which is vested "modal responsibility" – on which the validity of the writer's argument is made to rest, in each clause. This appears clearly when we add a response:

> Staffers stayed late into the night. – Did they?
> Media and public reaction has been incredible. – Has it?
> We urgently need your help. – Do you?

It is even clearer in the imperative, where "modal responsibility" means responsibility for providing the goods-&-services in question:

> Please make a special contribution. – Must I?

Note finally that all ranking clauses have positive polarity. The message is a positive one; the only negatives are either ensconced in the lexicon (*ignore, uncontrolled*) or else used in nominal groups to heighten the positive effect (*we had no idea we'd get such an overwhelming response; reaction has been nothing short of incredible*).

4 Transitivity

Table 3 presents the analysis of transitivity, showing the process type and the items occupying the various transitivity functions: the process itself, and any participants and circumstances. These are shown for all clauses, including those that are embedded, since embedded clauses select freely in the transitivity systems. Embedded clauses are numbered .1, .2, .3, etc. following the clause in (a nominal group within) which they are embedded.

There are thus 55 clauses: the 36 ranking clauses already identified, plus 19 that are embedded. The distribution of process types is given in Table 4.

The clear preponderance of material processes (33 out of 55, constant across all clause statuses) would suggest that the text is largely concerned with actions and events; and so at one level it is. However, with the doubtful exception of *hold local officials accountable*, all these material processes, whether middle or effective, represent actions which are either abstract or, if concrete, then of a very general kind. We could categorize these as in Table 5.

These portray a realm where the action is abstract, bland and formulaic. Where there is agency, the Actor/Agent is typically some abstract object or process: calls or requests, a test or a study, pressures, decisions and problems. The only actions performed by human Agents are giving money, tackling problems, releasing results or completing forms (there is also arming activists – with data). Where there is no agency, and the Actor is just the Medium for the action or event, human Actors preponderate; and their actions are vague generalities, like planning, taking action, or making decisions and contributions.

Of the remaining 22 clauses, most (17) are either verbal or attributive. Thus one motif is that of verbal action, with seven instances of *answer, tell, hear, talk, report* or *warn*. The ten attributive include the four with *need* (see notes to Table 4), three with *be* (furious, critical, incredible) and three others (have an idea, get a response, and *criteria ranging from . . . to . . .*). Thus the motifs brought out by the transitivity patterns are those of abstract or generalized actions, verbal events, and attributes; the attributes being mainly prerequisites to such actions and events, or their consequences.

All the four most frequent clause types – material effective, material middle, verbal, and relational attributive – are distributed evenly throughout the text; there is no clear pattern of movement from one kind of process to another. This is perhaps partly why I felt that the

Table 3 Process types and transitivity functions

Clause no.	Process	Process type	Medium	Other participants and circumstances
4	ring	mat/mid	phones	Time: at 7 a.m. on October 25
5	jam	mat/effec	switchboard	Ag; calls Dur: all day
6A	stay	mat/mid	staffers	Dur: late into the night
B	answer	verbal	staffers	Range: question
C	talk	verbal	staffers	Accomp: with reporters
7A	released	mat/effec	results	Ag; we
B	have	rel: poss/attr	we	Atte: no idea
C	get	rel: poss/attr	we	Atte: response
8	be	rel: int/attr	media & public reaction	Atte: incredible
9	come	mat/mid	deluge of calls	Place: from reporters and public officials
9.1	tell	verbal	(reporters)	Atte: furious
9.2	be	rel:int/attr	(officials)	Range: whistle; Matter: on . . . their cities
9.3	blow	mat/mid	we	Place: from concerned citizens
10	hear	verbal	we	
10.1	know	mental:/cog	(concerned citizens)	Range: what
10.2	do	mat/mid	(concerned citizens)	
10.3	hold	mat/effec	local officials	Ag; citizens: Atte; accountable
10.4	tackle	mat/effec	problems	
10.5	threaten	mat/effec	public health & well-being	Ag; problems
11A	be	rel: int/id	the nation's first survey	
11A.1	affect	mat/effec	cities	Ag; ZPG's Urban Stress Test
B	create	mat/effec	(ZPG's Urban Stress Test)	Ag; pressures
12	rank	mat/effec	184 urban areas	Time: after months of research (Ag; ZPG's U.S.T.) Manner: on 11 critieria
12.1	range	rel: circ/attr	criteria	Atte: from crowding . . . to . . . toxic wastes
13	translate	mat/effec	data	Ag; U.S.T.; Atte: into an action tool; Cause: for concerned citizens and . . . leaders

14A	mat/effect	use	it	Manner: well
B	rel: poss/attr	need	we	Atte: your help
15A	mat/effect	swamp	staff	Manner/Ag: requests for information
B	mat/effect	stretch	resources	Dist: to the limit
16	rel: int/attr	be	support	Atte: critical
17	rel: int/id	be	the best opportunity	Ag: ZPG's Urban Stress Test
17.1	verbal	hear		Range: population message (Ag: we)
18	mat/effect	arm	activists	Ag: ZPG; Manner: materials
18.1	rel: poss/attr	need	they	Atte: materials
18.2	verbal	warm		Rec: leaders; Matter: about stresses
18.3	mat/mid	reach	stresses	Place: crisis stage
19A	mental: perc	ignore	national government	Phen: consequences
B	mat/mid	act	we	
C	mat/mid	take		Range: action; Place: at local level
20	mat/mid	make	officials	Range: decisions; Time: every day
20.1	mat/effect	affect	lives	(Ag: decision); Manner: drastically
21A	mat/mid	make		Range: choices
B	mat/mid	plan		Cause: for people
C	rel: poss/attr	need	officials and public	Atte: data
21C.1	mat/effec	reveal	(data)	Ag: our study
22	mat/mid	make	(you)	Range: contribution; Place: to ZPG; Time: today
23A	mat/effec	use	whatever you give	Ag: you
23A.1	mat/effec	give	whatever	Place: in hands of those who need it most
B	mat/effec	put	Urban Stress Test	(Atte: U.S.T.); Manner: most
B.1	rel: poss/attr	need	(those)	
29	verbal	report	newspapers, TV and radio	Range: results of test; Role: as top news
30A	mental: aff	hope	I	
B	mat/effec	monitor	media coverage	Ag: we; Instig: you
C	mat/effec	complete	reply form	(ag: you)

Table 4 Distribution of process types

	material		mental	verbal	relational		total
	effective	middle			identifying	attributive	
α-clauses	7	6	1	2	2	5	23
β-clauses	6	3	1	2		1	13
[[-clauses	8	3	1	3		4	19
	21	12	3	7	2	10	
Total	33		10		12		55

Notes:

1 The three clauses with *make* + Range (*make decisions, make choices, make contributions*) are all interpreted as material: (i) *make contributions*, even if "unpacked" as *contribute (money)*, would still be material; (ii) *make decisions, make choices* could not be unpacked here as *decide, choose* because they could not project: the attached clauses are clearly expansions (×β *in planning for people*; = [[*that could drastically affect the quality of our lives*), whereas if the congruent forms were mental they would be able to project – as they could if the nominal groups in question were singular, e.g. *make the (sound) decision/ choice not to pursue the matter further.*

2 The four clauses with *need* (*we need your help, the materials they need, the public need the data, put the test in the hands of those who need it*) are all interpreted as relational: attributive/possessive, 'must have'. Of these, the first could also be interpreted as mental + projection, congruently *we need you to help us*; but given that *help* is followed by a cohesive lexical chain *support – contribution – contribution – give – $25 $50 or $100*, it seems more appropriate to interpret this too as a possessive.

3 The clause *to hold local officials accountable* . . . might by itself be taken as mental, agnate to *hold that local officials are accountable* ('consider that . . .'); but this is precluded here by the preceding clause *what they can do*. In this context the interpretation must be as material process, with *accountable* . . . as resultative Attribute.

text lacked direction in its chosen field; it seemed not to be 'going anywhere', not even round in a circle.

5 Clause complexes

As noted in the introduction above, eight of the thirty segments (§ 1–3 and 24–28) consist of clausettes; we shall leave these out of consideration here, and consider the remaining 22 segments. These contain 36 ranking clauses; 13 standing alone (as clause "simplex"), 8 in 2-clause complexes and 15 in 3-clause complexes.

Table 5 Material processes

	abstract 'make/be busy'	'do research'	'create/affect/do'	'give/use'	general
effective (Medium/Goal; +Actor/Agent)	calls jam switchboard	we monitor media coverage	test is created	you give (money)	
	staff is swamped with requests	we release results	pressures affect cities	we arm activists with data	
	resources are stretched	stress data are revealed by study	decisions affect lives	(money) puts test in hands of	
	you complete form	test ranks urban areas	problems threaten health	you can (give money)	
	officials tackle problems	test translates data		(money) is used	
middle (Medium/Actor)	phones ring	we "blow the whistle"	we act	you make contributions	
	staffers stay		we take action		
	calls come		decisions are made		
	stresses reach crisis stage		officials make choices		
			officials plan		
			they do what		

Table 6 Tactic pairs, by taxis and interdependency

	Expansion			Projection	
	elaborating	extending	enhancing	idea	locution
hypotactic	1		9	2	
paratactic		2			

There are thus 14 tactic pairs – since a complex of two clauses has just one such pair, while a complex of three clauses has two. Table 6 shows the distribution by taxis and interdependency (logical-semantic relation). The favoured type is hypotactic enhancement; within these, four are clauses of Cause: Purpose, all non-finite with *to*: *to use it well, to take positive action, to make sound choices, to put the Urban Stress Test in the hands of those who need it most*. Three others are also non-finite: one Manner, *by completing the enclosed reply form*, one Matter, *in planning for people*, and one which could be interpreted as Time: Simultaneity ('meanwhile', *answering questions . . .*) or alternatively as not enhancing but extending ('and'). The other two are finite: one Time and one Concession.

Three of the four purpose clauses are associated with *need*: *to use it well we need your help, to make sound choices . . . elected officials . . . need the population-stress data, [your money] will be used immediately to put the Urban Stress Test in the hands of those who need it most*. This motif also turns up in one of the three embedded clause complexes (see below):

the materials [[they need ×|| to warn community leaders . . .]]

This co-occurrence of need (required possession) with purpose lends some sense of urgency to the discourse; and this is perhaps reinforced by the other two purpose clauses, which co-occur with *can do, can act*. Again, one of these sequences is in an embedded clause complex:

citizens . . . [[who want to know '|| what they can do ×|| to hold local officials accountable . . .]]

while the other is the quaintly worded *we can act to take positive action*. . . . But although purpose is clearly the single most favoured form of interdependency (six out of the seventeen tactic pairs), it is never highlighted: all six instances have the simple non-finite form with *to*, instead of a finite clause (e.g. *if we are to . . .*), or an explicit conjunction (e.g. *in order to . . .*).

Table 7 Ranking clauses: simplexes and complexes

Clause no.	Symbol	Boundaries (first and last word, with conjunction(s) if any; (seg.) = clause takes up whole of segment)
4		(seg.)
5		(seg.)
6 A	α	staffers … night
B	$^{x}\beta1$	answering questions
C	$\beta^{+}2$	and talking … country
7 A	$^{x}\beta$	and we … test
B	$\alpha\alpha$	we … idea
C	$\alpha`\beta$	we'd … response
8		(seg.)
9		(seg.)
10		(seg.)
11 A	α	ZPG's .. <<…>> … cities
B	$<<^{=}\beta>>$	created … research
12		(seg.)
13		(seg.)
14 A	$^{x}\beta$	but to use … well
B	α	we … help
15 A	1	our … information
B	$^{+}2$	and our … limit
16		(seg.)
17		(seg.)
18		(seg.)
19 A	$^{x}\beta$	even though our … growth
B	$\alpha\alpha$	we … act
C	$\alpha^{x}\beta$	to take … level
20		(seg.)
21 A	$^{x}\beta\alpha$	to make … choices
B	$\beta^{x}\beta$	in planning … people
C	α	both … study
22		(seg.)
23 A	α	whatever … immediately
B	$^{x}\beta$	to put … most
29		(seg.)
30 A	α	I hope
B	$`\beta\alpha$	you'll … coverage
C	$\beta^{x}\beta$	by completing … form

Table 7 identifies each of the ranking clauses in the text, showing the tactic status and logical–semantic relationship (interdependency) of those entering into clause complexes. Table 8 identifies the clauses and clause complexes which are embedded in nominal constructions throughout the text.

Table 8 Embedded clauses and clause complexes

Clause no.	Symbol	Boundaries (first and last word, with relative or conjunction if any)
9.1	= [[ ]]	eager ... results
9.2	= [[	who were furious
9.3	'‖]]	that we ... cities
10.1	= [[	who want ... know
10.2	'‖	what ... do
10.3	ˣ‖	to hold ... accountable
10.4	ˣ‖	for tackling ... problems
10.5	= [[ ]]]]]]]]	that threaten ... well-being
11A.1	'[[ ]]	how population-linked ... cities
12.1	= [[ ]]	ranging ... wastes
17.1	ˣ[[ ]]	to get ... heard
19.1	= [[	they need
18.2	ˣ‖	to warn ... stresses
18.3	ˣ‖]]	before they ... stage
20.1	= [[ ]]	that could ... lives
21C.1	= [[ ]]	revealed ... study
22A.1	= [[ ]]	whatever you ... can
22A.2	ˣ[[ ]]	as you can
22B.1	= [[ ]]	who need ... most

6 Lexical cohesion

The main lexical bonding in the text, as is to be expected, is provided by reference to ZPG itself and to the Urban Stress Test. Either *ZPG* or one of its reference items *we, our* occurs in almost all segments in the substance of the letter (16 out of 22, and also in the Address); the *U.S.T.*, or *it*, is mentioned eight times.

The remaining lexical items cluster mainly into seven sets, which we could label "action, research, publicity, concerns, stress factors, people, and places". The items entering into these sets are all nominals (nouns or other constituents of nominal groups), and the chains are purely lexical, not lexico-referential: the only reference item is *such* in § 7.

Taken together, the items in these nine sets (the seven above, plus ZPG and the Urban Stress Test) account for 65% of all occurrences of lexical words in the text (162 out of 250). The remaining 35% include all the verbs and adverbs; high frequency and general lexical items like *idea, limit, trends, day, night*; and items such as *overwhelming, eager, furious, drastic, outraged, remarkable, special, incredible* where the linking motif is interpersonal rather than experiential.

Figure 4 shows the pattern of occurrence of items from the major sets in each of the 22 segments. Either ZPG or the U.S.T. (or both) occurs in all but three (§ 8, 16, 20 – the *our* in § 20 is not referring to ZPG); these connections are not shown. All other co-occurrences are shown by lines labelled with the serial numbers of the segments in question; thus, items from both "action" and "research" motifs will be found in § 13, 18, 21. It will be seen that six out of the seven motifs are strongly bonded: apart from "publicity – concerns", all possible cluster pairs are represented in at least one segment, and the mean number of occurrences of each such pair is three (that is, given six clusters, there are fifteen possible cluster pairs, and the number of pair occurrences in the text, by segment, is 45).

This strongly centripetal bonding, with each motif co-occurring with all the others and with ZPG and the Urban Stress Test, tends to keep the text in one place. There is a slight drift away from 'publicity' in the first part towards 'action' in the second, with a brief return to 'publicity' at the end – the two being then conjoined for the first time in the prosaic appeal to *help us monitor this remarkable media coverage by completing the enclosed reply form*. But there is little other movement. The motifs of research, concerns, places and people occur throughout the text, and there are no less than five segments in which three out of these four occur together (§ 9, 10, 11, 18, 19; *ZPG* also figures in all five).

The exception is the stress factors. These are mentioned only once, in § 12; and they co-occur here only with the motif of place (*184 urban areas*), and with the Urban Stress Test, referred to here as *it* (the only time it is not spelt out in full). ZPG does not occur in this segment. This insulation of the stress factors from the rest of the discourse keeps technical matters firmly at a distance; the effect is somewhat paternalistic, with some such message as 'keep the funds

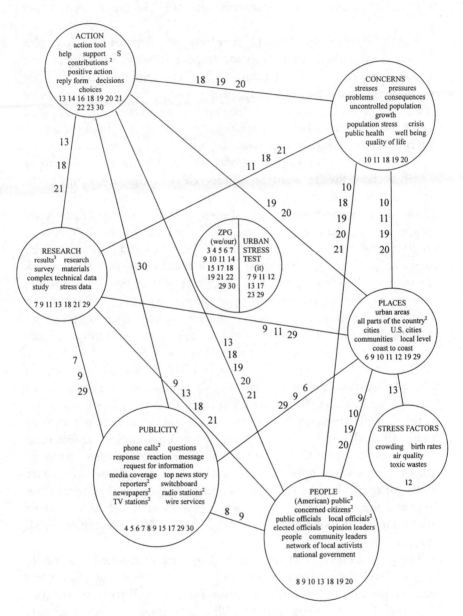

Figure 4 Lexical sets (nominals only) and their co-occurrence patterns

rolling, but don't bother your heads with the difficult stuff – we'll look after all that'. (Compare *translates complex technical data into an easy-to-use action tool.*)

7 Nominalization and grammatical metaphor

As one way of exploring the grammatical metaphor I reworded the text in a more congruent form, using the strategy of "how would I say this to a 12-year-old?" Here is the result:

KEEPING THE POPULATION NO BIGGER THAN IT IS NOW

4 At 7 a.m. on October 25, our phones started to ring.

5 So many people were telephoning us that the switchboard was jammed all day.

6 Our staff stayed (working) late into the night, answering questions and talking with reporters from newspapers, radio stations, wire services and TV stations in every part of the country.

7 When we told everyone what we had found out by our Urban Stress Test in 1985 (which shows how people get tired and upset if they live in cities) we'd no idea we'd have so many people taking notice.

8 It was incredible how (much?) the TV, radio and newspapers, and also ordinary people, talked about it.

9 At first the ones who kept telephoning us were mainly reporters, who were eager to tell people about the results of the stress test, and public officials, who were furious because we had "blown the whistle on" what it's like to live in their cities.

10 But now we're hearing from ordinary citizens from all parts of the country who are worried and want to know what they can do to get local officials to accept that it's their job to tackle problems coming from overpopulation, if this is (these are?) making people unhappy.

11 When we were creating this Urban Stress Test we had to research persistently and very thoroughly for months; it's the first time anyone in the country has surveyed how much difference it makes having so many people around if you live in U.S. cities.

12 We put 184 urban areas in order according to 11 different properties which we measured, including how crowded they are, how many children are being born, how good or bad the air is, and how much poisonous waste there is around.

13 What we found out with this test is complicated and technical; but

219

we've made the test (the results?) easy to understand so that citizens who are concerned about these things, and elected officials, and people whose opinions count, can use it (them?) to get things done.

14 But to use it well we urgently need you to help us.

15 We have only a small staff, and they've been swamped by being asked so many questions. We haven't enough resources to deal with any more.

16 You have to support us now so that we can survive.

17 The Urban Stress Test may be our best opportunity ever to get people to listen to what we are saying about population.

18 We can use the money you contribute for sending out to the more and more people who are working for us in different places all the information (?) they need in order to warn important members of the community that people are already beginning to suffer (?) because of overpopulation, before this becomes a crisis.

19 Even though our national government still ignores what happens if the population goes on growing without being controlled, we can try to do something about it in our own neighbourhoods.

20 Every day local officials in our communities are deciding things which will make a difference to the way we live.

21 So that they can choose properly when they plan for people (plan for the population?), both elected officials and the American public need to know what we found out when we studied stresses coming from overpopulation.

22 Please contribute extra money (?) to ZPG today.

23 Whatever you give – $25, $50, $100 or as much as you can – will be used immediately to tell the results to the people who most need to know them (give the test to the people who most need to use it?).

29 The results of the test were reported as a top news story by hundreds of newspapers and TV and radio stations from coast to coast.

30 I hope you'll help us to keep a record of all this remarkable number of reports, by filling in the form I'm enclosing for you to reply on.

When the text is approached from this angle three features seem to stand out: clichés, ambiguities, and grammatical metaphors. As a final step, we will discuss each of these in turn.

(1) Clichés. The clichés seem to cluster around four motifs:

(i) 'we are under pressure', e.g. *calls jammed our switchboard, the deluge of calls, swamped with requests, resources stretched to the limit;*

(ii) 'we amaze people', e.g. *met with an overwhelming response, reaction nothing short of incredible, remarkable media coverage;*

(iii) 'crisis threatens', e.g. *threaten public health and well-being, your support is critical, reach crisis stage, affect the quality of our lives;*

(iv) 'arm and act', e.g. *arm our growing network of local activists, act to take positive action at the local level.*

It looks as though all these clichés serve a function: that of easing the somewhat awkward disjunction (which appears in the theme and information structures; cf. Sections 1 and 2 above) between two apparently contradictory messages: 'look what we've done – we're great!' and 'we're puny and weak – so help us!' The use of wordings which are so hackneyed that they have lost much of their experiential meaning may help to paper over this contradiction.

(2) Ambiguities. Ambiguity and grammatical metaphor are closely interconnected: grammatical metaphors tend to leave many semantic relationships implicit and by the same token to neutralize certain distinctions. Ambiguities arose in this text particularly in relation to three issues: the nature of the problem, the status of the test, and the kind of assistance requested:

(i) (§ 10, 18) *population-related problems that threaten public health and well-being; emerging population-linked stresses . . . reach crisis stage*: is it the size of the population that is becoming threatening and critical, or other factors that arise from this?

(ii) (§ 13, 23) *translates complex data into an easy-to-use action tool; to put the Urban Stress Test in the hands of those who need it most*: is it the test itself, or the results of the test, that are to be made available?

(iii) (§ 22) *make a special contribution to ZPG today*: are we being asked to do something to further the aims of zero population growth, or to give money to a particular organization?

There are other, less salient ambiguities; for example in § 8 and elsewhere referring to the media response (is it the quantity of the reactions that is remarkable, or their nature and quality – many people responded, or people responded favourably?), and in § 21 *in planning for people* (does this mean planning on behalf of the public, or planning what to do as regards the growth of population?).

The word *population* in fact occurs seven times; and every occurrence is framed in one particular kind of grammatical metaphor: where nouns representing processes or attributes function as Head of the nominal group and are preceded by premodifying elements whose semantic relationship to the Head noun is unclear. The examples are:

> zero population growth
> population-related problems
> population-linked pressures
> the population message
> emerging population-linked stresses
> uncontrolled population growth
> population-stress data

It will be seen that the word *population* never occurs as Head; it is either a Modifier or else a part of a compound Modifier, and if the latter then followed either by another noun (*population-stress*) or by a verb in V^n form (*population-linked, population-related*). Thus quite apart from the vagueness of the last two, where the sense is 'having some (unspecified) connection with (the) population', each one of these instances is problematic. Population-stress data might be data about the stress caused by the population, or undergone by the population; the population message might be a message about how matters are, or about how they should be, and either concerning or addressed to the population; and even population growth, which presumably must mean people becoming more in number rather than becoming taller and fatter, is introduced in the contradictory context of zero. Nowhere is the concept of 'too many people', overpopulation, made explicit.

It could fairly be said that those to whom the letter is addressed will "get the message" in all these instances and reject interpretations that are inappropriate; and that it is of no consequence if they are misinterpreted or not understood by others. But, apart from the fact that this seems rather shortsighted – surely the message is one that is intended to be spread? – there is a deeper problem with these rather oblique forms of discourse: that they become so bland as to lose all impact. If the grammar creates a universe of pseudo-objects, like easy-to-use action tools, population-related problems, emerging population-linked stresses approaching crisis stage and positive action at the local level, then all of reality is held at a safe distance; and when these objects are further disneyfied by the use of pseudo-intimacies like dear friend of ZPG, our phones started to ring, our small staff is being swamped, with your contribution, and I hope you'll help us, the underlying message is that life can go on being just one long Happy Hour.

(3) Grammatical metaphors. As is clear from the rewording at the beginning of this section, the text displays a considerable range of grammatical metaphor: not extremely dense, but varied (cf. Jones et al., 1989, pp. 268–9, 302–4). It would take a separate paper to categorize and describe it in detail; instead, I shall look at some of its consequences by examining one segment (§ 18).

The following is an informal account of the major decisions that have to be made in interpreting this segment. Not all of these would necessarily be accounted for as grammatical metaphors; some involve lexical metaphor (i.e. metaphor in the usual sense of the term), while others are neutralizations by the grammar of semantic distinctions that are typically not, in fact, made explicit (e.g. *of, -ist* below). Each instance is discussed, and a decision taken among the possible interpretations; the number of possibilities is given in square brackets, usually [2]. A less ambiguous rewording is suggested.

(i) With your contributions, ZPG can arm our network . . .

(a) Who are *your* and *our*? 'You' is obviously the recipient of the letter. Assuming that 'we' are the writers, is this *our* anaphoric to ZPG or not? [2] (It is, although the structure is unusual; it would be more usual to write *We at ZPG can arm our. . . .*)

(b) *With your contributions*: does this *with* mean "giving", as in *with your guns we can arm our militia*, or does it mean "using"? [2] (It means "by using your contributions".)

(c) *Your contributions*: is 'you' here a possessor, as in *your property*, or is it a participant in some transitivity relation, like *your role* "the part you play"? (The second; "you" is Actor in a process of giving, i.e. "giver"). In that case, has the action been performed or not – that is, is the giving in the past or in the future? [3 options altogether] (The action is in the hoped-for future.)

Rewording: By using the money we hope you are going to give us, we at ZPG can arm our network . . .

(ii) . . . arm our growing network of local activists with the materials they need . . .

(d) *Arm our network with materials*: does this mean "give our network supplies of weapons" or "give our network materials which can be used as (if they were) weapons"? [2] (The second.)

(e) What are *materials*: goods-&-services, or information? [2] (Information.)

(f) Who or what are *activists*: people who support activism (cf. *communists*), or people who believe in activity (cf. *relativists*), or people who are active (cf. *sensualists*)? [3] (We ignore "people who act"! – presumably, people who are active.)

(g) *Our activists*: is 'we' possessor, or in some transitivity function (cf. (c) above)? [2] (The latter: "on our behalf", "in our cause".)

(h) Are *local activists* those in different localities, as in *local representatives*; those in our locality, as in *local doctors*; or those operating within a small area, as in *local government*? [3] (Probably the first.)

(i) In *network of activists*, what is *of*: ownership, as in *house of her parents*; constituency, as in *house of three storeys*; description, as in *house of ill repute*; material, as in *house of cards*; container, as in *house of antiquities*; or collective, as in *house of representatives*? [6] (Presumably the last of these.)

(j) Is the *growing network* expanding in size, like the network surrounding a ball that is being inflated; or is it increasing in numbers? [2] (The latter.)

Rewording: . . . we can supply those who are active on our behalf in different localities, now that they are organized into a network and are growing in number, materials that can be used as weapons . . .

(iii) . . . materials they need to warn community leaders about emerging population-linked stresses . . .

(k) What is *to* in *they need to warn*: "materials they need to warn community leaders about (i.e. that community leaders must be warned about)", or "materials that they need in order that they can warn community leaders"? [2] (The second.)

(l) Are *community leaders* "people who lead the community", "people who hold leading positions in the community" or "leaders who live in the community"? [3] (Perhaps the second, rather than the first of these.)

(m) What are *emerging population-linked stresses* (cf. the discussion of *population* above)? Are they "stresses linked to emerging population" or "emerging stresses linked to population" (i.e. which is emerging, the population or the stresses)? [2] Is *linked to* "causing", "caused by" or "co-occurring with"? [3] Is *emerging* "coming out", "beginning to show" or "increasing"? [3] (Combining the appropriate selection each time we get "stresses which are caused by population, and which are beginning to show".)

(n) Is *population* the kind of people, or the number of people? If it is the number, are there too many, or too few? [3 altogether] (Too many.)

Rewording: . . . materials that they need to use in order to warn those who hold leading positions in the community about stresses caused by there being too many people, stresses which are now beginning to show . . .

(iv) . . . before they reach crisis stage.

(o) Who is *they*: the activists, the community leaders, or the stresses? [3] (We can choose "stresses", because it is the nearest, and because of the collocational relation between *stress* and *crisis*.)

(p) Is *crisis stage* the stage which is a crisis, or the stage where crises occur? [2] (Uncertain.)

(q) If stresses *reach crisis stage*, is this a time, a place, or a degree of intensity? [3] (Probably a degree of intensity; in combination with (p) above, perhaps "a degree of intensity where crises occur", rather than "a degree of intensity which is a crisis".)

Rewording: . . . before the stresses become so intense that crises will occur.

It would be possible partially to "repack" this wording in a way which eliminates some at least of these alternatives; for example:

Any money that you contribute to ZPG can pay the cost of sending out information to supporters in different localities, so that armed with this information they can warn leading members of the community about the increased stresses brought on by overpopulation before these stresses start to cause a crisis.

Any interpretation of a text involves decisions. Most of these do not engage our attention; we reject improbable alternatives without ever noticing them. In this particular segment we should probably not envisage that *reach . . . stage* might refer to a play performed at a theatre, or that *growing network* could be a network for growing plants on, although neither of these is totally impossible. Here I have tried to include only alternatives which seemed reasonably plausible. Note that this is not a composition exercise for purposes of "improving" the text; there are far too many variables in discourse construction for any operation – even that of reducing ambiguity – to guarantee improvement. (The rewording of the text at the beginning of this section was different again; it was an intuitive venture at making the text more accessible – something that is connected with "less ambiguous" but by no means identical with it.)

The present exercise in unpacking and repacking one segment does suggest, however, that this text is somewhat problematic: not so much in the number of possible interpretations as in the number of plausible interpretations offered by its lexicogrammar. If we treated all of those enumerated above as independent of each other we should have a little over 4×10^7 acceptable readings. This is probably more than would be typical of a sentence of comparable length in most kinds of discourse. But it may be typical of this particular register, which we could perhaps characterize as the discourse of the "soft touch".

8 Summary

In this paper I have adopted a grammatical perspective on discourse, interpreting the text simultaneously as object and as instance. By bringing a text under attention we assign to it value as an object; this is the activity which turns a text into "literature" (not thereby implying 'good' literature, of course). By bringing it under grammatical attention we display its properties as an instance; this shows how it means, since every feature it displays is located in the context of its alternatives. These agnate forms, representing what might have been meant but was not, constitute an infinity of shadow texts against which the one in focus achieves its reality.

Among the grammatical systems instantiated in any text we can identify some where the choices made are likely to assume significance: very general categories of theme, transitivity and so on, and also syndromes of features like grammatical metaphor. Selections made within these systems will give the text its distinctive flavour and determine how we evaluate it relative to its sociosemiotic context. We could have examined other features, or explored these ones further – indefinitely further – in delicacy; in stylistic studies we may be treating of choices that are very delicate indeed. But we also have to make choices of our own, especially that between depth and breadth; and in the absence of obvious foregrounding of any one grammatical system it seemed preferable to aim for breadth.

I have not offered more than brief evaluative comments, although no doubt the wording of my own discourse construes an attitude towards its object. What I have tried to do rather is to show the grammar at work creating meaning in the form of written text. We tend to think of grammar as simply taking its orders from above; our own discourse has to make it strange, to show it de-automatized in the text under review. The patterns we bring out create meaning both at their own level and at each "higher" level that they realize – with which they are related by metaredundancy, in the terms of Lemke's explanatory model (Lemke 1984). I have concentrated on the meaning of the grammar at its own level, trusting others to explore the various realms of meaning that lie beyond.

Notes

1. For the grammar and its application to discourse analysis, see Halliday 1985a, 1985b.
2. The following symbols are used:

interdependency: logical-semantic relations:

parataxis 1 2 3 ...   = elaborating ⎫
hypotaxis α β γ ...   + extending   ⎬ expansion
                              × enhancing   ⎭
                              ' idea   ⎫
                              " locution   ⎬ projection

3. The Subject is realized as that element which, together with the Finite verbal operator, constitutes the mood-marking element of the clause; hence, in a declarative clause, the element that is recapitulated in the tag, e.g. *there* in *there's no danger of that, is there*? The unmarked pattern in a declarative clause is that in which the Subject is also thematic.

Chapter Eight

"SO YOU SAY 'PASS' . . . THANK YOU THREE MUCHLY" (1994)

1 Preamble: third party

A text is a process of sharing: the shared creation of meaning. Those who share in this process are the 'you' and the 'me' of the text. Our status as co-actants is made explicit in the text itself – in the grammar, which distinguishes between the speech roles (me and you) on the one hand, and everyone and everything else (him, her, it, them) on the other. Thus 'you' and 'me' are not only **creators of** the text; we are also **created by** it. 'You' and 'me' are brought into being by language.

It should be made clear that this sharing is a purely textual consensus. 'You' and 'me' agree to share in the semiotic process; without that, there can be no text. There is no implication of consensus of any other kind; we may be creating text in order to quarrel. Co-actants often sense the inherent contradiction in this situation, and try to destroy the textual consensus as well: "I'm not talking to you any more", palms pressed on the ears to block reception. In this way they can stop being 'you' and 'me', until a new text creates them afresh.

Every text defines its insiders and its outsiders. In principle the outsiders have no access to the text. In practice, they may overhear it; but the role of the eavesdropper is problematic, because the grammar does not admit a role of "third party **to a text**". The "third person" comes in as a participant in its experiential structures, alternating with "first" and "second person" in the functions of Actor, Goal, Agent, Medium, Beneficiary, and the like; but in relation to the text, this

First published in *What's Going on Here? Complementary Studies of Professional Talk*, edited by Allen D. Grimshaw. Norwood: Ablex, 1994, pp. 175–229.

'something or someone else' is simply a non-person. Such a one is clearly excluded from the text by the grammar. Even if there was no **overt** "person" system (as in some languages there is not), the third party is always defined cryptotypically, and in a way which shows it to be an outsider: the third party has no access to the modalities. So in English, for example, *perhaps* can mean 'I think it possible', as in *perhaps they've gone away*; or it can mean 'do you think it possible?', as in *have they gone away perhaps?* But it can never mean 'he or she thinks it possible'. Modalities are absolutely tied to the insider roles in the discourse.

Thus, while the grammar gives only superficial recognition to the Jakobsonian opposition of 'me (first person) versus the rest of the universe', it provides abundant and significant evidence for setting off 'you and me' (first and second person) against the rest – so making explicit the essentially dialogic nature of discourse. The 'you and me' share the context of situation within which the text is enacted; we are the co-actants – for us the text is a form of action, whereas for the others, the hims and the hers, it is not. The roles of you and me are interchangeable: the 'me' of one moment is the 'you' of the next – but they are not interchangeable with those of him and her. Our status as creators and creations of the text is institutionalized by the grammar, and constantly reiterated throughout the proceedings.

Because you and me are sharply defined in this way we tend to behave towards the text in proprietorial fashion, as if we owned it. A text is a form of private property; in bringing it into being we also establish title to it. In some cultural contexts the ownership of the text may be vested solely in me, excluding even you from part possession. This particular conception of ownership is associated with written text, and arises with the monologic notion of the "author": If I am an author you have to pay for the text by buying 'my' book, and if you figure out ways of getting round this constraint there are copyright laws to stop you threatening my livelihood. In the "process writing" current in the primary schools of the 1980s, children have been actively encouraged to claim ownership of their written texts, as if private property was the ultimate realization of power.

With spoken text, which does not (or did not until recently) take on the form of an alienable object, the sense of text as private property is tuned to privacy rather than to property. The text is open to you and me, but closed to all outsiders; if there are any third parties **situated** by the text they are not just overhearing, they are eavesdropping. Of course, privacy is also a product of the culture; in societies where there are no categories of public and private there could be no significance attached to private discourse. In others it exists, but as a marked option: institutionalized, for example, in the inviolability of the confession. But in our highly privatized cultures of today the outsider is typically excluded from the text. The text is confidential to you and me; 'they' have no right to be "listening in".

But since society cannot function if all discourse is private, there has to be some provision for listening in. Again, it is the marked option that comes to be institutionalized. We see this happening in the forms of dramatic art, the theatre and cinema, where the "audience" plays the eavesdropper role. Other kinds of text may of course be staged for the benefit of third parties, from politicians negotiating arms limitation agreements that are "meant" for the ears of their constituents back home, to the muttered asides that enrich domestic rhetoric. And where the power sources of society need to listen in, we have high technology eavesdropping: telephones are tapped, encounter spaces bugged and monitored. There are rewards and punishments for these actions, giving a high social value to discourse that is overheard.

One class of eavesdropper that is now well established is that of ethnographers, equipped since the advent of the tape recorder with a resource for surreptitious listening in. This in its turn has engendered a special variety of text, signalled by "do you mind if I record you?", where the interactants are creating what would have been private discourse except that they already know that eavesdroppers are around. All this of course has an effect on the nature of the discourse itself: what is "spontaneous, un-self-conscious, natural speech" any more?

The present text is one on which we have been invited, as ethnographers, to listen in. We feel somewhat embarrassed at this – or one of us does, at least – not because we are intruding into the privacy of the text; the interactants knew they were being recorded, and the text was in fact enacted, if not for that purpose, at least with that particular subplot in view. I felt embarrassed more in the way that one does when invited to sit in on a ceremony where I could not be sure of understanding what was happening. What do all these complex moves express? How many levels of interpretation are going to be needed as we try to penetrate the multiple semiosis of the text – and in so doing, to uncover our own role as its ethnographer? And how was that role to be acted out? – in the traditional ethnographic stance of the invisible observer, whether extraterrestrial being or professional sociologist? or as observer/participant, recognizing as semioticians the inevitable impact of our observation on the discursive processes themselves, and hence reflecting on the meaning-making nature of our own allotted enterprise?

2 Orientation

I decided to behave as a grammarian, since that is what I am, and I have been studying the grammar of conversation for a reasonably long time. The text thus became for me an *instance* of a particular *register*: that is, typical not just of "text in English" but of text in a particular functional variety of English. This is a semantic characterization: functional variation, as embodied in the concept of register, refers to the orientation towards certain areas of meaning, which can be interpreted theoretically as a setting of the probabilities in the content-plane systems of the language. The register, in turn, is associated with a particular situation type, particular settings of the parameters of field, tenor, and mode, which in the present instance could be summarized as follows:

Field Education: tertiary: university: postgraduate: research degree: PhD; social science: sociology: examination: thesis: defence.

[examiners] assessment of candidate's qualifications (knowledge and ability) to be admitted to the profession; negotiation of own views in order to arrive at consensus

[candidate] convincing examiners of her suitability for award of degree

Tenor Teacher/student: examiners/examinee: dissertation committee/candidate; four/one.

[examiners] three male/one female; three external members/one internal, chair: one more "expert" (senior, specialist in field)

[candidate] female; mature age

Mode Spoken: unrehearsed (impromptu); institutionalized: interview: judgemental, with reward dependent on outcome; bounded (opening-closing) and time-constrained.

Structured: interview proper + deliberation + enactment

[structure of subtext discussed in present chapter: problem (enunciation + proposals + complication) + decision (decision proper + summing-up) + post-mortem (problem$_2$ + closure)]

The institutional term that had been given to us was "dissertation defence"; as an outsider to the culture I had come to recognize that there was no translation equivalent of this expression; rendering it as "PhD oral" was more confusing than helpful. But in any case such generic labels are of limited value in enabling us to make predictions about the register: it has to be assumed that they are a shorthand for typical clusterings of field, tenor, and mode.

Out of the major systemic components of a systemic-functional grammar I selected three for detailed study: modality, the clause complex, and theme. The clause complex combines an interdependency system of TAXIS (parataxis/hypotaxis) with a logical-semantic system of expansion/projection; the two together would construct the combination of (1) spoken mode, with (2) the field of academic assessment. The modality features, including both modalization and modulation, would construe the tenor, the interpersonal relations among those taking part. The thematic organization would carry the planning of the discourse, its method of development as an interview. It seemed likely that these three taken together would give a reasonably revealing account of how the discourse was organized to function effectively in a context of situation of this kind – and some explanation of where it was (or was not) successful.

There was no possibility of covering more than a small proportion of the whole text; so I decided to focus on the designated "core" passage of approximately 12.5 minutes, beginning at Adam's *So you say* "*pass*". I shall refer to this passage as the "subtext". It shares many features with the remainder of the text, but departs from it in respect of others: specifically, it contrasts with all that precedes it in that it stands to the preceding discourse in the relation of a conclusion. No detailed analysis has been made of the previous portions; but a few points of contrast are noted in the discussion that follows.

I found I had to make a new transcription, in order to put in the intonation and the rhythm: these are necessary to any grammatical interpretation of speech. At the same time I was able to leave out various features that had been included in the original, "conversational analysis"-type transcription, which are not necessary for my purposes. (I was also able to correct a few errors in the original transcription.) The version of the subtext in this form of systemic text notation is included as an appendix to this chapter (Appendix 1).

I then made a clause-by-clause analysis of the subtext in respect of the systems of theme, information, transitivity, mood, modality, and key; and an analysis of each clause complex by interdependency and expansion/projection. The transcription (Appendix 1) shows the information structure, since this is carried by the intonation and rhythm. The worksheets (Appendix 2) show (a) the structure of each clause complex; then for each clause (including any that are embedded) (b) the functional components of the theme (textual, interpersonal, topical); (c) the mood and polarity; (d) the modality (modalization and modulation), and (e) the transitivity (process type, and any grammatical metaphor).

The analysis of the subtext shows that it contains 267 clauses, distributed over 116 turns. These form a rather coherent structure, which will be presented in the section that follows.

3   Structure of the subtext

Hasan (1985) has shown that, given a particular "contextual configuration" of field, tenor, and mode, it is possible to derive a "structure potential" which represents the predicted limits within which the structure of texts of that situation type will fall. The "structure formula" for any one instance – any particular text in that register – will be a variant of that potential, incorporating all features that are obligatory (elements that must be present, or constraints on the ordering of elements) and making some selection from among the remaining options.

This comprehensive "macro-structure" may in turn comprise smaller, micro-structures; hence there is a great deal of variation. Some of these are more constituent-like, such as those Sinclair and Coulthard (1975) were able to establish in their studies of classroom discourse. At other times the micro-structures are more prosodic: they represent co-occurrent motifs, like the "phasal" structures recognized by Gregory (1985). Both may be present simultaneously, the more constituent-like structures being typically field-derived (having to do with the nature of the social activity, 'what is going on'), the more prosodic ones typically tenor-derived (having to do with the relationships among the interactants, 'who are taking part'). Berry (1981) has shown that text structure is not determined solely by considerations of field.

I have not attempted any overall characterization of the macro-structure of the present text. I shall assume that the subtext selected for detailed treatment is itself a functional element in the structure of the text as a whole, and shall refer to it simply as "conclusion". In this subtext, the interactants are reaching, and also enacting, a joint decision;

both the process and its outcome are critical to the effective functioning of the text in the defined context of situation.

The subtext, in turn, has its own micro-structure deriving from this culminative function that it performs in relation to the text as a whole. The most general structure that we could postulate for such a culminative subtext would be that of

(Problem ˆ Resolution ˆ) Decision

– that is, a decision component either alone or preceded by the raising and disposing of one or more problems. In this instance all these elements are present, with perhaps three cycles of problem plus resolution; but there is an additional element following the decision, which would not have been predicted and which may or may not figure as an optional element within this text type (the alternative being that it falls outside it and indicates a shift of register). In the absence of evidence either way we shall adopt the simpler solution and treat it as an optional element that is part of the same text.

Within this there is a further layer of micro-structure which is still reasonably constituent-like, though as the subtext proceeds it becomes more a structure of interpersonal motif and hence more prosodic in its realization. The "problem and resolution" sequence begins with an enunciation of the problem, which is followed by proposals for its solution; then there arises another problem, in the form of a challenge followed by a defence. Focusing more delicately still, we can recognize two proposals for the solution of the initial problem, and then two cycles of challenging and defending. The "decision" component turns out to consist of a decision proper (itself comprising enunciation plus symbolic enactment – the enunciation incorporating a motif of "comic relief"), followed by a summing-up. At this point the subtext proceeds beyond the decision to a "post-mortem"; the post-mortem, in turn, engenders another problem, which is, however, shelved, not resolved. This post-mortem imparts to the subtext an incipient cyclicity which presumably could become severely dysfunctional; but it is inhibited by an *ex machina* closure, and it is this that allows us to treat the entire subtext as an element of the "dissertation defence", at least for purposes of the present exercise.

The movement of the subtext is set out in Figure 1.

4 Relation of text structure to clauses and turns

At this point we need to specify the sequence of turns in the subtext, and the sequence of clauses in each turn, to show how the text structure is made manifest. The subtext consists of 116 turns. (There is a gap on the recording between nos. 82 and 83, which are actually by the same speaker but are treated here as separate turns because of the gap.)

The distribution of turns and clauses in the second-order elements of structure (those numbered 1–7 in Figure 1) is shown in Table 1. It will be noted that the elements numbered 4 and 6 are interleaved; these two motifs are enacted in alternating bursts. The "post-mortem" phase is actually initiated by the last clause (clause 141) in turn 45: Sherm's (speaker S) *I must say that her nineteen sixty-eight story shocks me,* immediately following the summing-up. The problem raised in the post-mortem is then pursued alongside, and despite interruptions by, the symbolic enactment of the decision. Figure 2 shows the pattern of the subtext with turns and clauses related to third-order elements of structure.

Before closing this section it may be of interest to summarize the distribution of turns and clauses among the different speakers (Table 2).

5 Commentary on the structure of the subtext

If we consider the subtext simply as the culminative phase of a dissertation defence, then the "problem" is very simply stated: decide on a joint recommendation. If we take account of the separate roles of the different interactants, however, then the problem will appear in more specific terms.

For Adam, the problem is to get the committee to initiate and support, in consensus, the recommendation that he considers appropriate. For the other members of the committee, the problem is to arrive at this recommendation in the appropriate way: that is, while fulfilling their role as adjudicators, which requires demonstrating their severity by making critical comments on some aspect of the work. There is thus a partial conflict of aims as the other members raise minor but nevertheless repair-demanding challenges.

Thus, following Adam's initial feedline *so you say pass,* the other members bring up critical comments; and these come in two stages. First, there are the riders to the proposals themselves (2: James, turns 8–12; Sherm, turn 14); then there are the distinct challenges (3: James,

I (upswing)

Problem ˆ Resolution:

1 Enunciation of problem
2 Proposals for resolution:
   J – proposal
   S – proposal
3 Complication (challenge and defence):
   time factor:
    challenge
    A – defence
   scope factor:
    challenge
    A – defence

II (downswing)

Decision

4 Decision proper:
   enunciation of decision (incl. comic relief)
   enactment
5 Summing-up

III (return upswing)

Post-mortem:

6 Problem
7 Closure

Figure 1 Movement of the subtext

Table 1   Distribution of turns and clauses in elements of structure

Element of structure	Turns		Clauses	
	N	Numbers	N	Numbers
1. Enunciation of problem	7	1–7	8	1–8
2. Proposals for resolution	10	8–17	62	9–70
3. Complication(s)	15	18–32	38	71–108
4. Decision proper	20	32–38; 46–47; 76; 79–81; 106–113	43	109–127; 142–143; 188–189; 191–194; 245–260
5. Summing-up	7	39–45	13	128–140
6. Post-mortem: problem	57	45; 48–75; 77–78; 82–105; 114–116	102	141; 144–187; 190; 195–244; 261–266
7. Closure	0	116	1	267
	116		267	

turns 18 and 20; Pat, turns 22–31). Each of these calls forth a response from Adam in defence of his supervisee. The choreography is as follows:

2. *James*:   recommends 'pass'
    but qualifies 'judgement defective'
Adam: counters 'has learnt something'
Sherm: recommends 'pass'
    but qualifies 'vision too narrow'
    Adam: counters 'has to produce something'
3. *James*:   challenges 'timing too slow?'
    Adam: defends 'not really slow'
    Pat: challenges 'coverage too restricted?'
    Adam: defends 'not really restricted'

Adam has now countered all reservations and challenges, aided by some temporary alliances (e.g. with Sherm on the question of scope). He now comes to the hinge of the subtext, clause 109 in turn 32: *So I can tell her that – you know, I . . .*, where the introductory *so* functions as internal causal conjunctive: "as a result of (causal) the preceding discourse (conjunctive) I conclude (internal). . . ." The conventions of this particular register require that the sponsoring magus should not actually pronounce the magic spell. He can set it up, create the context

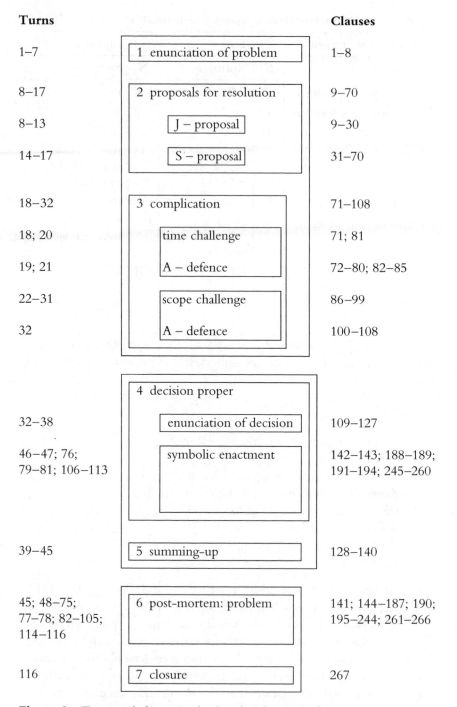

Turns		Clauses
1–7	1 enunciation of problem	1–8
8–17	2 proposals for resolution	9–70
8–13	J – proposal	9–30
14–17	S – proposal	31–70
18–32	3 complication	71–108
18; 20	time challenge	71; 81
19; 21	A – defence	72–80; 82–85
22–31	scope challenge	86–99
32	A – defence	100–108
	4 decision proper	
32–38	enunciation of decision	109–127
46–47; 76; 79–81; 106–113	symbolic enactment	142–143; 188–189; 191–194; 245–260
39–45	5 summing-up	128–140
45; 48–75; 77–78; 82–105; 114–116	6 post-mortem: problem	141; 144–187; 190; 195–244; 261–266
116	7 closure	267

Figure 2   Turns and clauses in third-order elements of structure

Table 2 Distribution of turns and clauses by speaker

Interactant	No. of turns	No. of clauses	Clauses per turn (mean)
Adam	26	76	2.92
James	16	31	1.94
Lee	25	45	1.80
Pat	11	12	1.09
Sherm	38	103	2.71
Total	116	267	

for it; and this Adam does, as far as the formulation of a projecting clause *I can tell her that . . .*; but he must not complete the projection. What Adam does is to keep the formula open with a holding expression *you know* and then wait for the visiting druids to come in with the words themselves. This they do, in turns 33 and 34 – Sherm: *she's won*; James: *she's overcome*.

Adam's role now becomes that of the jester; he provides some comic relief. Phases 1–3 have involved a certain amount of tension: not in relation to what would be decided – the decision has already been arrived at; but in relation to what processes would be gone through on the way to its being adopted. Each of the interactants has to mould the discourse in a certain patterning, to use it to achieve certain prescribed ends; and this has entailed a modest degree of conflict – or at least of incompatibility, such that they have had to manoeuvre, take up positions, and monitor the direction in which they were going. The resolution of the problem is at the same time a resolution of the tension, an audible sigh in the discourse; and Adam adopts the textbook strategy for such occasions – he tells a funny story, one that has himself as foil and that is relevant to the business in hand. This role naturally falls to the **local** druid: it is his novice who is being initiated, so it is he who plays the clown at this critical juncture in the proceedings.

There remains the final symbolic act: the execution of the charter. This is performed in a series of self-consciously casual little rituals that are strung throughout the remainder of the subtext (turns 46–47, 76, 79–81, and 106–113). I have interpreted these as a continuation of Phase 4 because they constitute the formal enactment of the decision; but they do not in fact begin to appear until after the completion of Phase 5, when Adam has gone out and then returned accompanied by the candidate.

Meanwhile, in Adam's absence, the three visiting magi have proceeded to talk about the novice; and they have been doing so in noticeably different terms – seeing her now as an initiate, "one of us", who has duly performed the rites. They have discussed her future in the order, the important work she has already been doing, and how to ensure her continued participation. This has contributed further to relaxing the tension, and might well have been the final sequence in the discourse. But – perhaps partly prompted by the need to keep the text alive for the symbolic enactment of the decision – one of the interactants, Sherm, has by now become personally involved. His own uprightness, and that of the institution itself, has been called into question by this newcomer to the order; and he probes the issue in a lengthy exchange extending over 57 turns, a total of 102 clauses. The debate rests inconclusive; partly because it is extraneous to the matter in hand – it cannot affect the main business of the text – and partly because in any case it cannot be resolved without going and looking up the records.

Once again it falls to the sponsor of the candidate to de-fuse the tension and bring the business to a close. This he does by again providing comic relief; again, in fact, referring to the past, but this time in very general terms: *all those changes depended on how some mothers behaved in 1937.* Then, before anyone can come back to the topic anew, he signs off, smartly, with an uncompromisable closing formula: *O.K. Thank you three muchly.* This has the appropriate "coefficient of weirdness" recognized long ago by Malinowski (1923/1959) as a necessary feature of the spell.

In the next three sections I shall examine certain features of the grammar of the subtext, interpreting these in terms of a systemic-functional grammar. For a summary of the relevant aspects of the grammar of English see Halliday (1985a). For an example of other discourse studies embodying the same approach see Hasan (1985) and Martin (1992).

6   Grammar (1): the clause complex

The "sentence" of our linguistic tradition arises from the recognition, by those who learnt to write language down, that there is structure in the grammar above the clause. A sequence of clauses may be tactically related – by parataxis and/or hypotaxis – so as to form a clause complex; and it is this clause complex that is encoded in writing in the form of a sentence.

I will refer to the clause complex here by the more familiar term. But – since this is a spoken text – it must be remembered that the

Table 3 Turns, clauses, and sentences in each phase

Phase	No. of turns	No. of clauses	No. of sentences	Clauses per sentence (mean)
1	7	8	7	1.1
2	10	62	28	2.2
3	15	38	19	2.0
4	20	43	32	1.3
5	7	13	11	1.2
6	57	102	73	1.4
7	0	1	1	1.0
Total	116	267	171	1.6

sentence is defined by the tactic relations among its constituent clauses. The limiting case is a sentence consisting of one clause: the "simple sentence" of traditional grammar. Table 3 shows the number of turns, clauses, and sentences in the seven phases of the subtext. Table 4 sets out the comparable figures for the different speakers.

Taken by itself, the average (mean) number of clauses per sentence in a dialogue signifies little, because it is constrained by the nature of the turns: rapid dialogic exchanges are characterized by short turns in which typically one turn = one clause = one sentence, as in turns 1–5 and 22–28, and the mean therefore tells us little about the grammar of the longer monologic passages. What is of more significance is the extent to which a speaker exploits the potential of complex sentence formation in those environments where it is possible for him to do so; and since the sentence is, overwhelmingly, bounded by the turn, this means in those turns which consist of two or more clauses. In the discussion that follows, therefore, we shall consider particular speakers

Table 4 Turns, clauses, and sentences by speaker (totals as in Table 3)

Speaker	No. of turns	No. of clauses	No. of sentences	Clauses per sentence (mean)
Adam	26	76	38	2.0
James	16	31	23	1.3
Lee	25	45	30	1.5
Pat	11	12	11	1.1
Sherm	36	103	69	1.5

at particular phases of the text, concentrating on passages where the turns are mainly longer than a single clause.

When James and Sherm are making their proposals, in Phase 2, stating why the candidate should be commended despite her faults, their clause-to-sentence ratio averages between 2 and 2.5 (James 17:9; Sherm 32:15, or 32:13 if two short turns are discounted). The structure is predominantly paratactic, though Sherm's becomes more hypotactic towards the end as he becomes more critical. During this same phase, Adam's ratio is just under 4 (11:3); one of his turns is the single word *Sherm?* (asking for Sherm's opinion), so that the remaining ten clauses are structured into just two sentences, one of 3 clauses and one of 7. Both of these, which are largely paratactic, show Adam on the defensive, somewhat urgently marshalling his clausal reinforcements with *ands* and *buts* and *therefores*.

In Phase 3, the positive rating of the candidate is explicitly challenged, first by James and then by Pat. In each case, the challenge occupies one turn (turns 18, 22); the turn is just one sentence, and the sentence is just one clause. Thus the challenges have the simplest possible sentence structure and a very high lexical density, with the embedding and grammatical metaphor that typically accompany it. For example,

> *James:* Adam, along these lines does she see the length of time [[it took her [[to finish this thesis]]]] as predictive of [[what she – her production record?

Even Pat's rather less ponderous *To what extent are these – the three theories that she selected truly representative of theories in this area?* is still much more marked in these respects than is typical of the text as a whole. The challenges are set in the grammar of more formal, written discourse. Adam's defence, in each case, is in striking contrast. Again, he relies more on the grammatical resource of sentence structure, with a clause-to-sentence ratio of 13:3 in the one case and 14:5 in the other – omitting his one-clause turns, 22:4 overall (see, in particular, Adam's turns 19 and 32). Given the high degree of hypotaxis in these instances we might well refer to this as a defence in depth.

It might appear from this that the greater degree of grammatical intricacy is characteristic of Adam as an individual speaker. But in Phase 6, where Adam is less personally involved, his clause-to-sentence ratio is only around 1 (15:13), whereas Sherm and Lee, who are now expounding positions in which they are personally concerned, go up to 1.5 (Sherm 45:30, Lee 33:22) – still a low figure for informal speech,

Table 5 Summary of clause-to-sentence ratios (entire subtext) in five segments identified by mode and tenor

Dominant mode	Tenor [main interactants]	cl:sent (unadjusted)	mean c/s	cl:sent (adjusted)	mean c/s
	Defence against challenge [Adam]	38:11	3.5	32:6	5.3
monologic	Challenge [James, Pat]	51:26	2	49:24	2
	Light relief [Adam]	15:7	2.1		
dialogic	Confrontation [Sherm, Lee]	78:52	1.5		
	Other turns	85:75	1.1		

but again allowing for the very short length of many of the turns; and higher than the three other interactants, whose contributions are almost entirely one-clause sentences. It is the roles in the development of the discourse, not the individual qualities of the speaker, that are being realized through the lexicogrammatical organization of the sentences. When Adam's role shifts to that of light relief, in Phase 4, his clause-to-sentence ratio goes up again to 2 (15:7): not as high as when he is defending the candidate, but higher than when he is largely uninvolved. At the same time the dominant form of interdependency becomes parataxis, instead of the more structured hypotaxis of the defensive passages.

The number of instances is not large, and these figures could arise by chance. But it is a general principle of spoken discourse that the more spontaneous, un-self-monitored the speech, the more intricate the tactic structure of the sentences; and it seems likely that this is what is being reflected here, as summarized in Table 5.

Thus, as expected, if we simply measure the overall ***intricacy*** of the sentences – their mean length in terms of the number of ranking clauses – this is primarily determined by the mode: where turns are short (that is, the mode orientation is dialogic) the sentences will average out as less intricate, because many turns will consist of one clause only. But if we break the text up according to mode orientation into its predominantly dialogic and predominantly monologic portions, and consider these separately, then within each mode the intricacy of the sentences appears as a function of the degree of personal involvement: the more the speaker is "wrapped up" in the discourse, the more complex the sentence grammar becomes. The depth of the sentence is a realization of (and metaphor for) the depth of the feelings.

This is not because of any **conscious** organization of the discourse. On the contrary, in highly self-monitored discourse the sentences tend to be **less** intricate – it is the *lexical density* that goes up under such conditions. Rather it is a feature of its spontaneity. What makes the grammar stretch in this way is the **unconscious** rhetoric of sustained commitment: to a topic, a position, or a goal. Nor is the complexity simply a matter of stringing together paratactic sequences of "andings". Parataxis does play a part (and is, in any case, itself a form of grammatical relationship); but the intricacy of these portions of text is characterized as much by hypotaxis as by parataxis. It is the combination of the two that gives the sentence (in this sense of a clause complex) the remarkable power that it has in spoken language. The present text does not display this intricacy to any very great extent; the speakers are monitoring themselves too closely for the grammar to get too far off the ground. But it does embody some of the kind of variation that is characteristic of such shifts of mode and of tenor.

7   Grammar (2): Modality: modalization and modulation

Modality is the judgemental component of the meaning of the clause: the opinions – offered by the speaker, or sought from the listener – regarding the likelihood (modalization) or the desirability (modulation) of the thesis. It is best considered along with polarity (positive/negative) as forming a single, complex semantic space.

Consider the proposition *it is*. If we vary this along the dimension of "probability" we get a semantic range as in Figure 3. The polar terms *it is, it isn't* are simply the limiting cases of the dimension of probability. In similar fashion we can expand the proposal *do!* along the dimension of obligation, as in Figure 4.

Thus, modality covers the intermediate space between the positive and negative poles: the speaker is explicitly selecting some band that lies between 'is' and 'isn't' (his judgement of how things are) or between 'do!' and 'don't!' (his judgement of how things should be). Of course, the speaker is also making a judgement in selecting one of the polar terms; what the modality system does is to specify certain intermediate values. The grammar identifies three of these: a median value ('probably'/'supposed to', where the polarity is equally balanced:

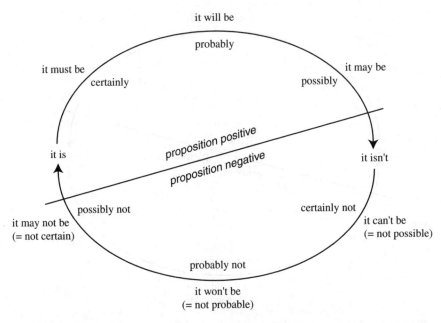

Figure 3 Modality: modalization (scale of probability)

'probable that . . . not' = 'not probable that', 'supposed not to . . .' = 'not supposed to . . .') and two outer values where it is skew: high ('certainly'/'required to': 'certain that . . . not' = 'not possible that . . .', 'required not to . . .' = 'not allowed to . . .') and low ('possibly'/ 'allowed to'; 'possible that . . . not' = 'not certain that . . .', 'allowed not to . . .' = 'not required to . . .'). There are other, more delicate distinctions within these three, and there are also other dimensions joining positive to negative; but these can be ignored for purposes of the present analysis.

In Phase 2 of the subtext the distribution of modalized clauses is as shown in Table 6.

The numbers are small; but this does represent a rather high concentration of modalities in relation to the subtext as a whole (and apparently also in relation to the remainder of the text). No distinction is being made here among the various sub-systems of modality: thus *they're probably away, it's probable/likely they're away, they're likely to be away, I think they're away*, are all being taken together as instances of "median probability"; and so on. These all embody more delicate semantic distinctions; but the text is too short to warrant our treating them apart.

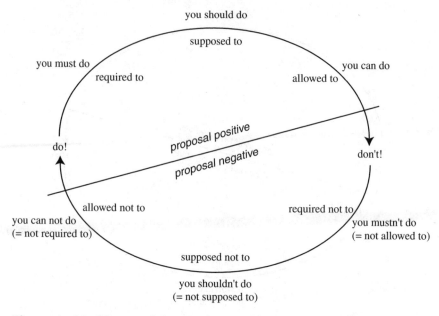

Figure 4   Modality: modulation (scale of obligation)

Let us consider the 17 clauses of James' proposal first. Nine of these contain modalizations; these are almost all median value (six include the form *I think*), and are either qualifications of his own assessment (*I think my sense is that she has done a good job, I think though she felt this compulsion about that*) or predictions of the candidate's future performance (*that may just come with exp[erience], she probably has to develop that sense*). These are matched by six clauses containing median- or high-value modulations – for example, *everything and more that a dissertation should be; she'll have to develop some sense of what stones aren't worth lifting; she can't publish a monograph of that* – from which there emerges a strong sense of the expected norms of scholarship, and of what a dissertation ought to be. The two motifs are combined in the *certainly she ought to*

Table 6   Modality in Phase 2 (James, Sherm)

	Total no. of clauses	Clauses with modalization	Clauses with modulation
J – proposal	17	9	6
S – proposal	31	13	3
Total	48	22	9

Table 7 Modality in Phase 3 (Adam)

	Total no. of clauses	Clauses with modalization	Clauses with modulation
time–defence	13	10	–
scope–defence	9	4	3
Total	22	14	3

be commended, where the *certainly* is a blend of both types of modality: with regard to the obligation to commend her (modulation: *she ought to be commended*), (1) I consider it more than probable that we are under such obligation (*certainly* as modalization), and (2) I insist that we are required to carry it out (*certainly* as modulation).

By contrast, the 31 clauses of Sherm's proposal include only three with modulations, and all of these are hedged around with a modalization: *I think it's important for her to quickly move . . .; it may be wise to restrict her vision; it'd be better it seems to me if she would expand her vision a little bit* (the last of which is followed by *well – let me take it back*). The keynote here is much more one of tentativeness: another ten clauses contain modalizations, which are mainly of "low" value, and are not simply attached to evaluative propositions. Examples are *what alternative meanings might be given to the class variable; the class variable is interpreted as a socialization variable but that's not necessarily the case; she could I think write some of this stuff up; she may well not think of herself as a young person initiating a research career; in the shorter run I'm not so sure.*

When we come to Phase 3, the challenge and defence, it is Adam, as defender, who displays the concentration of modalities, as shown in Table 7. Of the three modulations, two are negative (*you don't have to worry about cognitions; without having to get into their heads at all*) and all three are projected, as what "a real social structuralist . . . would say"; Adam is explicitly removing the motif of obligation from the discourse. Instead he uses a large number of subjective modalizations (*I think, I don't know*, etc.); and most of his modalizations (9 out of the 14) are thematic, for example, *I don't know that it was that slow, I think that Mel may encourage her* (see Section 8 below). The overall impact is one of deference and tentativeness, as Adam deftly leads up to the critical modulation: 'have I your permission to say she's passed?'.

The other section of the subtext in which modality plays a prominent part is Phase 6, where Sherm and Lee are negotiating towards a mutually acceptable version of past events. The proportion of the clauses that are modalized is about one in four (23 out of the 102 in question); but their effect is strongly enhanced, partly by the presence of some interrogative and tagged declarative clauses (e.g. *and didn't Jennifer Bird teach? but Jennifer was married, wasn't she?*), but more by the large number of clauses in which the modality itself becomes the thesis, for example, *that's not true, I'll test that hypothesis too, I prefer not to believe it, there's a further assertion*, and so on.

Sherm begins with a thematic high-value modulation *I must say* in its formulaic function of emphasizing an opinion; and the clause introduced by it turns out to be the point of departure for the whole discussion:

Sherm: I must say that her nineteen sixty-eight story shocks me.

He goes on with a double high-value modalization:

Adam there had to be female AIs pre-nineteen sixty-nine –
    I just don't believe I spent the first . . .

As he becomes less sure of himself the certainty of his grammar goes up:

these people taught classes for us, I'm absolutely certain

– followed by *I'm going back and check*. Lee counters with a clause that is doubly modalized but at median and low value:

I think you might find they were married

and maintains the same level with *I think you were acting chairman in sixty-four were you not?* By a few turns later, the modalities have begun to take over:

James: And didn't Jennifer Bird teach?
Sherm: Jennifer? I'm sure – well, again: I don't know, I'm not sure.
Adam: I think she taught; but then I'm not sure.
Lee: But Jennifer was married wasn't she?

until Sherm, following a Phase 5 interruption, resumes with:

Sherm: What you're implying may indeed be true

in which modality figures three times over: (1) the thesis of the attributive clause '*x* is true', (2) the embedded thesis in the Carrier 'what you're implying', and (3) the modalization itself 'may be'.

Once the modality has become foregrounded in this way Sherm holds on to it as a topic:

> *Sherm*: I don't like what's being said . . . I prefer to believe it's not really true . . . therefore I shall look for evidence that it's not true . . . and it may turn out that I won't find that evidence.

This last clause establishes the basis for an amicable closure through the use of the low-value modalization *may*: this then becomes a keynote for Lee and Adam:

> *Lee*: Well you may find it; and if you do . . . [ ]
> *Adam*: Well and there may be others too . . . [ ]
> *Lee*: Well that may have been a personal thing . . .

At this point it becomes possible to disengage, and for Adam to move to the final closing turn.

Modulation, therefore, appears as a significant feature only in Phase 2, the proposals for the evaluation of the thesis, which are essentially judgemental in character: there is a norm, against which the present offering has to be judged. The grammar of obligation expresses this characteristic, both directly in instances such as *should you have examined* −?, and symbolically as in *she ought to be commended*, where the obligation is on our part − we have the duty to commend her − but the motif of the maintenance of norms is clearly present.

Modalization, on the other hand, characterizes especially those parts of the text involving some degree of interpersonal negotiation: the examiners expressing their views, to arrive at a consensus, in Phase 2; Adam coming to the defence, his special pleading showing the delicacy that is expected of a candidate's sponsor, in Phase 3; and in Phase 6, Sherm exploring a politically sensitive area in which both he and the candidate are personally and professionally concerned. This final phase, which I have interpreted as "post-mortem" in the subtext, is at the same time a further subtext in its own right; as it moves away from the business of the oral examination, the extended modalization allows it to function as an armistice, terminating the preceding encounter while at the same time providing a foretaste of the cold war that is obviously going to come. .

8   Grammar (3): thematization

The system of THEMATIZATION is the textual component in the grammar of the clause: it is the system from which the clause derives its organization in the form of a message, as a Theme followed up by a Rheme. In each ranking clause, one of the elements in the process (i.e. an element in the transitivity structure: a participant or circumstance, or occasionally the process itself) is assigned the status of topical Theme.

So, for example, in

in this literature the class variable is interpreted as a socialization variable

the topical Theme is *in this literature*. If we changed it to *the class variable is interpreted in this literature as a socialization variable* then *the class variable* would become the topical Theme.

The thematic organization is realized by the ordering of the elements: that which is put first functions as Theme. The first element in the clause that has a function in **transitivity** (as Actor, Goal, Location, Manner, etc.) is the **topical** component of the Theme; whatever **follows** it functions as Rheme. It may be preceded, however, by other, nontopical elements, in which case these elements also contribute to the Theme of the clause. They are of two kinds: textual and interpersonal. For example, in

Well I think she has done a good job

well is textual Theme, *I think* is interpersonal Theme, and *she* is topical Theme. Most textual Themes are items which have to come first if they occur in the clause at all.

The significance of thematization is twofold. (1) In the clause itself, the Theme is the point of departure. In the case of the topical Theme we can interpret this in content terms: it is 'what the clause is about', following the explanation offered by the ancient Greek rhetorical grammarians. The textual Theme is the point of departure in another sense: it is the deictic element in the clause, that which makes explicit its relation to its environment. Textual themes are either continuative (like *well, oh, I mean*), conjunctive (like *on the other hand, after that, in point of fact*), or structural (paratactic or hypotactic conjunctions such as *and, but, so; if, because, while*). The interpersonal Theme is the point of departure in the sense that it signals the value the speaker assigns to the clause in the dialogue: this may be a mood element (e.g. a WH-item signalling 'I am asking you a question'), a modality or comment (giving

250

the speaker's angle, e.g. *perhaps, unfortunately*), or a vocative, making explicit who is being addressed. Unlike the textual Themes, such interpersonal elements are not obligatorily thematic; they may occur elsewhere in the clause, so that if they do occur in thematic position (i.e. preceding the topical Theme), their status as Theme is being foregrounded – although not very strongly, since for many of them it is the **unmarked** condition of their occurrence.

(2) The choice of Theme in the clause also has significance in the discourse (Fries 1995; Ghadessy 1995): if we examine, clause by clause, the thematic organization of the text, we find that the clausal Themes are carrying the text along and guiding the direction in which it is going. This does not mean the same element occurs repeatedly in thematic function: this may happen in some registers (for example, a participant recurring as Theme throughout a narrative), but in other registers the pattern may be established by systematic **variation** in the choice of Theme (e.g. Rheme of one clause becoming Theme of the next in the dynamic of a technical description). What is noticeable, however, is that when a text appears disjointed and directionless this is often due to a kind of thematic drift, an apparent randomness in the choice of Theme such that no pattern of any kind is set up. The effect is a statistical one; it is not the case that every clause will contribute to a particular pattern. But if a significant number of the ranking clauses in a text – and in particular those that are independent, since they possess the full range of thematic potential – displays a dominant thematic orientation, then the text will maintain a significant sense of movement that is clearly related to its function in the context of situation. Like everything else discussed here, these patterns are typically below the conscious awareness of speaker or listener; they need to be revealed by the processes of linguistic analysis.

In the present text what the linguistic analysis reveals is singularly predictable once the context of situation is given. Here are the prevailing topical Themes of Phase 2 (Table 8). The dominant Theme is clearly *she*, with *it/the dissertation* appearing as subsidiary Themes. The organizing principle of this portion of the text is clearly the "third party" of the discourse: the candidate and her work. First or second person Themes hardly appear at all – until Adam's defence at the end of the Sherm proposal (turns 15, 17). I was puzzled, looking at my analysis, to find Adam suddenly talking about himself at this juncture; but he is not doing, he is playing the candidate's part. Of the five occurrences of *I* as clausal Theme, four are functioning as projections of the candidate's view of herself.

Table 8 Topical themes in Phase 2

	Total no. of clauses	Clauses with "candidate" Theme	Clauses with "dissertation" Theme
James proposal	17	10	3
Sherm proposal	31	16	3
Total	48	26	6

The candidate remains as dominant clausal Theme (8 out of 15 clauses) throughout the first part of Phase 3, the time challenge. When it comes to the scope challenge, however, the pattern changes. Following Pat's initial Theme *to what extent*, which sets in motion the development of the whole passage, the Theme in the six clauses she exchanges with Adam is 'the three theories that she [the candidate] selected', referred to by Pat as *they* and by Adam collectively as *that*. This reflects a shift in orientation from the candidate ('she works slowly') to the content of her thesis. In his defence, particularly to the second challenge, Adam operates by changing the thematic basis of the discussion: he introduces various impersonal Themes, including three nominalizations which are almost the only nominalized clause Themes in the entire subtext:

one thing that'll happen
the only thing that would be substantially different
what you have to do

These are all Value in the Value ⁀ Token structure of an identifying clause (a thematic equative, or "pseudo-cleft construction"); what Adam is doing here is using the resources of the grammar to shift the grounds of debate away from the candidate and her writings.

As might be expected, there is no clear thematic patterning in the scattered segments of the decision and accompanying light relief; while in the summing-up (Phase 5) the dominant Theme is either *she* (the candidate) or *the position* (her appointment). In Phase 6, however, a new progression emerges. Sherm and Lee have now changed roles; it is not quite a reversal, since Lee cannot take on the mantle of power, but a role switch whereby she has become the accuser and he the accused. Moreover he accepts this role not merely as a symbol of past discrimination but as one who is seen to have been personally culpable (turns 57–64). This marked shift of tenor is achieved by personalizing the Theme: *I* and *you* become the primary motifs in the development of this new phase of the discourse. Then follows a passage in which other persons come in as topical Themes: *Ann, Jennifer,* and so on, serve as examples of the topic under discussion. For the final movement of this phase, the Themes are once again *I* and *you*, but now interspersed with impersonal *it, that, there*, as Sherm and Lee manoeuvre towards an acceptable compromise: one which involves an elaborate thematic interplay between themselves and sections of their own ongoing discourse – for example, *it* referring to *what you're implying, that* referring to *Ann eventually taught too*, and so on. As a coda, Adam comes in once again with a nominalized Theme *what's really critical*; this puts all their *I*s and *you*s and *it*s and *that*s to shame – and so has to be softened with the aid of a Rheme that is yet another piece of light relief. Then, before Sherm and Lee can continue – or else both turn on him – Adam closes the session.

Adam began this closing Theme by means of the continuative *well* – a form of textual Theme, as noted earlier. This typically introduces a new direction, either predicted (e.g. 'I'm now answering the question you've just asked me') or unpredicted; here, it is what enables Adam to get his overriding move accepted by the others. An interesting feature of this subtext is how small a range of nontopical Themes occur. A number of the modalizations in Phase 2 were thematic (6 out of 9 of James', 5 out of 13 of Sherm's; cf. Section 6 above), showing James and Sherm using 'in my opinion' as a method of development; but other than these, interpersonal Themes were extremely rare. As far as textual Themes are concerned, there were some continuatives (mainly *well* and *oh*) at critical points, and the usual paratactic and hypotactic conjunctions such as *and, so, then, but, if, because,* and *that*, which have to be thematic if they are there at all (and hence appear in every clause complex); but hardly any conjunctive expressions – *in that sense, along those lines, that is to say* were almost the only ones to occur. And within the topical Themes there are scarcely any circumstantials (time, place, manner, matter, cause), such as are very frequently found in many other varieties of text. The subtext studied here is developed almost entirely around two motifs: first, the (then absent) candidate and her work, and second, the interlocutors themselves and their own discourse on the issue that concerns them. The exception throughout is Adam, who uses the potential of thematic variation to bring about the resolutions, the transitions, and finally a conclusion to the discourse.

253

9 Summary

So to my own conclusion, which must be (like Adam's) brief. My aim
has been, in intention at least, a modest one: that of showing the
language at work in the creation of meaning. A text **is created by** its
context, the semiotic environment of people and their activities that
we have construed via the concepts of field, tenor, and mode; it also
creates that context. The relationship that we refer to as *realization*
between *levels* of semiosis – situation (doing) realized in semantics
(meaning), semantics realized in lexicogrammar (wording), and so on –
is a dialectic one involving what Lemke (1984) interprets as n-order
metaredundancies. A semiotic event is an event on many levels.

In this chapter, the focus has been on wordings: on patterns of
selection at the lexicogrammatical level. It is important not to think
of the lexicogrammar as a kind of outer clothing, as the "expression" of
meanings that somehow pre-exist the text. There is no prior meaning
that is then encoded into wording: there can be no dissertation defence
(and, needless to say, no dissertation) except as lexicogrammatical
events.

In looking at patterns in the wording I have of course been highly
selective; I have said nothing about cohesion, mood, transitivity,
information structure, tense, grammatical metaphor, the verbal and
nominal groups, or derivational morphology, nor about the lexical
choices that represent the more "delicate" regions of the lexicogrammar. All these and other systems would have repaid equally detailed
analysis, and more: a rich interpretation of the grammar of any text
would itself constitute a text of vastly greater length than the original.
I chose to discuss one or two systems that related rather clearly, as it
seemed to me, to the functions of the text in its particular context of
culture. The text before us – and the subtext picked out for closer
attention – exemplified the power of discourse to change the environment that engendered it. In particular, Lee emerges from the text as a
changed persona; and in the process, her relation with all the others has
undergone a change. We might want to think of the entire text as a
kind of expanded performative: 'We dub thee PhD.' But this would
obscure a more fundamental point, which is that **every** text is performative in this sense. There can be no semiotic act that leaves the world
exactly as it was before.

APPENDIX 1
TRANSCRIPTION OF "SUBTEXT"*

* Numbers in this transcript refer to turn numbers, not to lines. The text is that of the complete or shared text, i.e. lines 1491–1778.

Legend

//	tone group boundary (always also foot boundary)
/	foot boundary
^	silent beat
bold	location of tonic prominence (focus of information)
...	pause (sufficient to disrupt rhythm)
—	incomplete clause

1	tone 1 (falling tonic) 1 + wide fall 1 − narrow fall
2	tone 2 (rising tonic) 2 variant having sharp fall-rise
3	tone 3 ('level' tonic, realized as low rise)
4	tone 4 (falling-rising tonic)
5	tone 5 (rising-falling tonic)
13	tone 1 followed by tone 3 in compound tone group
53	tone 5 followed by tone 3 in compound tone group

1 A. // 1 ▲ so / you say / **pass** //
2 J. // 1 **oh** yeah //
3 A. // 2 ▲ is / that a ... // 1 that's a / **neutral** / term //
4 J. // 1 ▲ I'm / not **sure** //
5 S. // 1 what are you / **looking** for / Adam //
6 A. // 4 well I ... ▲ I / guess I / have in the / back of / **my** mind that

— // 1 ˌ that I / want to be / able to con/vey / some sense of
. . . ˌ the com/mittee's res/**ponse**//

7 S. // 1 ˌ the com/mittee's res/ponse to the / enterprise as a / **whole**//

8 J. // 1 **well** I // 4 think / **my** sense / is that . . . // 1 ˌ she has / done
ˌ a / good / **job** // 4 ˌ and she / certainly / has — // 4 ˌ I mean
/ this / project for / **her** has been // 1 everything and / **more** I
/ think that a // 1 dissertation / **should** be // 1 and at the / stage
of her pro/fessional de/velopment I / think this is / really a /
good / **job** and she // 1 ought to be com/**mended** // 1 certainly
she / ought to be com/mended for the / very thing that / Peg /
mentioned // 1 no / stone was / left un/**turned** // 4 ˌ I / think
in the / **future** she'll // 4 have to de/velop / some / **sense** of //
1 what stones / aren't worth / **lifting** you / know but // 1 ˌ but
/ that may just / come . . . / come with exp — // 1 ˌ I mean she
/ can't ˌ she / can't / **publish** a // 1 **monograph** of / that //

9 S. // 4 problem with / that in the / disser/**tation** / James is that if she
// 1 didn't / turn them / someone on this com/mittee would
have said / should you have ex/amined —

10 J. // 1 **right** // 5 ˌ but / I think / I think though / she felt this
com/**pulsion** about / that

11 S. // 1 ˌ her/**self** //

12 J. // 1 **yeah** // 1 ˌ her/**self** she // 5 wasn't really / worried about us /
looking over her / **shoulder** // 4 ˌ and so / she probably / has
to develop / **that** sense but I // 1 think / that'll just / come with
a — / you know with / more . . . / more / **research** //

13 A. // 4 ˌ oh I / think / **part** of it / was that // 3 ˌ you / **know** // 4 ˌ
that the / question that / **you** raised early / on and // 4 some of
the / questions that / **I** raised // 1 she got to / thinking about /
kinds of / **questions** // 1 not / necessarily a/bout spe/**cific** /
things but I / ˌ I / mean I // 1 think she's / learned something
about . . . ˌ the / kinds of / questions that / ˌ as / Sherm says / ˌ
people / **would** have asked // 2 **Sherm** //

14 S. // 4 ˌ it's a / fine / **job** // 4 ˌ by / **my** / lights // 4 ˌ I / would
have / **wished** it were / shorter // 1 ˌ I / have some / sympathy
for the twenty/five page / **psych** disser/tations . . . // 4 this . . .
ˌ the / one / **comment** I'd / have // 1 has to / do with her /
writing . . . this / **up** . . . // 4 her . . . the disser/tation was /
written . . . ˌ was / written within the / **frame** // 3 these are the
/ extant / **theories** let's // 3 use these to de/rive hy/**potheses**
and // 3 get some / **data** and // 1 cast them a/gainst . . . ˌ a/
gainst the / **theories** // 1 ˌ and / that's . . . / **fine** // 1 ˌ but it's

256

/ also a / **limit** // 1 + ˌ because it / leads her / ˌ for ex/ample /
not to // 1 ask such / questions as the / kind of thing I was /
pushing her on a / little bit // 1 what al/ternative / meanings
might be / given to . . . the . . . ˌ the / **class** / variable // 1 other
than the / sociali/**zation** it is // 4 true that / in this / **literature**
the // 1 class variable is in/**terpreted** as a / socialization / variable
// 1 ˌ but / that's not /ˌ / necessarily the / **case** if you // 4 start
from the more / **general** question of // 1 how can we ex/plain
/ **radicalism** // 4 rather than the / more par/**ticular** / question
of // 1 given the / theories / **currently** / used to ex/plain /
radicalism . . . // 1 ˌ she / **could** I think / write some of / this
stuff / up wi/thin the more // 1 **limited** / frame it'd be // 13
better it / seems to / **me** if she would // 1 ˌ ex/pand her /
vision a // 1 **little** bit // 1 ˌ so that she's / not / necessarily /
limited ˌ al/though I — . . . // 1 well / ˌ / let me / take it /
back // 1 ˌ in the / longer / **run** I would / want her to /ˌ / do
that // 4 ˌ in the / **shorter** / run I'm // 1 not so / **sure** // 1 ˌ it
/ may be /wise to re/strict her / **vision** // 1 ˌ in / order to . . . ˌ
to / get some things / **done** // 1 ˌ and / **out** I //I think it's im/
portant for / her to . . . ˌ to / quickly / move ˌ to / get at least /
one piece / out and in the / literature just to / give her the /
confidence that she can / **do** it // 1 ˌ I re/acted to that / forty
year old / **woman** comment // 1 ˌ because I think / that's . . . /
that's the / **danger** for / Pat — . . . // 1 ˌ for / **Lee** // 4 ˌ if she
/ **thinks** of her/self that / way she may / well not / think of
her/self as . . . // 3 ˌ you / **know** a // 3 young / **person** // 3 ˌ
in/itiating a re/search ca/**reer** // 3 getting things / **moving** // 1
ˌ and / **so** on that — //

15 A. // 13 **I** can / tell you what her / view on / **that** is and / that is //
4 ˌ I'm / **older** and // 4 therefore I'm in a / worse com/petitive
po/**sition** and I've // 1 **really** got to pro/duce //

16 S. // 1 ˌ but I'm / **smarter** //

17 A. // 1 and I'm / **going** to //

18 J. // 1 Adam a/long those /**lines** does // 2 she / see the / length of /
time it / took her to / finish this / thesis as pre/dictive of / what
she — ˌ her pro/**duction** / record //

19 A. // 1 actually it's . . . // 1 ˌ it's / not / all that / **long** / 1 given the
/ norm in soci/**ology** // 4 that — ˌ I / think that the . . . ˌ the
first / draft of her pro/**posal** // 1 ˌ was / less than / three years
a/**go** // 1 ˌ and / then she / did col/lect you / know a sub/
stantial a/mount of / **data** // 1 while she . . . ˌ and / she's been

257

/ **working** the full / time // 4 ˎ and / I don't / know that /
given that she / **did** collect her / own / data and // 4 did as we
/ all can / see a tre/mendous / search of the / **literature** // 4
and a tre/mendous a/mount of a/**nalysis** // 1 I don't / know
that it was / that / **slow** I / mean I // 4 don't think she was /
dragging her / heels very / **much** in this / period //

20 S.   // 1 James may be / thinking / more of her . . . ˎ her / total /
graduate ca/**reer**

21 A.   // ˎ but I / do / also — // 1 **yeah** // 1 ˎ that's / **true** // 1 — ˎ and
I . . . ˎ and I / think she's / a/**ware** of this and I / think you /
know she — . . . // 4 ˎ I / think one / thing that'll / **happen** I
/ think that . . . // 1 ˎ that / Mel may en/**courage** her // 1 ˎ and
I / think that'll be / all to the / **good** //

22 P.   // 4 ˎ to / what ex/tent are / these / ˎ the / three / theories that
she se/**lected** // 1 truly repre/**sentative** of / theories in this /
area //

23 A.   // 1 that's / **it** / ˎ // 1 that's /**it** //

24 P.   // 1 ˎ they / are in/**deed** //

25 S.   // 1 **yeah** //

26 P.   // 1 **oh** // 2 they are / **the** / theories //

27 A.   // 1 that's about / **it** //

28 P.   // 1 they are / not / **really** repre/sentative / then //

29 S.   // 1 **well** there are // 1 ˎ there are / vari/**ations** // 1 ˎ there are /
variations // 1 on / **themes** but . . . // 4 ˎ but / I don't know
of any / **major** con/tender ˎ there / may be // 1 ˎ well / I don't
/ know of / anything that / looks much / **different** from the /
things she's . . . ˎ she has / looked at in the spe/cific / time //

30 A.   // 4 ˎ ex/cept for the / sense that —

31 P.   // 1 ˎ so / nobody / nobody would at/tack her on / **that** ground /
then if she — //

32 A.   // 1 oh no / I don't / **think** so // 4 ˎ I think the / only / thing that
would be sub/**stantially** / different would be a // 1 real / social
/ **structuralist** who would / say // 4 ˎ you / don't have to /
worry about cog/**nitions** // 1 what you have to / do is / find
the lo/cation of these / people in the / social / **structure** // 1
— ˎ and / then you'll / find out how they're / going to be/have
with/out having to / get into their / heads at / **all** // 4 ˎ and /
that // 1 hasn't been / **tested** // 1 — ˎ ex/cept in / very / gross
/ kinds of / **ways** with // 1 macro / data which has / generally
/ not been / very satis/**factory** // 1 **yeah** / ˎ // 1 ˎ so I can /
tell her that — // 3 ˎ you / **know** I —

33 S. // 1 ˏ she's / **won** //

34 J. // 1 ˏ she's / over/**come** //

35 A. // 1 **yeah** // 1 ˏ I / told her the / story of when I / took my / **orals** // 1 ˏ it was / big Jack / **Bismark** and // 1 Jedley / Still/**well** and // 1 they came / out of the / oral and / Still/well says / you're going to / have to / **tell** him / Jack and // 1 Bismark says oh / no he says / go on / **you** tell him / Jedley // 1 ˏ it was / this whole / **business** // 1 ˏ she / already / **knows** so there's // 1 no / **point** //1 ˏ let me — / ˏ let me / go / **get** her and // 1 bring her / **in** //

36 P. // 1 yeah it was an / excellent / **job** I / think //

37 A. // 1 + got to / figure out / how to get / **out** of here //

38 S. // 1 someone / help / **Adam** //

39 P. // 1 + she's been / teaching new / **courses** // 1 + **too** / every se/ mester // 2 **hasn't** she //

40 S. // 1 **yeah** // 1 ˏ she / **has** // 3 ˏ they / teach I / think nine / **hours** //

41 J. // 1 ˏ for a / while she was in / danger of / losing her . . . / **slot** // 2 **wasn't** she //

42 P. // 2 ˏ well / wasn't the po/sition o/**riginally** just a / one year po/ sition //

43 S. // 4 ˏ yeah it / wasn't . . . ˏ it / wasn't that / **she** was in / danger of / losing the po/sition it was that the po// 1 + **sition** was in // 1 + danger of being / **lost** //

44 J. // 1 **yeah** //

45 S. // 4 ˏ and in / **point** of / fact I // 1 think it was / **opened** on the // 13 basis of an ap/**peal** which / **says** // 1 this is just too / valuable a / person to / **lose** she's an // 1 + **absolutely** / first rate // 4 **teacher** // 1 + really / **very** very / good // 4 ˏ I / **must** say that her // 4 nineteen sixty / **eight** story // 1 + **shocks** me//

46 A. // 1 ˏ well we / have something for you to / **sign** //

47 L. // 1 **couple** of / somethings //

48 S. // 1 Adam there / **had** to be / female A / I's pre / nineteen sixty / nine I // 1 just don't be/**lieve** . . . // ˏ I spent the / first —

49 P. // 2 ˏ you were in / **shock** / there for a / while //

50 A. // 4 ˏ there were . . . ˏ there were / certain / people who were . . ./ T / **A's** //

51 S. // 1 ˏ but the / A / **I's** //

52 A. // 3 Carol / **Collins** // 3 uh / Debbie / **what's** her name //

53 J. // 1 Sue / **Phillips** //

259

54 S. // 2 these people / taught /classes for / **us** // 1 — I'm / absolutely / **certain** // 1 — I'm going / back and / **check** //

55 L. // 1 **do** // 1 ˌ and I / think you might / find they were / **married** //

56 S. // 1 — ˌ I'll / test that hy/pothesis / **too** // I — ˌ I'm / curious e/ nough to / **check** //

57 L. // 1 ˌ and then I / think you / might . . . ˌ and then / check on a/ **nother** one // 1 check who was / acting / chairman when they re/ceived the . . .

58 S. // 2 ˌ ap/**pointment** //

59 L. // . . .ˌ ap/**pointment** //

60 S. // 1 ˌ I will / check / **that** one //

61 L. // 1ˌ I / think / **you** were //

62 S. // ˌ well I — //

63 L. // 1 ˌ cause I / think you were / acting / chairman in / sixty / **four** were you // 2 **not** //

64 S. // 4 ˌ I / was at / **some** point // 1 **yeah** // 4 sixty / four or / sixty / **five** //

65 P. // 2 ˌ dis/criminated in / **favour** of / married / women / Sherm //

66 L. // 1 ˌ the / girl who's / husband was in / anthro/**pology** //

67 J. // 1 + ˌ the / girl who's / husband was in / anthro/**pology** //

68 L. // 1 ˌ she's / now / down at the / **state** / unit // 1 **she** was / teaching before // 4 I taught //

69 J. // 1 **oh** yeah // 2 ˌ and / didn't / Jennifer / **Bird** teach //

70 S. // 4 **Jennifer** // 1 + ˌ I'm / **sure** // 1 well — / ˌ a/gain I don't // 1 **know** I'm not // 1 **sure** //

71 A. // 4 ˌ I / think / **she** / taught // 1 ˌ but / then I'm not / **sure** //

72 L. // 1 ˌ but / Jennifer was / **married** // 2 **wasn't** she //

73 J. // 1 **yes** //

74 S. // 1 **no** // 4 not at . . . /not at /**that** time // 1 **no** //

75 L. // 2 not at / **that** point // 1 **check** it be/cause — // 4 ˌ see the . . . ˌ the / reason I pre/**sume** that // 4 women were / **allocated** to / these po/sitions is because . . .

76 J. // 2 ˌ can we / **use** this // 2 do we sign re/**lease** forms // 2 **too** Adam //

77 L. // 1 ˌ of / **Clifford's** / teaching //

78 A. // 1 **oh** //

79 L. // 2 did you / already / **sign** them //

80 J. // 5 **no** // 5 **I** didn't / sign them //

81 A. // 1 ˌ that's / **right** // 1 + ˌ we've / got something / **else** for you to /sign // 1 **too** //

82 S. // 4 ˏ you know / ˏ / what you're im/plying may in/deed be / **true** // 4 ˏ but / if / ˏ it / **is** I . . . // 3 ˏ I'm / shocked by the / **fact** I'm // 1 also shocked by my / lack of a/**wareness** of it //

★ ★ ★ ★ ★ ★

83 S. // 1 that's not / **true** because // 1 **I** did // 3 ˏ when / Mary went / **out** —

84 L. // 4 ˏ when / **you** came / in // 1 they went /**out** // ˏ but you see / she was / looking about —

85 S. // 2 ˏ be/**fore** that / time //

86 L. // 1 **yeah** // 1 ˏ be/fore you were / **in** there //

87 A. // ˏ Ann —

88 J. // 1 **Wilder** //

89 L. // 1 **Lowell** //

90 S. // 1 **Wilder** //

91 A. // 2 ˏ did / **she** / teach // ˏ I / thought she —

92 S. // 1 no there's / this — / ˏ there's a / **further** as//1 **section** //

93 L. // 1 **Ann** e/ventually / taught // 1 **too** // 1 **yes** // 1 ˏ but / that just is / not des/criptive of the / situ/ation any / **more** and . . .

94 S. // 1 ˏ I / know but I . . . / frankly I don't / **like** what's being // 1 **said** // 1 it / **bothers** me it dis// 1 **turbs** me // 1 ˏ in the sense that I pre/fer not — . . . ˏ to be/lieve it's not / really / **true** //

95 L. // 3 o / **k** // 1 **fine** //

96 S. // 1 + therefore I shall / look for / evidence that it's / **not** true //

97 A. // 5 ˏ and / he'll / **find** it god/dammit // 4 **he** knows / how to be a / soci/ologist //

98 S. // 13 ˏ and uh / ˏ it / may turn / out that I won't / **find** that / **evidence** and // 1 then I'll / **really** be up/set //

99 L. // 4 well you / may / **find** it // 4 ˏ and / if you / **do** // 1 look for / **marriage** as the //1 ˏ differ/**entiating** / factor //

100 S. // 4 ˏ but / if I / **do** find it I —

101 P. // 1 + have an un/usual ef/**fect** then if / that's the / case //

102 L. // 1 + ˏ well / **I've** never been / able to / sort out the dis//4 crimination I've re/ceived as a / **woman** from the dis// 1 crimination I've re/ceived as a / **single** / person // 1 ˏ they get / inter/**twined** and they // 1 inter/**act** with each / other / sometimes //

103 A. // 1 well and there / may be / others / **too** // 1 other / kinds of dis/crimination as / **well** // 3 ˏ you / mentioned / **age** and // 1 that's that's / **clearly** a —

261

104 L. // 1 **oh** yeah //

105 S. // 1 **yeah** but // 1 that would / not have been / ˏ / **relevant** //

106 L. // 1 this is / not for / **signature** // 1 **wait** a minute // 1 **wait** a minute / ˏ // 1 this was / just a / double / **copy** // 1ˏ I / wanted a / copy of / what I / **did** //

107 S. // 2 ˏ then it's / **this** and // 2 **this** just the // 2 **two** things //

108 L. // 1 **yeah** //

109 A. // 2 ˏ just / **two** things //

110 L. // 1 one is the / **abstract** / 1 **yeah** // 3 one is the / **abstract** and // 1 one's the ac/**ceptance** //

111 S. // 1 that will be /ˏ pre/sumably / **duplicated** // 1 ˏ you'll need/

112 L. // 1 **yes** // 1 ˏ and they / will ac/cept the / **xeroxing** / of it //

113 S. // 1 + **good** they // 1 + save / **signatures** //

114 L. // 4 ˏ well / that / may have been a / **personal** / thing but the // 4 reason / **given** wasn't / based on / personal —

115 S. // 4 ˏ in / **that** sense it's // 1 + interesting how the / ˏ / climate and / circumstances have / **changed** / that is to say //4 if in/ deed there were . . . a / **personal** reaction / negative the // 1 last thing in the / **world** they would be / rationalized in / terms of would be . . . ˏ you know the //1 ˏ fact that it was a / **female** or / whatnot at // 4 **this** point //

116 A. // 1 ˏ well / what's really / **critical** is that // 4 all those / **changes** de/pended on // 1 how some / mothers behaved in / nineteen thirty / **seven** // . . . // 1 o / **k** // 1 thank you / **three** // 1 **muchly**//

APPENDIX 2
ANALYSIS OF "SUBTEXT"

Legend

CLAUSE
[n] clause broken off and not counted
[[rankshifted (embedded) clause
n- clause uncompleted but counted

CLAUSE COMPLEX

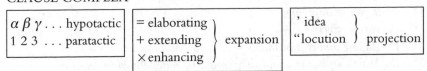

$\alpha\ \beta\ \gamma$ . . . hypotactic	= elaborating		' idea	
1 2 3 . . . paratactic	+ extending	} expansion	"locution	} projection
	× enhancing			

MOOD/POLARITY
declarative, interrogative: WH-, interrogative:yes/no, imperative, minor,
   non-finite
positive, negative   tagged ('+ tag'), untagged (others)

MODALITY

modalization: e.g.		modulation: e.g.
I think it is	subjective, explicit	I want you to
it may be	subjective, implicit	you should
it probably is	objective, implicit	you're supposed to
it's likely it is	objective, explicit	it's desirable for you to

263

TRANSITIVITY (PROCESS TYPE)

material; behavioural; mental: cognition, affection, perception; verbal; relational: attributive, identifying / intensive, circumstantial, possessive; relational: existential

effective (voice) shown where it is marked option

congruent process type shown where that selected embodies grammatical metaphor

Completion of Topical Themes

1 *at the stage of her professional development*
2 *problem with that in the dissertation*
3 *someone on this committee*
4 *the one comment I'd have*
5 *what alternative meanings*
6 *in the longer run*
7 *in the shorter run*
8 *the first draft of her proposal*
9 *one thing that'll happen*
10 *the only thing that would be substantially different*
11 *what you have to do*
12 *the reason I presume that women were allocated to these positions*
13 *what you're implying*
14 *the reason given*
15 *the climate and circumstances*
16 *the last thing in the world they would be rationalized in terms of*
17 *what's really critical*
18 *all those changes*

TURN	SPEAKER	CLAUSE	CLAUSE COMPLEX	FUNCTION IN CLAUSE COMPLEX	RANK SHIFT (EMBEDDING)	THEME			MOOD
						TEXTUAL	INTERPERSONAL	TOPICAL	
1	A	1				so		you	declar
2	J	2							minor
3	A	[3] 3					is	that that	int: y/n declar
4	J	4						I	declar
5	S	5					wh	at	int: WH
6	A	6 7	}	α 'β		well that	I guess	I I	declar declar
7	S	8							minor
8	J	9 10 11- 12	}	α 'β1 +2 1	=II	well and I mean that	I think	my sense she she this project a dissertation	declar declar declar declar
		13 14 15	}	+2 +3 1	=II	and and that	I think certainly	at...¹ she she	declar declar declar declar
		16 17 18- 19	}	'2 1 +2	'II	that but I mean	I think what	no stone in the future what stones that she	declar declar int: WH declar declar
9	S	20-			'II { × α1 α2	that if should		problem²... she someone...³ you	declar declar declar int: y/n
10	J	21 22				but	I think	she	minor declar
11	S	23							minor
12	J	24							minor

POLARITY	MODALITY				TRANSITIVITY		
	MODALIZATION		MODULATION		PROCESS TYPE		CONGRUENT
	VALUE	ORIENTATION	VALUE	ORIENTATION			
pos					vbl		
pos							
pos					rel	attr/int	
neg					rel	attr/int	ment:cog
pos					bhv/eff		
pos	medium	subj/exp			rel	attr/poss	ment:cog
pos			low	subj/imp	mat		vbl
pos	median	subj/exp			rel	id/int	ment:cog
pos					mat		
pos	high	obj/imp			rel	attr/int	
					rel	attr/int	
pos			median	subj/imp	rel	attr/int	
pos	median	subj/exp			rel	attr/int	
pos			median	subj/imp	vbl/eff		
pos	high	obj/imp	median	subj/imp	vbl/eff		
pos					vbl		
neg					rel/eff	attr/int	
pos	median	subj/exp	high	subj/imp	mat		ment:cog
neg					rel	attr/int	
pos	low	subj/imp			mat		
neg			high	subj/imp	mat		
pos					rel	id/int	
neg					mat		
pos					vbl		
pos			median	subj/imp	mat		
pos	median	subj/exp			ment:af		
pos							

TURN	SPEAKER	CLAUSE	CLAUSE COMPLEX	FUNCTION IN CLAUSE COMPLEX	RANK SHIFT (EMBEDDING)	THEME TEXTUAL	THEME INTERPERSONAL	THEME TOPICAL	MOOD
		25	⎱	1	'Ⅱ			she	declar
								us	non-finite
		26	⎰	×2		and so		she	declar
		27		+3		but	I think	that	declar
13	A	28–	⎱	11		oh	I think	part of it	declar
					=Ⅱ	that		you	declar
					=Ⅱ	that		I	declar
		29		=2				she	declar
		30		+2		but I mean	I think	she	declar
					=Ⅱ ⎰ ×β	as		that	declar
					⎱ α			people	declar
		31							minor
14	S	32						it	declar
		33	⎱	α				I	declar
		34	⎰	'β				it	declar
		35						I	declar
		36						the one... [4]	declar
					=Ⅱ			I	declar
					'Ⅱ			her	non-finite
		37	⎱	1				the dissertation	declar
		38		=21				these	declar
		39		×21				let's	imper
		40	⎰	+2		and			imper
		41		+3		and			imper
		42	⎱	1		and		that	declar
		43		+2α		but		it	declar
		44	⎰	×β		because		it	declar
					=Ⅱ			I	declar
					=Ⅱ		what	...[5]	int/wh
							it is true that	in this literature	declar
		45	⎱	1				that	declar
		46		+2α		but		you	declar
		47	⎰	×β		if		how	declar
					"Ⅱ		how		declar
					"Ⅱ ⎰ α				non-finite
					⎱ ×β				non-finite
		48						she	declar
		49		α		it'd be better	it	she	declar
		50		×β		so that		she	declar
		[51]		×β		although		I	declar

267

| POLARITY | MODALITY | | | | TRANSITIVITY | |
| | MODALIZATION | | MODULATION | | | |
	VALUE	ORIENTATION	VALUE	ORIENTATION	PROCESS TYPE	CONGRUENT
neg					ment: af	
pos					behav	
pos	median	obj/imp	high	subj/imp	mat	
pos	median	subj/exp			mat	
pos	median	subj/exp			rel	id/int
pos					vbl	
pos					vbl	
pos					behav	
pos	median	subj/exp			ment: cog	
pos					vbl	
pos					vbl	
pos					rel	attr/int
pos					ment: af	
pos					rel	attr/int
pos					rel	attr/poss ment: af
pos					rel	attr/circ
pos					mat	vbl
pos					mat	vbl
pos					vbl	
pos					rel	id/int
pos					mat	
pos					mat	
pos					mat	
pos					rel	attr/int
pos					rel	attr/int
neg					vbl/caus	
pos					mat	
pos	low	subj/imp			mat	ment: cog
pos	high	obj/exp			ment: cog	
neg			low	obj/imp	rel	id/int
pos					mat	vbl
pos			low	subj/imp	ment: cog	
pos					mat	
pos					ment: cog	
pos	median	subj/exp	low	subj/imp	mat	vbl
pos	median	subj/exp	median	obj/exp	mat	ment: cog
neg			low	obj/imp	mat	

TURN	SPEAKER	CLAUSE	CLAUSE COMPLEX	FUNCTION IN CLAUSE COMPLEX	RANK SHIFT (EMBEDDING)	THEME TEXTUAL	THEME INTERPERSONAL	THEME TOPICAL	MOOD
		51				well		let me	imper
		52						in...6	declar
		53						in...7	declar
		54	}	α	'II			it	declar
									non-finite
		55	}	×β		in order to			non-finite
		56		α	'II		I think	it	declar
		57	}	×β		for		her	non-finite
		58		×γ		just to			non-finite
					'II	that		she	declar
		59	}	α				I	declar
		60		×β		because	I think	that	declar
		61	}	×β		y		she	declar
		62	}	α				she	declar
					=II				non-finite
					+II				non-finite
15	A	63	1α					I	declar
		64	"β				wh	at	int: WH
		65	+21			and		that	declar
		66	"21					I	declar
		67	×2			and therefore		I	declar
		68	×3			and		I	declar
16	S	69				but		I	declar
17	A	70	+4			and		I	declar
18	J	71				along those lines	A(...) does	she	int: y/n
19	A	72				actually		it	declar
		73	1				I think	the...8	declar
		74	+2			and then		she	declar
		75	+3			and		she	declar
		76	+4α			and	I don't know	it	declar
		77	×β1			given that		she	declar
		78	+2α			and			declar
		79	×β			as		we	declar
		80	=5			I mean	I don't think	she	declar
20	S	81						John	declar

POLARITY	MODALITY				TRANSITIVITY		
	MODALIZATION		MODULATION		PROCESS TYPE		CONGRUENT
	VALUE	ORIENTATION	VALUE	ORIENTATION			
pos					mat		
pos			median	subj/exp	mat		
neg					rel	attr/int	ment:cog
pos	low	subj/imp			rel	attr/int	
pos					mat		behav
pos					mat		
pos	median	subj/exp			rel	attr/int	
pos					mat		
pos					mat		
pos					mat		ment:cog
pos			low	subj/imp	mat		
pos					ment:af		
pos	median	subj/exp			rel	id/int	
pos					ment:cog		
neg	low	subj/imp			ment:cog		
pos					mat		
pos					mat		
pos			low	subj/imp	vbl		
pos					rel	id/int	ment:cog
pos					rel	id/int	
pos					rel	attr/int	
pos					rel	attr/circ	
pos			high	subj/imp	mat		
pos					rel	attr/int	
pos					mat		
pos					ment:cog		
neg					rel	attr/int	
pos	median	subj/exp			rel	attr/circ	
pos					mat		
pos					mat		
neg	low	subj/exp			rel	attr/int	
pos					mat		
pos					mat		
pos			low	subj/imp	ment:per		
neg	median	subj/exp			mat		
pos	low	subj/imp			ment:cog		

TURN	SPEAKER	CLAUSE	CLAUSE COMPLEX	FUNCTION IN CLAUSE COMPLEX	RANK SHIFT (EMBEDDING)	THEME TEXTUAL	THEME INTERPERSONAL	THEME TOPICAL	MOOD
21	A	[82]				but		I	
		82		1		yeah		that	declar
		83		+2		and	I think	she	declar
		[84]				and	I think	one ..9	
		84		3			I think	Mike	declar
		85		4		and	I think	that	declar
22	P	86			=II	that	to what	extent she	int: WH
23	A	87		1				that	declar
		88		=2				that	declar
24	P	89						they	declar
25	S	90							minor
26	P	91				oh		they	declar
27	A	92						they	declar
28	P	93						they	declar
29	S	94		1		well		there	declar
		95		=2				there	declar
		96		+2		but		I	declar
		[97]						there	declar
		97				well		I	declar
					=II			that	declar
					=II			she	declar
30	A	98-							minor
31	P	99-				so		nobody	declar
32	A	100				oh no		I	declar

POLARITY	MODALITY				TRANSITIVITY		
	MODALIZATION		MODULATION		PROCESS TYPE		CONGRUENT
	VALUE	ORIENTATION	VALUE	ORIENTATION			
pos					rel	attr/int	
pos	median	subj/exp			rel	attr/int	ment:cog
	median	subj/exp			rel	id/int	
pos	low	subj/imp			vbl/eff		
pos	median	subj/exp			rel	attr/int	
pos					rel	attr/int	
					mat		
pos					rel	id/int	
pos					rel	id/int	
pos					rel	attr/int	
pos							
pos					rel	id/int	
pos					rel	id/int	
neg					rel	attr/int	
pos					rel	exist	
pos					rel	exist	
neg					ment:cog		
pos	low	subj/imp			rel	exist	
neg					ment:cog		
pos					rel	attr/int	
pos					behav/eff		
neg					mat		
neg					ment:cog		

TURN	SPEAKER	CLAUSE	CLAUSE COMPLEX	FUNCTION IN CLAUSE COMPLEX	RANK SHIFT (EMBEDDING)	THEME TEXTUAL	THEME INTERPERSONAL	THEME TOPICAL	MOOD
(32	A)	101		1α			I think	the...[10]	declar
					=⟦		(that)	that	declar
		102		=βα			(who)	isho	declar
		103		"β1				you	declar
		104		=2				what...[11]	declar
		105		×3α		and then		you	declar
		106		⟨βα				how	int: WH
		107		×β		without			non-finite
		108		+2		and		that	declar
					=⟦		(which)	which	declar
		109				so		I	declar
33	S	110						she	declar
34	J	111						she	declar
35	A	112				yeah		I	declar
					"⟦			when	
		113		1				it	declar
		114		+2		and		they	declar
		115		+31		and		Sh—	declar
		116		"2				you	declar
		117		+41		and		B—	declar
		118		"2		oh no	go on	you	imper
		119						it	declar
		120		1				she	declar
		121		×2		so		there	declar
		122		1			let	me	imper
		123		+2					imper
36	P	124				yeah		it	declar
37	A	125		α					declar
		126		×β				how	non-finite
38	S	127						someone	imper
39	P	128						she	declar
40	S	129				yeah		she	declar
		130						they	declar
41	J	131						for a while	declar

273

| POLARITY | MODALITY | | | | TRANSITIVITY | |
| | MODALIZATION | | MODULATION | | | |
	VALUE	ORIENTATION	VALUE	ORIENTATION	PROCESS TYPE	CONGRUENT
pos	median	subj/exp			rel · id/int	
pos					rel · attr/int	
pos					vbl	
neg			low	subj	ment:af	
pos			high	subj	rel · id/int	mat
pos					ment:cog	
pos					behav	
neg			high	subj	mat	
neg					mat	
neg					rel · attr/int	
pos			low	subj	vbl	
pos					mat	
pos					mat	
pos					vbl	
					mat	
pos					rel · id/int	
pos					mat	
pos					vbl	
pos			high	subj	vbl	
pos					vbl	
pos					vbl	
pos					rel · id/int	
pos					ment:cog	
					rel · exist	
pos					mat	
pos					mat	
pos	median	subj/exp			rel · attr/int	
pos			high	subj	ment:cog	
pos					mat	
pos					mat	
pos +tag					mat	
pos					mat	
pos	median	subj/exp			mat	
pos +tag					rel · attr./circ	

TURN	SPEAKER	CLAUSE	CLAUSE COMPLEX	FUNCTION IN CLAUSE COMPLEX	RANK SHIFT [EMBEDDING]	THEME TEXTUAL	INTERPERSONAL	TOPICAL	MOOD
42	P	132				well	wasn't	the position	int : y/n
43	S	133			=I	yeah		it wasn't	declar non-finite
		134			=II			it was	declar non-finite
44	J	135							minor
.45	S	136	⎫	α		and in point of fact	I think	it	declar
		137		=βα				which	declar
		138	⎬	×β	×[]			this	declar non-finite
		139	⎫	1				she	declar
		140	⎬	=2		really			declar
		141					I must say	her 1968 story	declar
46	A	142			=II	well		we	declar
								you	non-finite
47	L	143							declar
48	S	144					Alan	there	declar
		145	⎫	α				I	declar
		146-	⎬	β				2	declar
49	P	147						you	declar
50	A	148			=I			there	declar
								who	declar
51	S	149				but			minor
52	A	150							minor
53	J	151							minor
54	S	152						these people	declar
		153						I	declar
		154						I	declar
55	L	155							

POLARITY	MODALITY				TRANSITIVITY		
	MODALIZATION		MODULATION		PROCESS	TYPE	CONGRUENT
	VALUE	ORIENTATION	VALUE	ORIENTATION			
neg					rel	attr/int	
neg					rel	id/int	attr/circ
					mat		
pos					rel	id/int	attr/circ
					mat		
pos							
pos	median	subj/exp			mat		
pos					vbl		
pos					rel		
					mat		
pos					rel	attr/int	
pos					rel	attr/int	
pos	high	subj/exp			ment:af		
pos					rel		
pos					mat		
pos					mat		
pos	high	subj/imp			rel	exist	
neg					ment:cog		
pos					rel	id/circ	
pos					rel	attr/circ	
pos					rel	exist	
pos					rel	attr/int	
pos					mat		
pos					rel	attr/int	ment:cog
pos					ment:cog		

TURN	SPEAKER	CLAUSE	CLAUSE COMPLEX	FUNCTION IN CLAUSE COMPLEX	RANK SHIFT (EMBEDDING)	THEME TEXTUAL	THEME INTERPERSONAL	THEME TOPICAL	MOOD
55	L	155	}	1				do	imper
		156	}	+2α		and	I think	you	declar
		157	}	β				they	declar
56	S	158						I	declar
		159			×⟦			&	non-finite
57	L	[160]				and then	I think	you	declar
		160		1		and then		check	imper
		161		=2α				check	imper
		162		βα			who		int: WH
		163		×β		when		they	declar
58	S	↓							
59	L	↓							
60	S	164						I	declar
61	L	165	}	1			I think	you	declar
62	S	[166-]	}			well		&	
63	L	166	}	×2		'cause	I think	you	declar
64	S	167						I	declar
		168							minor
65	P	169							declar
66	L	170			=⟦			whose husband	minor / declar
67	J	171			=⟦			whose husband	minor / declar
68	L	172	}	α				she	declar
		173	}					she	declar
		174	}	×β		before		I	declar
69	J	175				oh yeah and	didn't	Janet Hunt	int: y/n

POLARITY	MODALITY				TRANSITIVITY		
	MODALIZATION		MODULATION		PROCESS	TYPE	CONGRUENT
	VALUE	ORIENTATION	VALUE	ORIENTATION			
pos							
pos	low	subj/exp			ment:cog		
pos					rel	attr/int	
pos					ment:cog		
pos					rel	attr/int	ment:cog
pos					ment:cog		
pos	median	subj/exp	low	subj/imp			
pos					ment:cog		
pos					ment:cog		
pos					rel	id/int	
pos					mat		
pos					ment:cog		
pos	median	subj/exp			rel	id/int	
pos +tag	median	subj/exp			rel	id/int	
pos					rel	id/int	
pos					mat		
pos					rel	attr/circ	
pos					rel	attr/circ	
pos					rel	attr/circ	
pos					mat		
pos					mat		
neg					mat		

TURN	SPEAKER	CLAUSE	CLAUSE COMPLEX	FUNCTION IN CLAUSE COMPLEX	RANK SHIFT (EMBEDDING?)	THEME TEXTUAL	THEME INTERPERSONAL	THEME TOPICAL	MOOD
70	S	176							minor
		177						I	declar
		178	}	1		well again		I	declar
		179		=2				I	declar
71	A	180	}	1			I think	she	declar
		181		+2		but then		I	declar
72	L	182				but		Janet	declar
73	J	183							minor
74	S	184							minor
75	L	185							minor
		186						check	imper
		187			=[[	see		the ...12	declar
							I presume	women	declar
76	J	188					can	we	int:y/n
		189					do	we	int:y/n
77	L	[-187]							
78	A	190							minor
79	L	191					did	you	int:y/n
80	J	192				no		I	declar
81	A	193						that	declar
		194			x[[			we	declar
								you	non-finite
82	S	195	)	1	α[[	you know		what ...13	declar
								what	declar
		196	}	+2 xβ		but y		it	declar
		197		α1				I	declar
		198	)	+2				I	declar

| POLARITY | MODALITY | | | | TRANSITIVITY | | |
| | MODALIZATION | | MODULATION | | | | |
	VALUE	ORIENTATION	VALUE	ORIENTATION	PROCESS TYPE		CONGRUENT
pos					rel	attr/int	ment: cog
neg					ment: cog		
neg					rel	attr/int	ment: cog
pos	median	subj/exp			mat		
neg					rel	attr/int	ment cog
pos +tag					rel	attr/int	
pos							
neg							
neg							
pos					ment: cog		
pos					rel	id/circ	
pos	median	subj/exp			mat		
pos			low	subj	mat		
pos					mat		
pos					mat		
neg					mat		
pos					rel	attr/int	
pos					rel	attr/pos	
pos					mat		
pos	low	subj/imp			rel	attr/int	
pos					vbl		
pos					rel	attr/int	
pos					ment: af		
pos					ment: af		

TURN	SPEAKER	CLAUSE	CLAUSE COMPLEX	FUNCTION IN CLAUSE COMPLEX	RANK SHIFT (EMBEDDING)	THEME TEXTUAL	THEME INTERPERSONAL	THEME TOPICAL	MOOD
83	S	199	}	α				that	declar
		200		×βα				I	declar
		·201		×β		when		Mary	declar
84	L	202	}	×β		when		you	declar
		203		1α				they	declar
		204		+2α		but	you see	she·	declar
85	S	205							minor
86	L	206		×β		yeah before		you	declar
87	A	207							minor
88	J	208							minor
89	L	209							minor
90	S	210							minor
91	A	211					did	she	int: y/n
		212						I	declar
92	S	213				no		there	declar
93	L	214	}	1				Mary	declar
		215		+2		but		that	declar
94	S	216	}	1	=Π			I	declar
		217		+2		but	frankly	I	declar
		218						what	declar
								it	declar
		219	}	α				it	declar
		220		×βα		in the sense that		I	declar
		221		×β				it	declar
95	L	222							minor
96	S	223	}	α		therefore		I	declar
		224		×β		that		it	declar

POLARITY	MODALITY				TRANSITIVITY		
	MODALIZATION		MODULATION		PROCESS TYPE		CONGRUENT
	VALUE	ORIENTATION	VALUE	ORIENTATION			
neg					rel	attr/int	
pos							
pos					mat		
pos					mat		
pos					mat		
pos					behav		
pos					rel	attr/circ	
pos					mat		
pos					ment:cog		
pos					rel	exist	vbl
pos					mat		
neg					rel	attr/int	attr/circ
pos					ment:cog		
neg					ment:af		
pos					vbl		
pos					ment:af		
pos					ment:af		
pos					ment:cog		
neg					rel	attr/int	
pos							
pos					mat		ment:cog
neg					rel	attr/int	

282

TURN	SPEAKER	CLAUSE	CLAUSE COMPLEX	FUNCTION IN CLAUSE COMPLEX	RANK SHIFT (EMBEDDING)	THEME TEXTUAL	THEME INTERPERSONAL	THEME TOPICAL	MOOD
97	A	225				and		he	declar
		226	}	α				he	declar
		227	}	β				how	non-finite
98	S	228	}	1α		and		it	declar
		229	}	×β		that		I	declar
		230	}	×2		and then		I	declar
99	L	231	}	1		well		you	declar
		232	}	+2 ×β		and y		you	declar
		233	}	α				look for	imper
100	S	234	–	×β		but y		I	declar
101	P	235	}	α					declar
		236	}	×β		y		that	declar
102	L	237				well		I	declar
					=[]			I	declar
					=[]			I	declar
		238	}	1				they	declar
		239	}	+2	and		they		declar
103	A	240				well		there	declar
		241	}	1				you	declar
		242–	}	+2	and		that		declar
104	L	243							minor
105	S	244				yeah but		that	declar
106	L	245						this	declar
		246	}	1				wait	imper
		247	}	=2				wait	imper
		248						this	declar
		249						I	declar
					=[]			what	declar
107	S	250				then		it	declar

POLARITY	MODALITY				TRANSITIVITY		
	MODALIZATION		MODULATION		PROCESS TYPE		CONGRUENT
	VALUE	ORIENTATION	VALUE	ORIENTATION			
pos					mat		
pos					ment : cog		
pos					rel	attr/int	
pos	low	subj/imp			rel	id/int	
neg					mat		
pos					rel	attr/int	ment : af
pos	low	subj/imp			mat		
pas					mat		
pos					mat		
pos							
pos					rel	attr/pass	mat
pos					rel	id/int	
neg					mat		ment : cog
pos					mat		
pos					mat		
pos					rel	attr/int	
pos					mat		
pos	low	subj/imp			rel	exist	
pos					vbl		
pos					rel		
pos							
neg	median	subj/imp			rel	attr/int	
neg					rel	attr/circ	mat
pos					mat		
pos					mat		
pos					rel	attr/int	
pos					ment : af		
pos					mat		
pos					rel	id/int	

TURN	SPEAKER	CLAUSE	CLAUSE COMPLEX	FUNCTION IN CLAUSE COMPLEX	RANK SHIFT (EMBEDDING)	THEME TEXTUAL	INTERPERSONAL	TOPICAL	MOOD
108	L	251							minor
109	A	252							minor
110	L	253	}	1				one	declar
		254	}	=21		yeah		one	declar
		255		+2		and		one	declar
111	S	256						that	declar
		257						you	declar
112	L	258				yes and		they	declar
113	S	259							minor
		260						they	declar
114	L	261	}	1		well		that	declar
		262-	}	+2	=[[	but		the... [14]	declar
									non finite
115	S	263	}	1	'[[	in that sense		it	declar
						how		the... [15]	declar
		264	}	=2×β		that is to say if	indeed	there	declar
		265	}	α				the... [16]	declar
					=[[			they	declar
					'[[	that		it	declar
116	A	266				well		what... [17]	declar
					=[[			what	declar
					'[[	that		all... [18]	declar
					'[[			how	int : WH
		267				o.k.			minor

POLARITY	MODALITY				TRANSITIVITY		
	MODALIZATION		MODULATION		PROCESS TYPE		CONGRUENT
	VALUE	ORIENTATION	VALUE	ORIENTATION			
pos							
pos					rel	id/int	
pos					rel	id/int	
pos					rel	id/int	
pos	median	obj/imp			mat		
pos					ment:af		rel:poss
pos			low	subj/imp	ment:cog		
pos					rel	id/circ	mat
pos	low	subj/imp			rel	attr/int	
neg					rel	attr/circ	
pos					rel	attr/int	ment:cog
pos					mat		
pos					rel	exist	ment:af
pos					rel	id/int	
pos					mat		ment:cog
pos					rel	attr/int	
pos					rel	id/int	ment:cog
pos					rel	attr/int	ment:cog
pos					rel	attr/circ	mat
pos					behav		

APPENDIX 3

Dear Friend of ZPG:

At 7.00 a.m. on October 25, our phones started to ring. Calls jammed our switchboard all day. Staffers stayed late into the night, answering questions and talking with reporters from newspapers, radio stations, wire services and TV stations in every part of the country.

When we released the results of ZPG's *1985 Urban Stress Test* we had no idea we'd get such an overwhelming response. Media and public reaction has been nothing short of incredible!

At first, the deluge of calls came mostly from reporters eager to tell the public about Urban Stress Test results and from outraged public officials who were furious that we had 'blown the whistle' on conditions in their cities.

Now we are hearing from concerned citizens in all parts of the country who want to know what they can do to hold local officials accountable for tackling population-related problems that threaten public health and well-being.

ZPG's *1985 Urban Stress Test*, created after months of persistent and exhaustive research, is the nation's first survey of how population-linked pressures affect U.S. cities. It ranks 184 urban areas on 11 different criteria ranging from crowding and birth rates to air quality and toxic wastes.

The Urban Stress Test translates complex, technical data into easy-to-use *action tool* for concerned citizens, elected officials and opinion leaders. But to use it well, we urgently need your help.

Our small staff is being swamped with requests for more information and our modest resources are being stretched to the limit.

Your supprt now is critical. *ZPG's 1985 Urban Stress Test* may be our best opportunity ever to get the population message heard.

With your contribution, ZPG can arm our growing network of local activists with the materials they need to warn community leaders about emerging population-linked stresses *before* they reach the crisis stage.

Even though our national government continues to ignore the consequences of uncontrolled population growth, *we can act to take positive action at the local level.*

Every day decisions are being made by local officials in our communities that could drastically affect the quality of our lives. To make sound choices in planning for people, both elected officials and the American public need the population-stress data revealed by our study.

Please make a special contribution to Zero Population Growth today. Whatever you give – $25, $50, $100 or as much as you can – will be used immediately to put the Urban Stress Test in the hands of those who need it most.

Sincerely,

Susan Webster
Executive Director

P.S. The results of ZPG's *1985 Urban Stress Test* were reported as a top news story by hundreds of newspapers and TV and radio stations from coast to coast. I hope you'll help us monitor this remarkable media coverage by completing the enclosed reply form.

BIBLIOGRAPHY

Bach, E. and Harms, R. T. (eds) (1968) *Universals in Linguistic Theory*. New York: Holt, Rinehart & Winston.

Benson, J. D. and Greaves, W. S. (eds) (1985) *Systemic Perspectives on Discourse, Vol 1: Selected Theoretical Papers from the 9th International Systemic Workshop*. Norwood, NJ: Ablex (Advances in Discourse Processes 15).

Berger, P. L. and Luckmann, T. (1966) *The Social Construction of Reality: A Treatise in the Sociology of Knowledge*. London: Allen Lane (Penguin Press).

Bernstein, B. (1971) *Class, Codes and Control, Vol. I: Theoretical Studies towards a Sociology of Language*. London: Routledge & Kegan Paul (Primary Socialization, Language and Education).

Berry, M. (1981) 'Systemic linguistics and discourse analysis: a multi-layered approach to exchange structure', in M. Coulthard and M. Montgomery (eds), *Studies in Discourse Analysis*. London: Routledge and Kegan Paul.

Birch, D. and O'Toole, M. (eds) (1988) *Functions of Style*. London: Pinter.

Braine, J. (1979) *J. B. Priestley*. London: Weidenfeld & Nicolson.

Bühler, K. (1934) *Sprachtheorie: Die Darstellungfunktion der Sprache*. Jena: Fischer.

Butt, D. G. (1984) 'Perceiving as making in the poetry of Wallace Stevens', *Nottingham Linguistics Circular* 13 (Special Issue on Systemic Linguistics).

Butt, D. G. (1988) 'Ideational meaning and the existential fabric of a poem', in R. P. Fawcett and D. Young (eds), *New Developments in Systemic Linguistics: Theory and Application*. London: Pinter.

Carter, R. (1982) 'Style and interpretation in Hemingway's "Cat in the Rain"', in R. Carter (ed.).

Carter, R. (ed.) (1982) *Language and Literature: An Introductory Reader in Stylistics*. London: Allen & Unwin.

Chabrol, C. and Marin, L. (eds) (1971) *Sémiotique Narrative: récits bibliques*. Paris: Didier/Larousse (Langages 22).

Chatman, S. (1968) 'Milton's participial style', *Publications of the Modern Language Association of America*.

Chatman, S. (ed.) (1971) *Literary Style: A Symposium*. New York: Oxford University Press.

Chatman, S. and Levin, S. R. (eds) (1967) *Essays on the Language of Literature*. Boston: Houghton Mifflin.

Cicourel, A. (1969) 'Generative semantics and the structure of social interaction', *International Days of Sociolinguistics*. Rome: Luigi Sturzo Institute.

Dalton, J. (1827) *A New System of Chemical Philosophy*. London: George Wilson. Facsimile edition, London: William Dawson.

Daneš, F. (ed.) (1974) *Papers on Functional Sentence Perspective*. Prague: Academia.

Darwin, C. (1859) *The Origin of Species by Means of Natural Selection*. New York: Avenel Books, 1979.

Douglas, M. (ed.) (1973) *Rules and Meanings: The Anthropology of Everyday Knowledge*. Harmondsworth: Penguin Books.

Dunne, J. W. (1934) *The Serial Universe*. London: Faber.

Duthie, A. (ed.) (1964) *English Studies Today, Third Series*. Edinburgh University Press.

Eco, U. (1976) *A Theory of Semiotics*. Bloomington, IN: Indiana University Press.

Elmenoufy, A. (1969) 'A study of the role of intonation in the grammar of English.' Unpublished PhD thesis, University of London.

Evans, G. L. (1964) *J. B. Priestley: The Dramatist*. London: Heinemann.

Ferguson, C. A. and Farwell, C. B. (1973) 'Words and sounds in early language acquisition: English initial consonants in the first fifty words', *Papers and Reports in Child Language Development* 6 (Stanford University Committee on Linguistics).

Firbas, J. (1964) 'On defining the theme in functional sentence analysis', *Travaux Linguistiques de Prague* 1.

Firbas, J. (1968) 'On the prosodic features of the modern English finite verb as means of functional sentence perspective', *Brno Studies in English* 7.

Firth, J. R. (1951) 'Modes of meaning', *Essays and Studies* (English Association). Reprinted in J. R. Firth, *Papers in Linguistics 1934–1951*. London: Oxford University Press, 1957 (Chapter 15).

Firth, J. R. (1953) 'The languages of linguistics', in F. R. Palmer (ed.), *Selected Papers of J. R. Firth 1952–1959*. London: Longmans.

Five to Nine: Aspects of Function and Structure in the Spoken Language of Elementary School Children (1972) Toronto: English Department, York University, and Board of Education for the Borough of North York.

Foucault, M. (1975–76) 'The units of discourse', in H. S. Gill (ed.), *Parole and Langue: Studies in French Structuralism*. Patiala, India: University of Patiala (Pakha Sanjam 8).

Fowler, R. (ed.) (1966) *Essays on Style and Language: Linguistic and Critical Approaches to Literary Style*. London: Routledge & Kegan Paul.

Fowler, R. (1981) *Literature as Social Discourse: The Practice of Linguistic Criticism*. London: Batsford Academic and Educational.

Fries, P. H. (1981) 'On the status of Theme in English: arguments from discourse'. *Forum Linguisticum* 6.1. Reprinted in J. S. Petöfi and E. Sözer (eds), *Micro and Macro Connexity of Texts*. Hamburg: Buske, 1983.

Fries, P. H. (1994) 'On theme, rheme and discourse goals', in M. Coulthard (ed.), *Advances in Written Text Analysis*. London: Routledge.

Fries, P. H. (1995) 'Patterns of information in initial position in English', in P. H. Fries and M. Gregory (eds).

Fries, P. H. (1996) 'Themes, methods of development, and texts', in R. Hasan and P. H. Fries (eds).

Fries, P. H. (1997) 'Toward a discussion of the flow of information in a written English text', in M. J. Cummings and M. Gregory (eds), *Relations and Functions in Language*. Amsterdam: Benjamins.

Fries, P. H. and Gregory, M. (eds) (1995) *Discourse in Society: Systemic Functional Perspectives*. Norwood, NJ: Ablex (Advances in Discourse Processes).

Garvin, P. L. (ed. and trans.) (1964) *A Prague School Reader on Esthetics, Literary Structure and Style*. Washington, DC: Georgetown University Press.

Genette, G. (1975–76) 'Structuralism and literary criticism', in H. S. Gill (ed.).

Ghadessy, M. (ed.) (1995) *Thematic Development in English Texts*. London: Pinter.

Gibson, W. (1958) 'Behind the veil: a distinction between poetic and scientific language in Tennyson, Lyell and Darwin', *Victorian Studies* 2.

Gill, H. S. (ed.) (1975–76) *Parole and Langue: Studies in French Structuralism*. Patiala, India: University of Patiala (Pakha Sanjam 8).

Golding, W. (1955) *The Inheritors*. London: Faber.

Gregory, M. (1967) 'Aspects of varieties differentiation', *Journal of Linguistics* 3.2.

Gregory, M. (1974) 'A theory for stylistics exemplified: Donne's Holy Sonnet XIV', *Language and Style* 7.2.

Gregory, M. (1978) 'Marvell's "To his Coy Mistress": the poem as a linguistic and social event', *Poetics* 7.4.

Gregory, M. (1985) 'Towards "communication" linguistics: a framework', in J. D. Benson and W. S. Greaves (eds).

Gutwinski, W. (1974) *Cohesion in Literary Texts: A Study of Some Grammatical and Lexical Features of English Discourse*. The Hague: Mouton.

Halliday, M. A. K. (1961) 'Categories of the theory of grammar', *Word* 17.3: 242–92. In Halliday 2002.

Halliday M. A. K. (1967a) *Grammar, Society and the Noun*. London: H. K. Lewis (for University College London).

Halliday, M. A. K. (1967b) *Intonation and Grammar in British English*. The Hague: Mouton. (Janua Linguarum Series Practica 48).

Halliday, M. A. K. (1967–68) 'Notes on transitivity and theme in English, Parts 1–3', *Journal of Linguistics* 3–4.

Halliday, M. A. K. (1970) *A Course in Spoken English: Intonation*. London: Oxford University Press.

Halliday, M. A. K. (1971) 'Linguistic function and literary style: an inquiry into the language of William Golding's *The Inheritors*'. [Chapter 3, this volume]

Halliday, M. A. K. (1974) *Language and Social Man*. London: Longmans (Schools Council Programme in Linguistics & English Teaching, Papers, Series II, 3). Reprinted in Halliday 1978.

Halliday, M. A. K. (1975) 'Language as social semiotic: towards a general sociolinguistic theory' in A. Makkai and V. B. Makkai (eds), *The First LACUS Forum 1974*. Columbia, SC: Hornbeam Press. Abridged version reprinted in Halliday 1978.

Halliday, M. A. K. (1977) 'Text as semantic choice in social contexts' [Chapter 2, this volume]

Halliday, M. A. K. (1978) *Language as Social Semiotic: The Social Interpretation of Language and Meaning*. London: Edward Arnold.

Halliday, M. A. K. (1985a) *Introduction to Functional Grammar*. London: Edward Arnold. [2nd (revised) edition, 1994]

Halliday, M. A. K. (1985b) 'Dimensions of discourse analysis: grammar', in T. A. van Dijk (ed.), *Handbook of Discourse Analysis*, Vol. 2, London: Academic Press.

Halliday, M. A. K. (1987) 'Spoken and written modes of meaning', in R. Horowitz and S. J. Samuels (eds), *Comprehending Oral and Written Language*. New York: Academic Press.

Halliday, M. A. K. (1988) 'On the language of physical science', in M. Ghadessy (ed.), *Registers of Written English: Situational Factors and Linguistic Features*. London: Pinter.

Halliday, M. A. K. (2002) *On Grammar*. London: Continuum.

Halliday, M. A. K. and Hasan, R. (1976) *Cohesion in English*. London: Longman (English Language Series 9).

Halliday, M. A. K., McIntosh, A. and Strevens, P. (1964) *The Linguistic Sciences and Language Teaching*. London: Longman.

Hasan, R. (1964) 'A Linguistic Study of Contrasting Features in the Style of Two Contemporary English Prose Writers'. Unpublished PhD thesis, University of Edinburgh.

Hasan, R. (1967) 'Linguistics and the study of literary texts', *Études de Linguistique Appliquée* 5.

Hasan, R. (1971) 'Rime and reason in literature', in S. Chatman (ed.), *Literary Style: A Symposium*. New York: Oxford University Press.

Hasan, R. (1973) 'Code, register and social dialect', in B. Bernstein (ed.), *Class, Codes and Control, Vol. 2: Applied Studies towards a Sociology of Language* (Primary Socialization, Language and Education). London: Routledge & Kegan Paul.

Hasan, R. (1975) 'The place of stylistics in the study of verbal art', in Hakan Ringbom (ed.), *Style and Text: Studies Presented to Nils Erik Enkvist*. Stockholm: Skriptor.

Hasan, R. (1984) 'The nursery tale as a genre', *Nottingham Linguistic Circular* 13. Abridged version reprinted in C. Cloran, D. G. Butt and G. Williams (eds), *Ways of Saying: Ways of Meaning: Selected Papers of Ruqaiya Hasan*, London: Cassell, 1996.

Hasan, R. (1985) *Linguistics, Language and Verbal Art*. Geelong, Vic.: Deakin University Press. Reissued Oxford: Oxford University Press, 1989.

Hasan, R. (1989) 'Semantic variation and sociolinguistics', *Australian Journal of Linguistics* 9.

Hasan, R. and Fries, P. H. (eds) (1995) *On Subject and Theme: A Discourse Functional Perspective*. Amsterdam: Benjamins.

Hill, A. A. (1953) *Report of the Fourth Annual Round Table Meeting on Linguistics and Language Study*. Washington, DC: Georgetown University (Monograph Series on Languages and Linguistics 4).

Hjelmslev, L. (1961) *Prolegomena to a Theory of Language* (Revised English edition, translated by F. J. Whitfield). Madison: University of Wisconsin Press. (Originally published as *Omkring sprogteoriens grundlaeggelse*. Copenhagen: Munksgaard, 1943.)

Huddleston, R. D. (1965) 'Rank and depth', *Language* 41.

Hudson, R. A. (1967) 'Constituency in a systemic description of the English clause', *Lingua* 18.

Hudson, R. A. (1971) *English Complex Sentences: An Introduction to Systemic Grammar* (Linguistic Series 4). Amsterdam: North Holland.

Hughes, D. (1958) *J. B. Priestley: An Informal Study of His Work*. London: Hart-Davis.

Hymes, D. H. (1971) 'Competence and performance in linguistic theory', in R. Huxley and E. Ingram (eds), *Language Acquisition: Models and Methods*. London: Academic Press.

Jones, J., Collin, S., Drury, H. and Economou, D. (1989) 'Systemic-functional linguistics and its application to the TESOL curriculum', in R. Hasan and J. R. Martin (eds), *Language Development: Learning Language, Learning Culture: Meaning and Choice in Language*. Norwood, NJ: Ablex (Advances in Discourse Processes 27).

Kennedy, C. (1982) 'Systemic grammar and its uses in literary analysis', in R. Carter (ed.).

Kinkead-Weekes, M. and Gregor, I. (1967) *William Golding: A Critical Study.* London: Faber.

Kress, G. and Hodge, R. (1979) *Language as Ideology.* London: Routledge & Kegan Paul.

Lamb, S. M. (1966) 'Epilegomena to a theory of language', *Romance Philology* 19.

Leech, G. N. (1965) '"This bread I break": language and interpretation', *Review of English Literature* 6 (New Attitudes to Style).

Leech, G. N. (1969) *A Linguistic Guide to English Poetry.* London: Longmans (English Language Series).

Lemke, J. L. (1984) *Semiotics and Education.* Toronto: Toronto Semiotic Circle.

Lemke, J. L. (1985) 'Ideology, intertextuality, and the notion of register', in J. D. Benson and W. S. Greaves (eds).

Levin, S. (1971) 'The conventions of poetry', in S. Chatman (ed.).

Lyons, J. (ed.) (1970) *New Horizons in Linguistics.* Harmondsworth: Penguin Books.

Malinowski, B. (1923/1959) 'The problem of meaning in primitive languages', in C. K. Ogden and I. A. Richards (eds), *The Meaning of Meaning.* New York: Harcourt Brace.

Malinowski, B. (1935) *Coral Gardens and Their Magic*, Vol. 2. New York: American Book Co. Reprinted as *The Language of Magic and Gardening*, Bloomington: Indiana University Press (Indiana University Studies in the History and Theory of Linguistics), 1965.

Martin, J. R. (1985) 'Process and text: two aspects of human semiosis', in J. D. Benson and W. S. Greaves (eds).

Martin, J. R. (1992) *English Text: System and Structure.* Amsterdam: Benjamins.

Matthiessen, C. M. I. M. (1985) 'The systemic framework in text generation: Nigel', in J. D. Benson and W. S. Greaves (eds).

McIntosh, A. (1963) '"As You Like It": a grammatical clue to character', *Review of English Literature* 4.2. Reprinted in A. McIntosh and M. A. K. Halliday (eds) (1966).

McIntosh, A. (1965) 'Saying', *Review of English Literature* 6.2.

McIntosh, A. (1966) 'Some thoughts on style', in A. McIntosh and M. A. K. Halliday (eds).

McIntosh, A. and Halliday, M. A. K. (1966) *Patterns of Language: Papers in General, Descriptive and Applied Linguistics.* London: Longman (Longmans Linguistics Library).

McKellar, G. B. (1985) 'Social Man: On the Foundations of a Contemporary Neurolinguistics: A Critical and Systematic Examination of Issues in the Science of Man'. Unpublished PhD thesis, University of Sydney.

Milic, L. T. (1967) *Styles and Stylistics: An Analytical Bibliography*. New York: Free Press.

Milic, L. T. (1971) 'Rhetorical choice and stylistic option: the conscious and unconscious poles', in S. Chatman (ed.).

Mukařovský, J. (1977) *The Word and Verbal Art: Selected Essays*, translated and edited by J. Burbank and P. Steiner (eds). New Haven, CT: Yale University Press.

Oakey, M. (1978) 'Sky watcher', *School Magazine*, 3 September.

Ohmann, R. (1967) 'Literature as sentences', in S. Chatman and S. Levin (eds).

Ohmann, R. (1971) 'Speech, action, and style', in S. Chatman (ed.).

O'Toole, M. (1982) *Structure, Style and Interpretation in the Russian Short Story*. New Haven: Yale University Press.

O'Toole, M. (1988) 'Henry Reed, and what follows the "Naming of Parts"', in D. Birch and M. O'Toole (eds).

O'Toole, M. (1995) 'A systemic-functional semiotics of art', in P. H. Fries and M. Gregory (eds).

Ouspensky, P. D. (1931) *A New Model of the Universe*. London: Kegan Paul.

Pike, K. L. (1959) 'Language as particle, wave and field', *Texas Quarterly* 2.

Priestley, J. B. (1937) *Midnight on the Desert: A Chapter of Autobiography*. London: Heinemann.

Priestley, J. B. (1939) *Rain upon Godshill: A Further Chapter of Autobiography*. London: Heinemann.

Priestley, J. B. (1948/49/50) *The Plays of J. B. Priestley*, Vols. 1–3. London: Heinemann.

Priestley, J. B. (1977) *Instead of the Trees: A Final Chapter of Autobiography*. London: Heinemann.

Prigogine, I. and Stengers, I. (1985) *Order out of Chaos: Man's New Dialogue with Nature*. London: Fontana Paperbacks (Flamingo). (Original French edition *La Nouvelle Alliance* (1979); revised.)

Ravelli, L. J. (1985) 'Metaphor, Mode and Complexity: An Exploration of Co-varying Patterns'. Unpublished B.A. Honours thesis, University of Sydney.

Reid, T. B. W. (1956) 'Linguistics, structuralism, philology', *Archivum Linguisticum* 8.

Sacks, H., Schegloff, E. A. and Jefferson, G. (1974) 'A simplest systematics for the organization of turn-taking in conversation', *Language* 50.

Sebeok, T. A. (ed.) (1960) *Style in Language*. Cambridge, MA: M.I.T. Press.

Sinclair, J. McH. (1965) 'Linguistic meaning in a literary text'. Paper read to the Philological Society, Cambridge, March.

Sinclair, J. McH. (1966) 'Taking a poem to pieces', in R. Fowler (ed.).

Sinclair, J. McH. (1972) *A Course in Spoken English: Grammar*. London: Oxford University Press.

Sinclair, J. McH. (1982) 'Lines about "lines"', in R. Carter (ed.).

Sinclair, J. McH. and Coulthard, R. M. (1975) *Towards an Analysis of Discourse*. London: Oxford University Press.

Sinclair, J. McH., Jones, S. and Daley, R. (1970) *English Lexical Studies*. University of Birmingham, Department of English.

Sinclair, J. McH., Forsyth, I. J., Coulthard, R. M. and Ashby, M. (1972) *The English Used by Teachers and Pupils*. University of Birmingham, Department of English.

Sinfield, A. (1971) *The Language of Tennyson's 'In Memoriam'*. Oxford: Blackwell.

Taber, C. (1966) *The Structure of Sango Narrative*. Hartford: Hartford Seminary Foundation (Hartford Studies in Linguistics 17).

Tennyson, A. [Alfred Lord Tennyson] (1849) *In Memoriam A.H.H.*, in *The Works of Alfred Lord Tennyson, Poet Laureate*. London: Macmillan.

Thibault, P. J. (1984) 'Narrative Structure and Narrative Function in Vladimir Nabokov's *Ada*'. Unpublished PhD thesis, University of Sydney.

Thibault, P. J. (1986) 'Thematic system analysis and the construction of knowledge and belief in discourse', in P. J. Thibault, *Text, Discourse and Context: A Social Semiotic Perspective*. Toronto: Victoria University (Toronto Semiotic Circle Monographs, Working Papers and Prepublications 3).

Thibault, P. J. (1991) *Social Semiotics as Praxis: Text, Social Meaning Making, and Nabokov's 'Ada'*. Minneapolis: University of Minnesota Press (Theory and History of Literature 74).

Thorne, J. P. (1965) 'Stylistics and generative grammars', *Journal of Linguistics* 1.

Threadgold, T. (1986) 'Semiotics – ideology – language', in T. Threadgold *et al.* (eds), *Semiotics – Ideology – Language*. Sydney: Sydney Association for Studies in Society and Culture (Sydney Studies in Society & Culture 3).

Todorov, T. (1971) 'The place of style in the structure of the text', in S. Chatman (ed.).

Ullmann, S. (1964) *Language and Style*. Oxford: Blackwell.

Ullmann, S. (1965), 'Style and personality', *Review of English Literature* 6 (April).

Vachek, J. (1966) *The Linguistic School of Prague*. Bloomington: Indiana University Press.

Whorf, B. L. (1956) *Language, Thought and Reality: Selected Writings of Benjamin Lee Whorf*, edited and with an introduction by John B. Carroll. Cambridge, MA: MIT Press.

Zumthor, P. (1971) 'Style and expressive register in medieval poetry', in S. Chatman (ed.).

INDEX